Sequel to the a
Perking the Pansi
move to

C000092577

TURKEY
STREET

Jack and Liam
move to Bodrum

JACK SCOTT

First Published in Great Britain 2015 by Springtime Books

© Copyright Jack Scott

All rights reserved. No part of this publication may be reproduced, stored in or introduced into a retrieval system, or transmitted, in any form, or by any means (electronic, mechanical, photocopying recording or otherwise) without the prior written permission of the publisher.

This book is sold subject to the condition that it shall not, by way of trade or otherwise, be lent, resold, hired out, or otherwise circulated without the publisher's prior consent in any form of binding or cover other than that in which it is published and without a similar condition including this condition being imposed on the subsequent purchaser.

ISBN: 978-0-9932377-2-0

Disclaimer
This book is based on actual events. To protect the privacy of the persons involved, and in the interest of narrative clarity, some names, characterisations, locations, conversations and timescales have been changed.

For Doreen and Agnes

And for Mark
(1972-2013)

What the critics said about Jack Scott's debut book, *'Perking the Pansies, Jack and Liam move to Turkey'*:

'A compelling and enjoyable read... empathetic, respectful and acute.'
Hugh Pope, international journalist and author

'Jack Scott's witty new book... the originality lies more in its honesty about the grubby reality of expat life that conventional travel literature prefers to gloss over.'
Pat Yale, Time Out, Istanbul

'An excellent book. Funny, insightful and poignant all at once.'
Rainbow Book Awards

'Exquisitely written, utterly candid and beautifully descriptive.'
Deborah Fletcher, author

'There is heartlessness and tragedy here but also a generosity of spirit and positivity, along with a dogged determination to see the best in humanity.'
Polari Magazine

'An entertaining story, told with wit and insight.'
Paul Burston, author

'At turns hilarious, saucy, witty, heart-warming and incredibly moving.'
Linda A Janssen, Global Living Magazine

'*Scott pulls no punches… these vignettes are unrelentingly accurate.*'
Jane Akatay, journalist

'*I can't heap any more praise on the book without gushing.*'
Roving Jay, author

'*A beautiful, tender and truly funny book, I can't wait to read it again.*'
Lou Kief, author

'*A delicious addition to the tradition which began with Gerald Durrell.*'
David Gee, author

Teşekkür Ederim

First and foremost, my eternal thanks must go to the magnificent land we called home for all too brief a time. Turkey broke the umbilical cord between wages and lifestyle, gave me time and space to write and somehow turned me into an accidental author. Who'd have thought? Certainly not me. The Bodrum Belles and our crazy neighbours in Turkey Street accepted us into the fold with warmth and without question. Annie Onursan, a vetpat of distinction, kindly checked my schoolboy Turkish and provided some of the images in this book. Kilian Kröll, my talented and erudite Yankee editor, knocked my manuscript into shape with skill and charm. Jo Parfitt's backing has been invaluable. She is a true force of nature.

Thank you one and all.

As always, my final gratitude goes to the man who has given me the happiest days of my life. I couldn't have done it without you, Liam. No, really.

'On no account learn the language: the more English you sound, the more likely you are to be believed.'
Quentin Crisp

PREFACE

POSTCARD FROM THE EGE

In the autumn of 2009, Jack and Liam, a work-weary middle-aged gay couple, fled the Smoke and dropped into Bodrum to claim their place in the sun. Turkey had become a destination of choice for thousands of desperados leaving behind the daily grind or snapping up a cheap bolthole for the summer sabbatical. Like Jack and Liam, most clung to the narrow strip running along the Aegean and Mediterranean coasts, the part of Turkey best suited to Western sensibilities. The country's burgeoning popularity had transformed large swathes of the chiselled coastline beyond recognition. Just as Spanish-style costas spread like a virus, conurbations of anonymous boxy resorts marched relentlessly up hill and down dale. The Land of the Sunrise gave up her Tiffany Blue waters and pine smothered mountains for the single-minded pursuit of jam today.

While Jack and Liam were pitching their tent, Recep Tayyip Erdoğan, the Prime Minister of Turkey, was taking his seat at the G20 Summit of the World's major economies in Pittsburgh. Erdoğan could be forgiven for looking a little smug. The great, the good and the baffled were scratching their heads trying to respond to the biggest financial crisis since the Great Crash of 1929. Yet Turkey was weathering the storm remarkably well and had just entered the top flight, the ultimate validation of Erdoğan's stewardship of the Turkish economy. A few years earlier, it had been all so different. Following decades of endemic financial instability, chronic inflation, wild runs on the currency and international bailouts, the Turkish banking system had finally snapped, suffering its own meltdown long before the subprime mortgage crisis in the United States set off a train of events that brought global capitalism teetering over the edge. Turkey may have been NATO's eastern anchor with its second largest army, but it was the IMF calling the shots. The Government of the day acted quickly and decisively, reforming the banking sector and restructuring public debt. Little good it did them. A few months on, Erdoğan's AK Party swept to power on a high tide of expectation. The new Islamic-leaning Government jump-started the economy with tax reforms and a round of Thatcherite privatisations. In just seven years, Turkey recorded the kind of spectacular growth the West could only fantasise about. With a competitive, robust and well capitalised financial sector and money worth the paper it was printed on, Erdoğan could afford to cock a snook at the flatlining European Union and drag his feet on Turkey's application to join the club. For the first time since the fall of the Ottomans, Turkey had a seat at the top table rather than standing at the end of it begging for a hand-out. Yes, Prime Minister Erdoğan had good reason to be smug.

He wasn't the only one. More by luck than judgement, Jack and Liam had stumbled into Yalıkavak, a former sponge diving village neatly tucked away behind a mountain pass twenty kilometres from Bodrum. Quickly ensconced in an oversized villa, three loos for two, gin clear skies and a supercharged view of the Aegean, it was all a perfect antidote to the no-time-to-talk, coffee-on-the-go culture of metropolitan London. But within weeks, a glorious autumn of sunset cocktails and moonstruck nights was sullied by an expat rat pack and drenched by the wettest winter Asia Minor had seen since Noah. Winter thundered violently ashore – all crash, bang and wallop – and as brutal winds battered the dream, al fresco hedonism gave way to herringbone slippers and sheepskin muffs. Warmed by logs, layers and vats of local plonk, they sidestepped the living dead in Primark fleeces and battened down the hatches. When a perfidious landlord tried to sell their home from under them, Jack and Liam knew the game was up. They repacked their saddle bags, abandoned swivel-eyed suburbia and rode to Bodrum Town for Earthly Paradise Number Two.

Welcome to the sequel of Jack Scott's award winning debut book, '*Perking the Pansies, Jack and Liam move to Turkey*'. Act Two brings their Anatolian affair, twisting and turning, to its surprising finale.

Editor's Note
For non-British readers who may be stumped (itself a cricketing term) by some of Jack's racy idioms and cultural references, you will find *A Word or Two in British* at the

end of the book. Likewise, readers who are unfamiliar with the language of the sultans will find *A Word or Two in Turkish* bringing up the rear. Jack likes to be educational as well as decorative.

CHAPTER ONE

THE GARDEN OF SIN

A small stone house in the heart of Bodrum Town sat prettily in a secret garden littered with cracked antiquities and dominated by a double-trunked olive tree older than God. It was the original homestead of Turkish gentry, but when the family grew in wealth and status they moved to grander pastures, leaving the estate to fade into quaint dilapidation. As time rolled by, marauding grapevines sunk their tendrils into the mud-mortared walls and wild flowers blanketed the courtyard in a twist of camomile and hollyhocks. For years, the tumbledown house remained hidden behind its sturdy garden walls, until, that is, the elders spotted a business opportunity targeted at a mushrooming community of expats. Selling off the family silver was decidedly un-Turkish, but renting it out to the moneyed infidels was an altogether different proposition: some *yabancılar* were more than happy to pay top dollar for a generous slice of authenticity. After months of wrangles with town planners and a spot of palm greasing on the side, the clan renovated their ancestral seat and on the same plot, built a larger reproduction cottage in reclaimed stone where a derelict barn had once stood. The two toffee-coloured houses stood out from the whitewashed norm, happy snapper delights peering over the garden wall at the hurly burly of a town on the march.

The varnish was barely dry when the spruced up manor attracted the attention of two evicted Brits looking for somewhere new to lay their hats.

'This is it,' I had said as we explored the renovated house. 'The real deal.'

The original family home had an unconventional higgledy-piggledy open plan charm and came with working fireplaces and a converted basement once used to corral livestock, the kind of place you'd imagine the Madonna pitching up to on Christmas Eve, heavy with the Messiah and looking for a budget manger.

Liam wasn't entirely convinced. 'Do I look like an ass?'

We tried the house next door. The larger and perfectly formed replica had been constructed in traditional Aegean style – thick stone walls, flat roof and exposed wooden beams – and came with newfangled luxuries like rooms and doors.

'Is special wood,' said our potential landlady, pointing down at the oak floor as we toured the mezzanine bedroom. 'From special forest.'

The special wood from the special forest came at a special price but as Bodrum had always provided refuge to the exiled and the unorthodox, we gambled on getting the going rate for 'theatrical' types. Supplemented by Liam's feeble but endearing attempts at Turkish, the gamble paid off and Hanife the Magnificent, the undisputed matriarch of an old Bodrum family, accepted us and our pink pounds with open hands. We paid our rent and two weeks later, moved into Stone Cottage No. 2 on the corner of Sentry Lane and Turkey Street. And so it came to pass that by happy coincidence we found ourselves living on the same road as the Mausoleum at Halicarnassus, one of the Seven Wonders of the Ancient World.

'I think,' Liam had said at the time, 'you would call that a result.'

Our new landlady was a tiny but formidable ex-teacher, a gutsy pensioner with a shock of silver running through a neat black bob. Hanife lived with her doting husband in a three-storey townhouse on the opposite side of Turkey Street, a nondescript concrete block with a side yard of rapacious chickens. She may have been pleased with her colourful new tenants and happy to put up with their aberrant ways, but Hanife was fiercely proud of her heritage and took every opportunity to educate her stooges in the ways of Turkish sensibilities.

'*Londra?*' she had announced as we handed over an envelope stuffed with fifty lira notes. 'Ha! You run like stupid rats in tunnels of metro. Is no life! In Turkey, we live!'

If Hanife appeared unruffled by our exotic union then she was equally nonplussed by the arrival, a few weeks later, of Beril and Vadim, a maverick and unwed Turkish couple who had escaped the conformity of Ankara to take possession of Stone House No. 1 and join us in the garden of sin. Vadim was a retired rock and roller, a portly, rosy-cheeked percussionist in his late fifties, obsessed with drums and wedded to his collection of Turkish *darbuka*s.

'What's the big deal?' said Liam after the first deafening assault on our eardrums. 'They're only bongos.'

Over time, we had both acquired a reverential respect for Vadim's musical bent and would occasionally spy him and Beril through an open window reclining Ottoman style on carpet-covered floor cushions, calves entwined, staring at the low Biblical beams and marvelling at the intricacies of a Hendrix wah-wah. It was Woodstock all over again – all that was missing were the joss sticks, doped up beatniks and Joni Mitchell in a kaftan.

Beril was a good decade younger than her rhythm and blues man and bore more than a passing resemblance to Kate Bush in her Home Counties years. She tolerated Vadim's banging with good grace but preferred the gloomy Gallic romanticism of Charles Aznavour to the guitar riffs of Eric Clapton. She also had a volcanic temper and a fuse the length of a Swan Vesta. Beril's capricious tendencies resulted in regular breaches of the peace, her full throttle explosions always directed at Vadim and always without warning. She may have been small but Beril had the operatic lungs of a Wagnerian Brünnhilde and didn't seem the least bit concerned that we could hear every high-octave salvo. Vadim took his punishment like a man and rarely responded in kind. It was clear that he adored his little firecracker and when the rows spilled out into the courtyard, he would lean up against the old tree and simply say, '*Evet, aşkım*, yes, my love.' When the volleys subsided, as they always did, he would smile and say sorry for something he hadn't done, and that was that. We were yet to discover the source of Beril's wrath.

Our efforts to learn Turkish had just about reached the 'mine's a large one' stage and their grasp of English was rudimentary at best. Besides, we were generally content not knowing what all the fuss was about. In many ways, our ignorance helped us cope with the intimacy of our cheek by jowl existence.

'It could be worse,' I had said when Beril and Vadim ran into the garden for the first time and hugged us like long-lost friends. 'We could have been lumbered with a couple of old stick-in-the-muds rolling out the prayer mats. Those two are as damned as we are.'

Our first Bodrum summer passed in a hot flash. Days, weeks and months raced by as we set up home, lolled our way through the hairdryer heat, explored the narrow network of lanes branching out like veins from the harbour or caught the breeze on our large first-floor balcony. Liam took every opportunity to improve his pidgin Turkish, pouncing on unsuspecting Bodrumites as they sipped their *çay* in the municipal tea house. It met with limited success. Nearly all of them wanted to practice their English, not listen to their mother tongue being savaged by a stuttering heretic.

Most evenings, Liam would fire up the lanterns swinging from the branches of the old olive tree, Vadim would crack open the *rakı* and the stage would be set for our regular Bacchanalia. We would dine to an eclectic soundtrack of Dylan, Santana and *Sing it Again Rod* courtesy of our newly acquired communards, sometimes sharing our al fresco tables, sometimes nesting on our side of the garden screened by a dusty clump of pink oleanders. Occasionally, Liam and his MP3 player would treat the neighbourhood to a sprinkling of Dusty, a medley from *Glee* or if they were really unlucky, Kathryn Grayson and Howard Keel warbling through *Stranger in Paradise* in crackled mono. We communicated with our new neighbours through a none too effective combination of grunts, mimes and dog-eared dictionaries or by taking advantage of one of the bilingual guests Beril and Vadim would occasionally invite along to the party.

Mini dishes of Turkish tasters flew out from Beril's kitchen as she launched her mission to spice up our bland English palates, something she approached with the unrestrained fervour of a TV evangelist. Like her parents before her, Beril had never ventured into Europe beyond the city limits of old Istanbul but had heard terrible tales about British cuisine, a culinary travesty, all fish 'n' chips, pork scratchings, over-boiled carrots, scurvy and mad cow disease.

'Eat!' she would scream, sliding another exotic sample onto our table. 'Is good. Eat!'

We would comply like scolded children, tucking into her braised artichoke hearts, garlic-roasted aubergines, sautéed spinach or white bean goo, salivating even before the first mouthful.

'*Süper!*' we would shout over to Beril as she puffed on a Black Russian Sobranie, looking on and waiting for every last scrap to be devoured. '*Le-zz-et-li!* De-li-cious!'

Now and then, our no-nonsense landlady would pop by with something to challenge the gag reflex – her speciality tripe soup, a lethal mixture of cow's stomach and mutton cheeks served with a tongue-stripping spoonful of garlic and vinegar sauce. We later discovered that Hanife's regular deliveries of *işkembe çorbası* said more about our drinking habits than her generosity. It was the local cure for hurricane hangovers.

'You stupid Engleesh,' she would bark at Liam when he clattered through the twisted gate of her urban farm to pay the rent. '*Şarap, şarap*! Is always wine! Drink our Turkish water!'

It was sage advice. Bodrum's south-facing aspect and natural amphitheatre of low hills pushed summer temperatures up to the mid-forties and when the onslaught continued, we wilted like parched pansies.

Autumn came as a merciful relief. Nights cooled, fans were packed away and we reacquainted ourselves with the inside of the house, lounging on the sofa, ploughing through our secret stash of chick lit or screaming at Liam's *Turkish for Idiots* CD as it confirmed and reconfirmed that our foreign language skills were close to tragic. Liam's assertion that Turkish was phonetic and mostly regular fell on deaf ears; my love affair with the language of the sultans was cooling as quickly as the weather. For his irritating party trick, Liam would belt out an absurd example of Turkish agglutination, revelling in its complexity as if he had suddenly discovered the secret to eternal youth.

'*Avustralyalılaştıramadıklarımızdanmışsınızcasına!*' he would bellow, pausing only to gauge my reaction before continuing with his equally irritating translation.

'As if you were one of those whom we could not make resemble the Australian people!' he would say, all wide-eyed and gushy. 'Isn't that amazing?'

'Yeah, amazing,' I would reply. 'So what's Turkish for *As if you were one of those whom we could not stop annoying the fuck out of your long suffering husband*? Give it rest, Liam, and pass the *şarap*.'

From time to time we would venture out from the comfort of our Sentry Lane haven and meander into town for an autumn mingle. As luck would have it, we accidently gate-crashed the infamous Ladies Lunch at the Marina, an annual handbag and shoes fest, top billing on the emigrey social almanac. Everyone who was anyone was there with their tits and teeth out on display. It was at the Ladies Lunch that we encountered a select group of Bodrum vetpats, a trio of irresistible women with irrepressible courage under fire. Through a drunken haze of vodka and pomegranate schnapps, they force-fed us chocolate torte and extracted our story. Tiffin and tittle-tattle with the three Bodrum Belles would become a regular feature of our Turkish days. Sometimes, we would ride out to the Peninsula, lunching by the water's edge or taking front row seats for the bittersweet Charlotte and Alan show as the turbulence of an adoption gone wrong swirled around them.

When the dial of the garden thermometer started its inevitable dip towards the low teens, Beril and Vadim gradually disappeared from view, abandoning outdoor life for the cosiness of their old stone house. Like all our neighbours, they were preparing for the big change, knowing all too well that autumn was on the wane. But nothing, not even the threat of Wuthering Lows blowing down from the Russian Steppes could upset the equilibrium of Jack Scott and Liam Brennan.

CHAPTER TWO

TURKEY STREET

It was still dark when Liam boarded the early morning bus to Bodrum Airport. Barely awake, he slumped into a window seat and adjusted his eyes to the cold light of the Havaş coach. A restless night of thunder and hard rain had left him dull-minded and he struggled to focus through the misted window. Outside, the storm had calmed to a penetrating drizzle as the wind squeezed the last drops of water from the clouds. Shopkeepers and bus drivers huddled together under the bulging awning of a small *kafe*, sipping steaming tea and swapping hearsay before another day of hard bargaining and short hops.

Liam spotted me in the small crowd of well-wishers and launched into a passable Mary Pickford, sobbing melodramatically and pressing his lips to the coach window.

You're an idiot, I mouthed. *A complete idiot.*

The driver turned the ignition and slowly reversed the bus from the bay, swinging round towards the *otogar* exit. Liam dashed to the opposite window and traced a sad face in the condensation. For the second time in a month, he was jetting off to deal with a family crisis and I waved goodbye as the airport express disappeared into the narrow streets of Bodrum. He may have been an idiot, but Liam was my idiot and I hated to see him go.

Tired and dripping, I waded past rows of sleeping *dolmuş* minibuses – 'dollies', as Liam called them – and splashed home along Turkey Street. Twenty-three centuries earlier, Alexander the Great had marched along the very same road to wrest old Halicarnassus from the doughty Persians, just before he went on to conquer half the known world. My ambitions were rather more modest: to survive the short stroll in one piece and jump back under the duck down duvet. Like many old Anatolian thoroughfares, Turkey Street was just wide enough for two emaciated camels to pass each other unhindered. This constraint never seemed to trouble the locals but for us, motorcades of Nissan tanks flanked by Vespas on amphetamines made for a testing pedestrian experience. Aided by the now-you-see-them-now-you-don't pavements, death or permanent disability lurked at every twist and turn of the perilous road.

At the first blind bend I was greeted by our neighbourhood *berber*, a man who crimped for a pittance six days a week and seemed as happy as a ringtone doing precisely that. In fact, we had never seen Ali without his unnerving perma-grin.

'Maybe he's just happy,' I had said to Liam.

'All of the time? And what's with the Ali Berber thing? Honestly…'

Despite the frozen smile, or maybe because of it, we became regulars at Ali's shabby but squeaky-clean barber shop, paying over the odds for our two minute crops. Through a mixture of Turklish and creative hand signalling, we would chat about the rising price of meat, the cycle of the seasons or the latest Government diktat.

Ali was sweeping out a paddling pool from the front of his shop. An obligatory picture of Atatürk was nailed above a cracked sink and the morning news blared from an old TV set hanging off the wall. I waved.

'*Yağmur*… rain!' he announced as I passed, his eyes raised to the heavens. '*Allah Allah*!'

I stumbled on a pothole outside the artists' café and cursed. The place was boarded up for winter and judging by the bowed and broken terracotta roof, the esoteric canvases hanging inside were unlikely to survive the monsoon unscathed. The tiny shoe shop opposite was never open at any time of year. A permanent display of shoe boxes was stacked high against one side of the plate-glass window and a solitary pair of red Mary Janes sat gathering dust on the other.

A sharp shower quickened my pace and powered me past Spring Lane and on to Halfway Square, a low-rise quadrangle with a rundown children's playground at its centre. On the corner, a miniature mosque was part buried in tarmac. Turkey Street had built up around it, year on year, layer by layer. Its single mini-minaret scored the rolling blanket of low cloud.

I checked my phone.

'Jack, there's a man on the coach with come to bed eyes and a one way ticket to Kurdistan. I've decided to

follow him and breed goats on the Iraqi border. See Ya. Liam.'

I hurried across the street to a small cluster of shops – a ladies *kuaför* with a trio of bonnet-hood hair dryers, a tatty laundrette with plastic chairs, a small market shop and the Stone Oven bakery – and sheltered under a wooden canopy. My stumpy thumbs struggled to reply to Liam's text. A young bread maker in a nylon hairnet, checked trousers and blue latex gloves took a break from his kneading, retrieved a cigarette from the flap of his flour-dusted apron and lit up next to me. He was soon joined by the owner of the market, a balding hippy, his side strands pulled back and fashioned into a pony tail. Marketman accepted a light from Breadmaker and they both nodded in my direction. We huddled in silent communion, together but quite separate.

'You'd look like an old drag queen mucking out goats as wife no. 3. Besides, your arse is way too skinny for saggy pantaloons. Back to Plan A.' Send.

Our attention was diverted by the rattling of a wooden cart steered by a humpbacked rag and bone man, his dusty brown suit two-toned by the rain. A frayed collar poked out of a patchwork cardigan, and an embroidered pillbox hat was balanced precariously on the side of his head. The old man stopped at a row of overflowing communal bins and saw off a cluster of alley cats with a brusque side swipe.

'Siktir git!'

A quick filter through the castoffs produced a battered coffee maker and he examined it forensically, rubbing it clean with the cuff of his jacket. He placed the swag into his cart and shuffled off to his next scavenge, whistling as he went.

Just get on with it, Jack. It could be worse. You could be working for a living.

By the time I had opened our wood-panelled gate at Sentry Lane, the rain had petered out and a reticent sun was peeking through a small crack in the clouds. I pulled up the sodden bath towel draped across the bottom of the front door and wrung it out into a flower bed. Bitter experience and floating rugs had taught us that Mad Mother Nature, or at least Turkey's madder twin sister, could douse the house like a crazy car wash, pumping water under every sill and transforming Turkey Street into a raging torrent. Sometimes, without hint or warning, blue sky dreams turned to black, and sometimes Liam would leave me to stoke the embers and wring out the sodding sodden towels.

Liam called in the small hours.

'Jack?'

'Who else would it be? What's up?'

'Nothing.'

'Are you crying, Liam?'

'No.'

'Where are you?'

'In bed.'

'On the Iraqi border?'

'North Finchley. I might be longer than I thought.'

'Oh?'

'Is that a good Oh or a bad Oh?'

'Take as long as you like, Liam.'

'I miss you.'

'It's only been a few hours.'

'I guess that means something, Jack.'

'You married me, didn't you?'

'I was drunk.'

I turned on the bedside lamp and sat up in bed.

'Liam?'

'What?'

'Call every day or I'll take up with Ali Berber.'

'The wife may have something to say about that.'

'As long as she gets the housekeeping, she won't care. Get some sleep, Liam.'

'I just wanted to say goodnight, that's all.'

'Who's stopping you?'

'You say it first.'

'Liam, just put the bloody phone down.'

CHAPTER THREE

HOME ALONE

'Eat, eat!' insisted Beril, pointing at a dish of spinach and eggs. 'Eat!'

My fiery courtyard companion was determined to keep my pecker up. With Liam a continent away and Vadim buying more bongos in Ankara, she doubled my rations. The offerings were left on our patio table, freshly cooked, spooned into earthenware bowls and artfully decorated with dill, parsley or chives. It was like meals on wheels for the lost and lonely and it became a daily donation. As promised, Liam called every day, assuring me that all would be well even though neither of us thought it would be. He nagged me to steer clear of Marketman's corked wine ('It'll give you gut rot'), take regular walks by the Aegean ('Sea air wards off dementia, I read it in *Marie Claire*'), and keep away from the boys at the *pazar* ('You'll only pick up a nasty discharge'). He also reminded me to switch the hot water supply. With winter lurking on the horizon and the first fat rains already upon us, it was time to shut off the solar panels and fire up the winter boiler.

When it came to the biannual flat roof shuffle, Liam had unilaterally decided that my nimble limbs were better suited for buildering up the side of the house without the aid of a safety rope.

'Look, Jack,' he had said, 'just climb onto the kitchen roof, shimmy under the canopy of the olive tree, leap across to Beril and Vadim's house and the stopcock's right there under your nose. It's not difficult. You know how to shimmy, don't you?'

When I asked Hanife about the hot water arrangement, she shrugged her shoulders and presented me with a crock of her tripe soup by way of compensation. Somehow, it didn't feel like a fair exchange for risking a broken neck. The unconventional set-up was one of life's great mysteries, like trigonometry, the Immaculate Conception and Donald Trump's comb over.

I retrieved the rotting ladder from the corner of the garden – a death trap held together by rusting nails – and dragged it across to the house. Beril dashed out to help with the climb, her screeches of encouragement only serving to scare off Bianca, her demented kitten, a ball of white fur riddled with neuroses and imaginary fleas. As my backside edged over the parapet, an olive branch snagged the waistband of my sweatpants and tugged them down to reveal the velvety cleavage of my milky white buttocks. I rolled my eyes, instantly regretting my decision to go commando. Beril gasped and shielded her eyes as I moondanced free from the offending branch. Eventually, it lashed back, horsewhipping my behind and cluster-bombing adolescent olives over me, the roof and the entire courtyard. Beril regained her composure with alarming speed, gathering up handfuls of olives and cackling wildly as she hurled them back at me.

'Yes, Beril,' I yelled down. 'Funny. Very funny.'

By the time I was back on terra firma and struggling to recover what was left of my dignity, Beril had prepared my reward: boiling hot *şekerli kahve* and a side order of mini Turkish delights. I had never quite developed a taste for sweet and gritty Turkish coffee, but it would have been churlish to refuse and besides, Beril was sitting opposite watching every teeth-rotting sip.

'So?' I said. 'What's with the look?'

'So?' she replied, mimicking me but doing her best not to smirk. 'Is good?'

I popped a Turkish delight in my mouth. 'Yes. Is very good. Thank you, Beril.'

'No problem. *Ark-a-daş-lar,*' she said slowly, offering her hand across the table. 'Friends. Yes?'

'Yes,' I answered, cupping her hand, suddenly touched by her warmth, not to mention her improving English. 'Friends. Has a nice ring to it.'

She took out a small package wrapped in an old cover of Turkish *Hello* from a bag by her side.

'And now… gift,' she said quietly. 'For you.'

'Why thank you, Beril. That's very kind.'

'And for Liam.'

'He's back tonight, Liam.'

'Is good?'

'Oh yes, Beril, is very good.'

Beril beamed and with job done leapt up from the table to gather up the empties.

'So,' she announced, 'I *telefon* Vadim. Ankara. Okay?'

'Of course,' I said. 'Say hello.'

'*Tamam*. Say hello. Okay.'

Within minutes, the sound of shrieking slammed through Beril's open door. Arsegate was out.

Liam arrived home just as the sun was setting. The dining table was dressed to perfection for his return. Long-stemmed candles cast shadows on the desert-coloured walls and an open bottle of red sat begging to be drunk.

'So?' I asked. 'How was it?'

'Oh, you know.'

Liam gazed over at the dining table.

'Quite a spread. Expecting royalty?'

'Just some sad old queen I know.'

A spicy aroma seeped from the kitchen.

'And you've cooked?'

'Not unless you call throwing a few chicken thighs into the oven "cooking", no.'

My culinary skills left a great deal to be desired, but even this ham-fisted line cook could rustle up a one pot wonder without sparking an international incident. My signature dish was a random medley of vegetables, spices and wine, flung into a Pyrex dish.

'And the excitement doesn't end there,' I said as we took our seats at the table.

I pointed to a dish of oily green gloop glistening in the candlelight.

'What is it?' asked Liam.

'Hanife made it.'

'That was nice of her. Is it edible?'

'Why don't you try?'

'So, has Jack been a good boy while Daddy's been away?'

'Actually, Jack's started a blog.'

Liam looked up from his supper.

'A blog?'

'Yes, Liam. A blog… about us.'

'Who the hell would want to read a blog about us?'

'No one apparently. Not yet anyway.'

'Oh.'

Liam dipped a teaspoon into Hanife's goo and yawned.

'Long day?'

'Long week, Jack.'

'So? How was it? You've hardly said a word.'

'It all went according to plan,' said Liam, screwing up his face as a layer of green gunk stuck to the roof of his mouth. 'Dad went in for his knee op and I stepped into the breach.'

'That's it?'

'That's it.'

'You know you can fly home whenever you need to.'

'Sure. At a cost.'

'Look, Liam. Some things are more important than money.'

Liam gave up on Hanife's gruel and heaped a pile of rice onto his plate.

'I do love you, Jack.'

'That, my husband, is the right answer.'

After dinner, we plumped up the scatter cushions and curled up on the sofa for a night at the movies, courtesy of Beril and her mystery package, an American import DVD. *Under the Tuscan Sun* was a touching tale of a Yankee lass whose marriage collapsed around her when she wasn't paying attention. She emerged from the wreckage to carve out a new life in Tuscany, all quite by chance. It was a ridiculous, sentimental, sugar-coated yarn about life regained in Expatland. We devoured it and cried like babies. It was 'boo' to the bastard who dumped her and 'hoorah' for the cast of colourful characters who picked her up, dusted her down and helped her start all over again. In real life, of course, not everyone was quite so nice. In our experience, the overeager Shirley Valentines who washed up like driftwood on Turkey's shores were often on a hiding to nothing. Plucked, banged then blown out when the cash dried up, the orchestra of ladies kept on coming anyway, scouting Turkey's resorts for love and orgasms. Hope over experience usually prevailed. But Beril's gift contained an altogether different kind of message. When the saccharin heroine first arrived in Italy, she found herself swept up in the middle of a gay coach tour, surrounded by a botoxed crew of clichéd clones with shiny veneers and Touche Éclat'd cheeks. Beril had picked up the subplot and was telling us something she had found difficult to say directly. *I know about you two. And it's cool.*

Liam retired as soon as the closing credits started to roll, flopping into bed and leaving a familiar stack of clothes piled on the floor, rising up like a Cappadocian cave house. At best, Liam's approach to domestic order had always been laissez-faire. During our salad days, I would return from work to find a shoe on the mantelpiece or a freshly laundered jockstrap in the fridge next to the crème fraîche. It was his way of telling me to lighten up. Eventually, I took the hint and as the years passed, Liam raised his game and I lowered mine. Now, when he cooked, it no longer resembled Sarajevo during the Balkan conflict and with my OCD seriously reined in, we had arrived at a contented compromise. Apart from one small thing. When Liam retired for the night, he would slip out of his clothes and leave them in a concertinaed heap. Shoes poked out from under crumpled jeans that sat untidily beneath a half unbuttoned shirt. It was as if he had disappeared through a trap door with David Blaine and a puff of white smoke.

I crept upstairs, stepped around the floordrobe, folded my clothes on the tub chair and slipped under the matrimonial covers. For a moment, Liam gripped me like a vice then turned over and dropped into a deep sleep. I stayed awake, staring at his shrouded outline and listening to the dull hum of Turkey Street.

CHAPTER FOUR

IN THE BLEAK MIDWINTER

As Christmas approached, night time temperatures plummeted to zero and we exiled ourselves to a corner of the sofa in front of an infrared heater. Our faces tanned while our backsides froze. Liam extracted his Dennis the Menace jimjams from the bottom of the wardrobe, unrolled the woolly socks, recommissioned the hot water bottle and upped the tog on the duvet. In bed, we weaved together, drawn to each other's body heat, our limbs knotted like a plaited loaf at the bottom of a tepid oven. Daytime activities were stretched to fill the time and chilly evenings kept us under wraps as we exhausted our extensive DVD library with regular showings of classics from good times past: *Priscilla Queen of the Desert, Beautiful Thing, Love Actually, The Holiday, Calendar Girls, Postcards from the Edge, Golden Girls* (Series 1-4), *Gimme, Gimme, Gimme* (Series 1-3) and a host of other manly favourites.

The Siberian cold front continued unabated and a viral dark fungus spread faster than the Black Death in the dank corners of our stone house. Cutting edge building technology – air bricks and cavity walls – had yet to catch on in Turkey, and Liam advised me to stop breathing and so prevent the evil spores from damaging my ageing lungs. His attempts at hitting back with a Domestos-filled water cannon met with limited success, and in the end we adopted the Turkish approach: utter resignation. We would let the place rot over winter and make good when we eventually came out of mothballs. Turkey being Turkey, sun and storms played good cop, bad cop and as the meteorological drama continued, it wreaked havoc on our power supply. Liam suspected water damage and when he threw open the door of the fuse box, a flimsy container inexplicably set into an outside wall, his worst fears were realised: lines of rainwater were dribbling down the live wires. Vadim rode to the rescue and attached Beril's Babyliss to an extension lead but after an hour blowing hot air at the saturated wires, he retreated to his bongos a defeated man.

We summoned the Royal Marines in the form of our indomitable landlady. Hanife the Resourceful swung into action and dispatched her half pint distant cousin, the youngest and tiniest electrician that side of the Aegean. No more than four and a half feet in his socks and with the hands of a foundling, the acne-faced sparky could only reach the fuse box by standing on a folding garden chair. We watched from the wings as he tiptoed precariously on the edge. Liam checked our liability insurance and I went for a lie down in a darkened room. Progress was slow but studious. Acneface fiddled with the fuses for hours, oozing confidence and reknitting the mass of wires like a seasoned village weaver. At last, his work was done and when he flicked on the kitchen light and the infrared heater fired up, young Faraday smiled a satisfied smile. His excitement reached disco pitch when the air-conditioning unit powered up as Liam switched on the kettle. Finally, through a tortuous process of trial and error, he concluded that the root of the problem was an unexplained surge in one of the ring circuits. To test his theory, he plugged in the Wi-Fi modem. Bang went the modem. He plugged in the TV. Bang went the surge protector. He plugged in the water heater. Bang went the circuit board. As a flume of smoke filled the house, bang went our tempers and we threw Acneface out onto the street.

Hanife and her charge returned early the next morning.

'He is cousin,' she said. 'But he is fool. I have extracted confession.'

'Extracted?' asked Liam.

'Yes. He will pay.'

'Thank you, but there was no need to waterboard the poor boy on our account.'

Hanife handed Liam a small dish containing an oblong of milky chicken jelly.

'Is gift. I make.'

'Thank you.'

'*Tavuk göğsü.*'

'I'm sure Jack will love it.'

'So,' said Hanife. 'My cousin, not electrician.'

'He's not?'

'*Yok.* No. Is water technician.'

'You mean he's a plumber?'

'Yes, plumber. He make electrics when we make house.'

'But he's just a boy.'

'Fifteen now, a man.' Hanife reconsidered her answer. 'Then, fourteen.'

Liam placed the pungent jelly onto the patio table and looked over at the boy.

'A fourteen year old plumber installed the electrics in this house? The house we're living in?'

'*Evet*. Yes. Is very dangerous. You must be careful when choosing house. Is not England.'

I stepped through the French doors to see what all the fuss was about.

'Ah, Jack. Look what Hanife's brought you.'

'Is it for the cat?'

'Just look pleased and thank the nice old lady. And, Jack…'

'Yes, Liam?'

'This house is a death trap and I hold you entirely responsible. Just so we're clear.'

As it turned out, temperamental electrics were the least of our worries. The following morning, Liam tuned the radio to *TRT Türkü,* cracked some eggs into a pan and it came to him, just in the nick of time. We had forgotten to renew our residence permits.

'Before we know it, we'll be clapped in irons and carted off in the back of a paddy wagon,' he said, plonking a flaccid omelette in front of me. 'Imagine that. We've got a fortnight and then… it's curtains.'

From the previous year's merry-go-round, we knew that obtaining the elusive blue book would be a bureaucratic whirl. Still, as it was impossible for most Turks to enter Britain at all, even for a holiday, the powers that be were quite forgiving, considering. That year, the bean counters in Ankara had upped the ante. As well as doubling the fee, presumably to raise a few extra bob for the national debt, they now required applicants to prove they were fit and proper persons who wouldn't offend the morals of the nation. We would have to make ourselves known to our local *Muhtar* and be subject to a cross-examination by an officer of the constabulary. Given our growing infamy, we thought the morality test might be a bit of a stretch.

'Let's face it,' I said as we sat at the dining table to fill out the applications, 'the game's up. They'll take one look at you and we'll be shoved on the first plane back to Sodom.'

'Have faith, my little pervert. This is Bodrum. It's got form. We just need to woo the local bigwig.'

'Us?'

'Ah, maybe not *us*,' said Liam, grabbing his house keys and flouncing off into the garden. 'Wait here. I've got an idea.'

A woman on a mission led us in single file along the edge of Turkey Street.

'Come!' Hanife commanded. 'Come!'

Passers-by waved to our redoubtable landlady as she weaved us through the stop-start traffic, and washer women hollered *merhaba* as they hung out their laundry in the winter sunshine. No knickers, of course. That *would* have offended the morals of the nation, even in Bodrum. When we reached Halfway Square, Hanife took a moment to pass the time of day with Marketman, thanked him for an impromptu gift of dried carob pods and nattered with Ali Berber when he emerged from the Stone Oven bakery clasping his sticky lunch. More locals appeared from the backstreets and mobbed our stately patron. It was like escorting the Queen on a walkabout and we kicked our heels until Her Maj was ready for the off.

When she was done, Hanife took a sharp right and frogmarched us along Spring Lane, stopping at a narrow shop unit set back from the street.

'In, in!' she barked, bundling us through the paint-chipped doorway. '*Muhtar!* Is *Muhtar!*'

The small den reeked of testosterone, sweat and ashtrays, and a thick fog of cigarette smoke hung in the air. The shabby rectangular room was dominated by a large desk and behind it sat the head man. He was no oil painting. Drooping cauliflower ears were stuck awkwardly to the side of his head and a bulbous nose was underlined by a Stalinesque moustache. The *Muhtar* was surrounded by courtiers lining the walls like a Papal conclave, each one a facsimile of their illustrious leader. Hanife cut through the smoke and the *Muhtar* jumped to his feet. When he flustered, fawned and flattered, we knew we were standing in the shadow of Bodrum royalty and looked on admiringly as Hanife pointed back at her new tenants and handed over our forms. With barely a cursory glance, our paperwork was officially stamped with the official stamp of the official stamper and our sponsor shooed us back out into the street. It was all done in an instant and, mission accomplished, Hanife trooped us back home and deposited us at the junction of Sentry Lane.

'Is done,' she said. 'Now Bodrum is home. Go!'

We filed into our courtyard. Voices murmured from the garden as we closed the gate behind us. Vadim was seated at our patio table, deep in conversation with a policeman and Beril was buzzing round them, uncharacteristically compliant, smiling sweetly and serving tea like the good housewife she wasn't. The copper, a strapping lad with deadly good looks and a deadly weapon stuffed into his holster, stood up and offered us his hand. Vadim beckoned us to join the table and Beril served more tea before retreating to her kitchen.

A protracted Turkish conversation ensued, obviously about us but not actually including us. We sat back, wrists rigid, feigning comprehension and nodding manly nods when it seemed appropriate to do so. We caught the odd word – *kardeşler, para, iyi, İngilizce* for brothers, money, good and English – but as the two men rabbited on at breakneck speed, there was little more we could do other than keep up our macho disguise. Our inquisitor appeared inquisitive rather than inquisitorial, curious rather than officious, occasionally glancing at the unlikely 'brothers' in amusement. At the end of the interrogation, he rose from his seat, shook us by the hand and swaggered off into Turkey Street. Somehow or other, Vadim had thrown the dashing bloodhound off the scent, presumably by passing us off as harmless lovey types with a few quid in the bank. Two weeks later, we laid our offending gay hands on our little blue residence permits, thin and flimsy things that looked like they had been run off on a Hewlett Packard and bound together with Pritt Stick. Just in time for Christmas. Glory be to God. Amen.

CHAPTER FIVE

A CHRISTMAS CAROL

We breezed past the hoi polloi like minor celebs and fast-tracked into the business class lounge of Bodrum Airport. Liam was less than impressed. It was the last few days of Advent and he was longing for *Hark the Herald* and a dressed Norwegian spruce straddled by a startled fairy. Our upgrade had come courtesy of Air Miles and our elevation to posh had raised Liam's expectations beyond all reason. The place looked like it had been styled by World of Leather and the much anticipated complimentary fodder turned out to be a narrow selection of local spirits and a bucket of dry croissants. We opted instead for coffee on tap and a two-man white leather pouffe. Liam looked around for a dollop of celebrity. Clare Balding would have done. The funny looking one from Little Mix, even. He took a sip from a chipped porcelain cup and spat it out.

'So this is it. Luxury. Vile coffee and nobody famous. Things can only get better.'

Things got marginally worse on the short hop to Istanbul, a frenetic hour that passed in a flash with a rushed slurp of flat bubbly, microwaved snacks and an assortment of fixed-grin waitresses. Still, the brief stopover at Istanbul's Atatürk Airport offered a visual feast of pick 'n' mix travellers, a heady blend of shiny business suits and ethno-religious finery.

Liam fixed his gaze on a troupe of silver-bearded oddballs wrapped in glo-white togas, milling around like extras from *The Ten Commandments*.

'Oh, Moses, Moses! Why of all men did I fall in love with the prince of fools?'

'That's a question I ask myself every single day of my life, Liam. Cut the biblical shit, you're no Nefrertiri.'

'And you're no Charlton Heston, more's the pity.'

'They're not even Jewish.'

'Look at the beards, look at the sandals. Think plagues of Egypt, think murderous asps.'

'The asp was Cleopatra, Liam.'

'But I am the Pharaoh's daughter and this is my son!'

'Just to be clear, Liam, when we get Christmas out of the way, you're dumped.'

Istanbul's faux Ottoman business lounge was up a notch or two from Bodrum but the leather luxury was more Las Vegas than Topkapı Palace. Disappointingly, the coffee was still vile and the limitless booze still limited. Liam passed the time by constructing a baby Jesus from pieces of cinnamon swirls while I dipped into a selection of international newspapers. The British choice was confined to *The Times* and *The Daily Mail*. Clearly, only Middle England travelled Club Class. Once on board, Turkish Airlines pulled out all the stops, delivering us to cattle class seats and disguising the gruel by slopping it into miniature china crockery. Liam took a shine to the toytown cutlery and contemplated sliding it into his man bag. When his spoon failed to puncture the nuked plum sponge and bent in half, he quickly thought better of it. The much vaunted entertainment selection was an obscure disaster movie that may as well have been subtitled *Bad Acting on a Runaway Train, Everyone Dies Except Denzel Washington* and when everyone started to die except Denzel Washington, we considered pulling the emergency cord.

'Ding Dong Merrily on High,' muttered Liam.

'Oh, come on, we've got the high,' I said, grabbing champagne from a disapproving trolley dolly. 'Let's work on the merry.'

The flight to Heathrow was our last chance to grab time together before the Christmas offensive and we made the most of it. Liam ordered Jägerbombs to accompany the fizz and by the time the Boeing had touched down, we were sated, horizontal and ready for the Queen's Speech.

'This is it, then,' I said to Liam at the Paddington Station taxi rank. 'Time for you to leave me. Again.'

'Don't be such a drama queen. It's just a few days.'

'And time for me to start my grand tour of the Capital relying on the kindness of strangers.'

'You're staying with your sister in Tooting, Jack.'

Behind us, a Sally Army band launched into *Good King Wenceslas* and above the taxi rank, the station tannoy blasted out a hissing version of *Little Donkey*. I groaned. I'd had a guts-full already. 'If I hear one more sodding carol...'

A plump, warm-faced woman passed by swathed in Horn of Africa robes, her lurid outfit puncturing the drabness. A young boy skipped next to her humming *Jingle Bells* over and over. Liam caught me crack a smile.

'So, Jack Scott does festive. Gawd bless yer, Mr Scrooge, gawd bless yer.'

'Liam, if there's one thing I hate, it's a smug do-gooder with a Tiny Tim story. Here's your taxi, say goodbye and sod off.'

We hugged hard and I disappeared into the crowd, ignoring the commuters and dragging my case through the mass of late Christmas shoppers and pissed up suits. Within minutes, I morphed into one of them, joining the cast of thousands in a recreation of the Blitz. Stoic Londoners pickled by corporate booze and emptied of Christmas cheer, descended into the Stygian gloom of the Underground like miserable lemmings. Stiff upper lips prayed to the baby Jesus for Armageddon, anything to get them through Judgement Day, soaring suicide rates and the hell that was about to pass. Christmas had barely begun, but I was already longing for the sound of Vadim's bongos.

An arctic snap promised snow but didn't deliver. In a North Finchley kitchen, *Fairytale of New York* piped out from an old radio as Liam fussed over the festive lunch. A small turkey lay resting on a serving plate, covered in foil. He opened the oven door to a swirl of hot smoke and the kitchen window steamed up spontaneously, masking the view of a frosted suburban lawn. He muttered to himself as he shook the Maris Pipers for the umpteenth time, slipping a tray of parsnips onto the top rack and transferring the hot muffin tin to a trivet by the side of the sink. *What a faff.* Saint Delia said Teutonic timing was the key to a slap-up Christmas lunch, but Liam reckoned his efforts were more British Rail than Deutsche Bahn. With the prepping done and the Yorkshires rising, he poured himself a beer and joined the others in the front room. Liam Senior was still cranky from the discomfort of his knee operation and grunted from behind *The Irish Times*. His wife sat opposite, giggling enthusiastically as an old video of *Mr Bean* jumped from one farcical scene to another. Cathleen had finally let the dye grow out of her hair and newly acquired silver curls swept down across her forehead. Liam's younger brother, Sean, was supported by a pillow in his high back chair, his wheelchair folded away in the corner of the room. He grinned at Liam and went back to flicking through the old photos and postcards he always kept by his side in a dented old biscuit tin. Liam took a seat at the dining table and played with the place settings. All was calm. Earlier in the day, Cathleen's attempt to coax Sean down from the bathroom had almost seen them both in a heap at the bottom of the stairs.

Cathleen looked up from the screen. 'It's about time you moved out, son. You can't stay here forever.'

'I haven't lived at home since my teens, Mum. I live in Turkey now, with Jack.'

'Course you do,' she said, picking up the remote control and turning up the volume as Mr Bean lost his wristwatch up the rear end of a large Norfolk Black. 'Jack. We like Jack.'

The oven pinged. Liam went back into the kitchen and strained the gravy. The prodigal son had returned, albeit briefly, to mop brows, smooth the edges and cook the perfect Christmas dinner.

CHAPTER SIX

TURKEY WITH ALL THE TRIMMINGS

Heavy skies hung over Turkey Street. A bare larder and a drained wine cellar forced us out into the cold and as we darted past Halfway Square, the stress of a London Christmas evaporated into the damp morning air. Locals crammed into the Stone Oven for their morning loaves, stubbly husbands queued for a chance appointment with Ali Berber's cut-throat razor and a racketeer set out his stall of fake Diesel tee shirts at the entrance to the *otogar*, praying not be moved on by the *Jandarma*. It was good to be home.

At the Tansaş supermarket, jabbering bands of last-minute shoppers shoved their way through the packed aisles to pick up their *Milli Piyango* lottery tickets and grab essential New Year supplies – chestnuts, *baklava* and lucky red knickers. At the front of the store, a small group had gathered to rummage through the discounted odds and sods of what appeared to be a Christmas trinket gondola. Not to miss a trick, Turks had appropriated the traditions of Yuletide and grafted them onto New Year.

Baubles, fairy lights, soft toy *Noel Baba* Santas, tinselled trees, they were all there at the seasonal stall, piled high like the secret stash of a magpie with a glitter fetish.

'It's all down to the Chinese,' said Liam, delving through the glitzy paraphernalia. 'This little lot was manufactured in Hong Kong.'

He was right. The enterprising Chinese had flooded the Turkish market and judging by the way the festive tat was flying off the shelves, they were onto a sure fire winner.

'Let's buy a wee tree,' said Liam. 'A Sino-Turkish tree.'

'And why would we do that? It's New Year.'

'To celebrate our own little Christmas. We've never had Christmas on our own. Ever.'

'That's hardly my fault, Liam.'

Liam ran his hand through a box of tinsel. '*Et tu, Brute?*'

'Christ. No idea where that came from. Sorry.'

Liam grinned and picked up a six-inch artificial tree. 'So? How about this one?'

'It's still a no.'

Liam removed the Christmas tree from its tiny cardboard box, set it down on the dining table and stared at the instruction leaflet. It was in Chinese. When he picked up his tweezers and began the painstaking task of placing each of the tiny baubles onto the pipe cleaner branches, I lost the will to live and went in search of Beril and Vadim. The soggy courtyard was strewn with broken branches and leaf litter. The winds had picked up and the mother of all storms was brewing out at sea. Bianca was the only sign of life inside Beril and Vadim's house, curled up on the kitchen windowsill, a single eye flashing open at the sound of my footsteps. On our patio table, a handwritten note poked out from under a wrought iron candle holder.

'So? What does it say?' asked Liam as he put the finishing touches to his miniature fake fir.

'We're to meet them in the Nazik Ana Restaurant just after midnight.'

'Odd.'

'And written in perfect English.'

'Nothing about those two will ever surprise me... Ta dah! Tree's up.'

'It's bent, Liam.'

'And your point is?'

'And half your balls are missing.'

The storm passed as quickly as it had arrived. The New Year's Eve parade was set fair and Bodrum was draped in a sea of red ribbons. Bubble-wrapped captains and their shivering passengers huddled together on deck to babble and booze by candlelight, restaurants poured out onto the pavements and tinny music blared from the municipal speakers. Harbour Square, the town's beating heart, was thumping hard, illuminated by a large virgin-white Christmas tree fashioned from plastic and aluminium. The crowd was a microcosm of Turkish society – mobs of shifty-looking likely lads leering at everything that moved, pantalooned grannies with their infant charges, trendy young things glued to their smart phones and teenage girls variously sporting elaborate headscarves or Santa hats. The Castle of St Peter, Bodrum's Crusader heirloom, kept watch over the festivities.

Liam downed a can of Efes, grabbed my arm and dragged me through the crowds to the heaving upper terrace of a harbourside bar. It was the perfect place to catch the headliner at the free concert, an energetic Turkish diva slapped up in enough war paint to scare off General Custer. Naturally, we had no idea who she was but the jostlers gave her an ecstatic welcome. She wailed her way through her back catalogue and with each song the volume increased, the lighting became more theatrical and the applause more frenzied. New Year beckoned and she pleaded with the audience to settle for a message straight from her Anatolian heart. Lights dimmed, the crowd hushed and a lone guitarist joined her centre stage to strum an intro, spot-lit by a large Super Trouper.

Nasıl anlatsam? she sang.
Nerden başlasam?
How can I explain?
Where do I start?
Bodrum, Bodrum.
Bodrum, Bodrum.
Feeling, a little feeling,
All I wanted was this,
Some sea, some sleep.
Once upon a time I was in love
But now, I forget, what was her name?
Bodrum, Bodrum.
Bodrum, Bodrum.

The famous ballad hypnotised the home team from the first note. They swayed in unison, chanting '*Bodrum, Bodrum*', transfixed by the electricity of the moment and interlocking arms as emotions soared. Liam looked about the crowd and his eyes flooded. At the stroke of midnight, we hugged and kissed, masked by the crush as an explosive pyrotechnic bonanza lit up the night sky and a thousand *mutlu yıllar* reverberated around the harbour.

With gunpowder spent and low smoky clouds hanging in the air, we edged our way into Nazik Ana for our rendezvous with the neighbours. A petite figure emerged through the giddy revellers, propped up by a forty-something heavyweight, a wide shouldered bouncer-type with a thick handlebar moustache and an oily black wig nesting on his head.

'My darling boys, you came!'

'Sophia?' said Liam. 'It was *you* who left the note?'

'Now, my year is complete,' slurred Sophia. 'Now, my restless heart can sleep.'

Sophia was our eccentric part-time neighbour on Sentry Lane, an aristocratic Turk with RADA-trained English and pretentions to match. As a ravishing young thing in Swinging Sixties London, the would-be starlet had courted fame and fortune but had never quite made the grade. When the penny finally dropped that she was destined for the cutting room floor, a determined Sophia had leapt up from the casting couch straight into the arms of a dashing Turkish diplomat twenty years her senior. For years, Sophia had travelled the world, living the cossetted life of an ambassador's consort until one day the man who 'worshiped' her met his untimely end at a bridge party in Milan.

'It was a dreadful and merciless stroke,' Sophia had explained. 'I have no doubt that Allah had his reasons but he failed to communicate them to me. Me, the grieving wife!'

A decade on, Sophia had remained resolutely single, a well-appointed Turkish widow with dazzling white hair fashioned into a bun and a 'heart in a million pieces'. In winter she would decamp to Istanbul for a warm slice of urban living and underfloor heating, abandoning her draughty Aegean cottage until the warmth of spring lured her back to the coast.

'What an unexpected pleasure,' I said. 'Happy New Year, Sophia.'

'The pleasure is all mine, my darling. Embrace me!'

A long line of spit dribbled down Sophia's chin and splattered onto her companion's shoes.

'Off her tits,' whispered Liam.

I held out my arms. 'Back for good, Sophia?'

'Alas, no. One night only. How could I resist this night of nights? Turkey embraces you, Jack, Bodrum embraces you and I embrace you!'

Sophia's embrace missed its target.

'My country adores people like you,' she muttered, anchored to her mysterious friend as he gathered her up from the restaurant floor. '*Different* people... it is our tradition.'

'And your friend?' I asked.

'Ah! My Onur!' said Sophia, staring into the eyes of her guardian. 'He is a marvel, an absolute marvel.'

'With an iron grip,' I said as my fingers recovered from a crushing handshake.

'Oh yes. My Atlas... he helps me with business. Just business, you understand.'

'You look radiant, Sophia,' I said provocatively, staring at her flawless complexion. This was not the sixty-five-year-old face I remembered from our last encounter. 'How *do* you do it?'

'Do it? Genes, dear. And a *soupçon* of Clarins. My mother was the same. I am blessed.'

Onur stroked Sophia's cheek and whispered into her ear. She shuddered in pleasure and drifted off, slobbering like an infant, relaxed in the grip of her companion, her shoulders dipped and her lips curled. As they swayed together, their hips gently rocking, tutting waiters rushed past and partying diners took photos for Facebook.

Liam coughed. 'You still with us, Sophia?'

'Yes, dear,' she replied, trance-like, her body limp in the arms of Onur. 'Still here, dear.' Her eyes sneaked open. 'But now I must leave. I must sleep. We shall meet again. In the Bodrum spring.'

She cupped her hand and attempted a royal wave.

'Goodnight, darlings. And remember. The darkest hour is just before the dawn... just before the dawn.'

Onur dragged sleeping beauty out to the street to be swallowed up by the milling crowd and Sophia's first performance of the year faded into the night.

We headed east into Tavern Alley, a narrow lane off the *pazar* and home to a collection of small crush bars. The place was packed and the mood was bawdy. A sequined rah-rah skirt twerked on a table top and packs of wolf-whistling boys looked on as she swung her booty and her sisters downed the booze. If alcohol consumption, particularly by women, was frowned upon in wider Turkish society, there was little evidence of it among the tequila slammers of Tavern Alley.

'So,' said Liam as we snaked around a busking band of minstrels, 'what do you make of Sophia?'

I laughed. 'A nip and tuck.'

'Joan Rivers?'

'Peggy Lee, more like. That face has been stretched tighter than one of Vadim's bongos.'

'And Onur?'

'Cha-ching.'

We settled at a bench table and ordered beers from one of the harassed waiters circulating through the commotion. Our neighbour on the congested bench was instantly smitten with Liam.

'I run man's club,' said the admirer, a fifty-something sot in a wide-lapelled cream suit.

'That's nice,' said Liam, heaving at his aniseed breath.

'For man, you understand?'

'Like the Masons, you mean?'

Liam stared at the man and considered basic fashion tips. The greasy shoulder-length hair, open-necked shirt and chunky gold medallion dangling below the sweep of his vest screamed cartoon mafia.

'Tonight, you come,' he said, tonguing his finger suggestively. 'Yes, you come with me. We drink, we eat.' He smirked. 'You like shish?'

Defeated by the cold night air and in need of bladder relief, we abandoned the Loony Tunes lothario and ventured inside the bar opposite, only to be pinned up against the wall by a swirling maelstrom of grungy hipsters with messy shag cuts. The music was refreshingly unsophisticated and the anti-fashionistas whirled around just as enthusiastically to Depeche Mode dirge as they did to disco Kylie. When they whooped at the intro to *It's Raining Men*, Liam reached spiritual enlightenment and jumped into the mêlée to join them.

'Forgive them, Father, they know not what they do!' he screamed from the dance floor. 'Picture it, Jack. New Year's Eve. Turkey. Two old fairies, a bunch of pogoing mop heads and the biggest gay anthem ever written. I love this place.'

Maybe this wasn't Turkey, not really, but it was one small slice and like me, Liam had fallen under its spell. As an arm appeared from within the writhing scrum and pulled Liam further into the fray, I took a seat at the bar and prayed the spell would last.

CHAPTER SEVEN

THE BODRUM BELLES

While Bodrum nursed its New Year hangover, the town received broad side-swipes from a small division of mechanical diggers. These CATs didn't purr and it was a sound that echoed through the land. With a green light from Ankara and purse strings loosened, the entire country was in the mood to spend, spend, spend, buoyed by a new self-confidence and a tidal wave of foreign investment. Bodrum's elders weren't about to let the grass grow and certainly had no intention of letting their Aegean sisters steal a march. Along Marina Boulevard, a long line of mismatched terraces was torn down with such haste that some doorways were left hanging in midair. Supping and shopping required a grappling iron and a pioneering spirit, more grab the rope than mind the step. Within days, the Town Hall was stripped down to a skeleton and the old fish market was hauled off to the tip in the back of a truck. Bar Street, with its hassle shops, drinking dens and overpriced *lokantalar*, became a cratered dirt track impassable in the rain and an entire three-storey building was razed, revealing a view of the Aegean not seen since Mausolus was on the throne. Shopkeepers cranked down the shutters and fled the war zone hoping for a spring revival and seasonal workers were sent back to their villages to hibernate, marry their cousins and breed.

'Your hole's blocked,' said Doc, pointing at a pool of rippling rainwater catching the sun on the flat roof of our single-storey kitchen. 'You need to sort it.'

Doc Muswell was always matter of fact in matters of fact. Liam's favourite Bodrum Belle was a walking-talking Wikipedia with an engineer's bent and a string of qualifications. Doc wasn't her real name, of course, but soon after her arrival in Bodrum, her shrewd eye for detail earned her the apposite nickname. It stuck. From then on, Jilly, the name on her passport, was reserved only for officialdom and her elderly mother.

'It's that woman's fault,' said Liam, 'the hammer thrower in Crimplene. She scaled the walls and thrashed the hell out of the olive tree. Still, nice crocheted twinset in lilac DayGlo.'

'Well it needs a jolly good poking, otherwise you'll get seepage,' said Doc hovering indecisively over a milk chocolate Hobnob.

'Don't worry,' I said, 'Liam's used to bit of seepage. It's an age thing. That Tena Lady moment's just around the corner.'

We were taking tea sugared with hot gossip on our first-floor balcony and shooting the breeze with cross-talking enthusiasm. Our Belles were in gobby mode. If we'd wanted to shy away from the curtain-twitchers, we couldn't have chosen a worse position, overlooking Turkey Street like the balcony at Buckingham Palace.

I picked up the teapot and offered the spout to Jess.

'Shall I be mother?'

Ex-model Jessica Holt looked ravishing as usual. But then, she could climb into a bin liner and still look like Hepburn in her Unicef years. She had baulked when I called her my 'Lotus-eating sophisticate' and when Liam declared her a 'fine lady of a certain age, a model past and an elegant carriage,' she had whacked him hard with her clutch bag.

'SHALL I BE MOTHER?'

'There's no need to shout, Jack, I may be getting on but I'm not deaf. Does that dog ever shut up?'

'No. Nor the other three. It's the price we pay for living in the oldest ward in town.'

'You get used to it,' said Liam. 'In the end, you just yell above the yapping.'

The residents of Bodrum enjoyed a purely pragmatic relationship with man's best friend. Most dogs were strategically installed at the front of a house to perform the traditional guard and protect function, lashed to rusty poles and fed on kitchen slop. It was something Western softies found hard to take and the incessant yapping was a constant reminder of the casual neglect. Occasionally we would see some best of breed on leads but they tended to be leashed to the best of breed in heels.

'Count yourself lucky,' said Victoria. 'I've got a pride of alley cats round my way. It's like Sodom and Gomorrah.'

Victoria Hastings was our dolly drop Belle with the look and allure of the blonde one from ABBA before she went all Greta Garbo.

'Postman's been,' said Liam as an envelope flew over the garden wall and landed in the borders. 'It'll be last year's credit card statement.'

'Well at least we get mail these days,' said Victoria. 'Remember the old days, girls?'

As I poured the tea and Liam went to retrieve the post, the three Belles raided the biscuit barrel and reminisced with gusto. Bodrum had once been a laidback kind of town, they said, a backwater on hold. They talked animatedly about contraband, cold-water flats, power supplied on a wing and a prayer and queuing up for hours at the old post office for the weekly call home to mother.

'And don't even go there with the dancing bears,' said Jess.

The Belles made it sound heroic. In their own way, each of them had been a trailblazer, buccaneers with bras to burn and points to prove.

'Well I couldn't do without my iPhone,' said Doc. 'Or Facebook.'

Victoria tutted. 'Erdoğan's banned it, Doc.'

'No, that's YouTube.'

'So, the sour-faced old fart can block the internet but he *still* can't keep the power on,' snapped Victoria, pulling her fishtail plait over her shoulder and twisting the end round her finger.

'Careful Victoria,' I said. 'Don't want to get deported now, do you?'

'The old girl next door to me used to have a cow,'

said Jess, distractedly. 'Every day, she would lead it up to the hills above Bodrum to graze, even after they built the bypass. She nearly caused a pile-up. And then... it all ended when she was sent to the knacker's yard.'

'I do hope you mean the cow,' said Doc, stealing the last of the Hobnobs. 'The hills are alive with the sound of cement mixers, these days. Illegal, a lot of it, all done with a nod, a wink and a brown envelope stuffed with cash.'

Victoria nodded. 'I blame the planners.'

'They can't all be bent,' said Liam, jumping back into his seat.

'If an ugly thug in a shiny suit strutted into your office, placed a loaded gun on your desk and made thinly veiled threats to you and yours, what would you do?'

'Take the bung and reach for the stamp,' said Liam.

'Exactly.'

Jess fondled the ripe black olives on what was little more than a twig planted in a glazed pot to the side of the sofa.

'Your sapling's done well, Jack. I had no idea you had green fingers.'

'John's tree,' I said. 'Cute, isn't it?'

'Who's John?' asked Jess.

'My dead boyfriend.'

A temporary pause in the traffic noise offered the perfect opportunity for a tragic fairy tale. I looked at Liam for approval.

'Once upon a time,' I began as the Belles settled around me, 'far, far away... I was already a seasoned old pro with more notches on my bedpost than the wicked stepmother. But then, I fell under the spell of this... well, extraordinary young man, a handsome prince with razor sharp wit and a wry smile. We collided by the coat check in Copacabana, a knocking shop in Earls Court back in the day. The glamour of it all. He stayed the night and never left. Eight years in, he fell ill, quite suddenly and within six weeks he was gone.'

'Bloody hell, Jack,' said Doc. 'You could have dressed it up a bit.'

'He died in my arms, quite a Hollywood moment. Not that I'd care to relive it. And that was that, the end of the fairy tale and the end of John.'

Victoria sighed. 'So how did he die?'

'Badly.'

Liam flinched.

'Pneumonia,' I said.

'Oh,' said Victoria. 'Horrible.'

'He was thirty-six.'

'That's no age at all.'

'No. A victim of his time.'

'And you?'

'Oh, I was lucky.'

'And now you have Liam,' she said.

'Yes. Now he's the lucky one.'

Liam raised his eyebrows. 'Wherever Jack lives, he plants a tree in John's memory.'

'I've moved so often, I'm doing my bit for reforestation.'

'Well you should bottle the olives,' said Doc. 'They're almost past it.'

'My dear Doc, if there's one thing John taught me, it's that life is way too short to bottle olives. I'll pass 'em to Beril. She's good at that kind of thing.'

Right on cue, Beril's shrill voice bounced over the garden wall from Turkey Street.

'*Yavaş! Yavaş!*'

A muddied pickup truck overladen with boxed vegetables was inching past, tailed by a convoy of tetchy drivers and biker boys in replica World War Two German helmets.

'*Yavaş! Yavaş!*' Beril screeched again.

We peered down from the balcony as the truck scraped against the wall and its load became snared by the spikes of a giant bougainvillea. Beril yelled at the driver to reverse. As he did so, the truck gouged out a chunk from the wall and the bougainvillea branches recoiled, showering the waiting motorcade with unfledged leaf litter. What Beril screamed next was something of a mystery. Not even our multilingual Belles could interpret the tirade, but judging by the reaction of the stunned driver, it might well have involved his mother and a goat. Content she had saved the estate from wanton destruction, Beril looked up at the balcony and bowed theatrically.

'Not a woman to be messed with,' said Jess clapping politely.

With the drama over, a weak winter sun finally dipped behind the house and the sleeveless Belles shivered in the late afternoon chill. We rushed through any other business and the meeting came to a reluctant close.

'I found it in the bedding,' said Liam, as I cleared the balcony table. 'With the credit card bill.'

He tossed me a gold-embossed invitation from the Honorary British Consul. Judging by the quality of the card and Her Maj's coat of arms, the invitation to 'take cocktails and canapés with the captain aboard HMS Cumberland,' seemed genuine enough. After a lengthy tour of duty chasing Somalian corsairs across the Indian Ocean, the frigate was sailing up the Red Sea towards the Suez Canal and was due to dock at the Port of Bodrum on a rare courtesy visit.

'So,' said Liam. 'Shall we go?'

'Go? Of course we shall go. Sponge down the sailor boy outfits. It's time we copped a feel of the captain's jib.'

'I bet you've got a whole load of those up your sleeve?'

'One or two. Fancy examining the captain's log? A sneaky peek at his magnificent greased piston?'

'It's just drinks and nibbles, Jack.'

'A little Cumberland sausage on the quarterdeck? That'll sort me out.'

Liam rolled his eyes as he picked up a tray of empties. 'It's the roof that needs sorting, Jack. Just get on with it.'

'Aye aye, Cap'n.'

With Liam humming the chorus to *In the Navy*, I clambered onto the kitchen roof and set about draining the unwanted paddling pool with the handle of a wooden spatula. The undammed waters spewed like a mini Niagara onto the newly turned vegetable patch of our Amazonian neighbour. Her chained-up dog, one quarter of our quadrophonic sound system, and the kind of mutt that would bark at the sound of a sparrow's fart, was so thrown by the sudden gush that it was stunned into silence. As Liam finished wiping down the kitchen and launched into a flat rendition of *I Am Sailing*, I only wished it had affected him in the same way.

CHAPTER EIGHT

THE SISTERHOOD

For Jessica Holt, there was nowhere quite like Bodrum, even in winter. The winds were howling as she closed the door of her apartment and rushed down the steep hill into the night. At the corner of Turkey Street, she turned up the sable collar of her camel coat and headed east past a jumble of shops – an illegal gambling den where many a punter had lost a shirt on the three thirty at Veliefendi Races, the dry cleaners with the baggy-faced seamstress who sat in the window every day except Friday, and the Tiny Tots *butik* with its display of petrified *Children of the Damned* dummies. By the time she had reached Newtown Mosque, a far more imposing affair than its elder sister on Halfway Square, mini tornadoes were waltzing along the tarmac, spinning debris into the air. She tucked in her chin and scurried past the Mausoleum gates, taking temporary shelter at the entrance to an internet café serving up Google with Black Sea tea. Jess had retraced this route a thousand times on autopilot and after fifteen years had never tired of it. At the junction of Old Hamam Street she stopped abruptly and took a call under the light of a street lamp.

'No, I can't, I'm busy. Don't say that, my darling… no really, don't say that. It's got to stop. This is the last time, you hear?'

She switched off her phone, dropped it into her market-bought Mulberry and tore along Turkey Street, pausing briefly to put up her umbrella as another sharp shower waterbombed the already saturated streets. *Really, of all the times to call.* When she finally arrived at Sentry Lane, she stepped through the open gate, scanned her reflection in a candlelit window and rapped on the door of No. 2.

'Lively weather we're having.'

'Forget the pleasantries, Jack. Take me to your wine.'

Jess shivered into the house and hurried over to the infrared heater. A treacherous gust had inverted her brolly and the wind and rain had battered her carefully teased hair.

'Nice look, darling.'

'Shut it, Jack.'

'Well if it isn't an angel from heaven,' said Liam, emerging from the kitchen with a plate of goats' cheese tartlets and a large *bulgur* salad.

'Just get me a bottle, Liam,' snapped Jess, handing me a dripping coat and the twisted remains of an umbrella. 'This is an emergency.'

'How thrilling,' said Liam. 'What's up?'

'Nothing I should tell you two about.'

Jess sat at the table and poured herself a large red.

'It's a bit delicate.'

'You're not up the duff?'

'I'm nearly sixty, Liam.'

Jess leaned forward and lowered her voice.

'It's Cristal.'

'Crystal DeCanter, the Stoke-on-Trent drag queen?' asked Liam.

'For pity's sake. Cristal from Torba. The Brummie girl.'

'Not had the pleasure, have we, Jack?'

'Well you'd like her. Cristal's a sweetie. And a right looker. She was a model back in the day. It's how we met.'

'On the catwalk?'

'Not exactly, no. She went down the glamour route. Rugby calendars mainly.'

We froze.

'You mean Cristal Cologne, the topless model,' I said. 'The ditzy redhead on Blankety Blank.'

'That's just it,' said Jess. 'It was all an act.'

Liam topped up Jess's glass and shoved the plate of collapsed tarts to her side of the table.

'Tuck in, Jess. They taste better than they look.'

'Have you never heard of muffin trays, Liam?'

'So,' I said eager to get on with it. 'What's the dirt on our Cristal?'

'Well, she left England when her lingerie company folded.'

'Slutz Unlimited?'

'It was Kinky Nicks, Jack.'

'Classy outfit then?'

'Quite. Anyway, she came to Turkey on holiday and fell into the arms of a deckhand.'

'Don't tell me, another Shirley Valentine laid at low tide.'

'It really wasn't like that, Jack. Well, not entirely. They got married. I must say, Liam, your tarts are surprisingly good.'

'So what's the problem?' I asked.

'He's knocking her about, that's the problem. It breaks my heart.'

'Have some salad, darling,' said Liam. 'It's my own dressing.'

'So she just needs to dump the bastard,' I said. 'End of.'

'It's not that simple, Jack. She's not ready.'

'What for? His fists?'

'It gets worse. In the end she denies it all, despite the bruises.'

'The walked into a door syndrome.'

'Exactly. What the hell's in this dressing, Liam? It's divine.'

'*Sumak*. You like?'

'Look, Jess,' I said, glaring at Liam. 'I'm sorry if this sounds harsh, but the lady needs to wake up and smell the hummus.'

Jess buried her head in her hands and groaned. 'She loves him.'

'Oh come on, when your boat's holed beneath the waterline, head for dry land. It's no use bobbing about in the water like flotsam just because the sea's warm. What's the point in being in love if you're just a VOMIT?'

'One of Jack's ever so clever acronyms,' said Liam.

'Victims of Men in Turkey,' I said. 'A phrase I picked up in Yalıkavak.'

'Very clever, Jack, but it's not that simple. My husband left *me* and I'm no VOMIT.'

Jess's revelation came as a bit of a shock. We may have shared bawdy boat trips and drunken nights with our three Belles, but deep down, our relationships were as thin as a Sun editorial.

I sighed. 'So what happened?'

'Not much. We moved here to run a scuba diving business. He met a pretty young thing in figure-hugging rubber and left me in dry dock. He took everything.'

'So that's why you work all the hours God sends.'

'It was ten years ago. I survived. I get by.'

Liam slipped Gloria Gaynor into the CD player and went to make coffee.

'I guess we've all been through the ringer,' I said. 'One way or another.'

'Yes, Jack, but I'm no bloody victim. Besides, if it wasn't for Liam, you might be one of your VOMITs.'

'I don't think so.'

'I wouldn't be so sure if I were you. What if you were past your sell-by date and a handsome young man said he loved you, said you were beautiful. It might well turn your head.'

'I wouldn't fall for it,' I insisted.

'Even if it was the first time you'd heard it in years?'

'Even then.'

'You'd shag him though,' said Liam from the kitchen.

'I'd hide my wallet first.'

'All I'm saying is that Cristal needs our help,' said Jess. 'And she's going to get it.'

'Saved by the Belles?' asked Liam.

'If you like. Why not? We look out for each other. And some of us turn out okay in the end, you know. We're survivors, not victims, and there's a whole tribe of us scattered around the Aegean. Round the world, probably.'

'The Sisterhood,' I said. 'Ladies who lunch and learn.'

'The Sisterhood,' said Jess. 'I like it. Much nicer than VOMITs.'

And so we continued to debate the plight of Juliets and the occasional Julian who lost their heads, hearts and life savings to the caravan of pretty Romeos with loaded pants and empty pockets.

When every last scrap of food had been eaten, we clinked coffee cups and Liam begged to become an honorary member of the newly constituted Sisterhood.

'It's a ladies only club,' said Jess. 'You don't qualify.'

'You'd be surprised,' I said. 'There's more to Liam than meets the eye.'

'Oh come on, Jess. No exceptions? Not even for me?'

'Not unless you can think of a way to earn your stripes, Liam, no.'

'I'll walk you home?'

'It's a start. A very small start.'

'Protecting Jess from the hooded claw,' I scoffed. 'What a hero.'

'Ignore the sarcastic little shit, Jess. Grab your muff and follow me.'

Safely home, Jess blew Liam a goodnight kiss and locked the heavy metal gate behind her. Liam retraced his steps down the unlit hill, turned the sharp corner back into Turkey Street and headed home. The streetlamp by the Mausoleum was flickering as it always did. He stopped to light a cigarette. It was gone three a.m. The rain had passed and Bodrum was as quiet as falling snow. Liam checked his phone, stubbed out his cigarette, considered lighting another but decided against it.

That rakı chaser was a mistake. Go home. Get some sleep.

A car parked by the side of the street sparked into life and exhaust fumes billowed into the nippy air. Liam scurried off towards Sentry Lane, momentarily lit by the beam of the car's headlights but then darting back to the safety of the shadows.

Bloody idiot.

The car purred, dipped its headlights and tailed Liam, step for step. When Liam stopped, it stopped, and when he picked up speed, it picked up speed. It revved its engine. Liam looked over his shoulder.

The bastard's playing with me.

He considered escaping into one of the side streets but opted instead for the home straight. When the car sped past and came to a screeching halt at the top of Sentry Lane, it was checkmate and Liam froze.

He knows where I live.

A shadowed head peered out from the driver's window and shouted back to Liam.

'Hey! You want ride? I have money.'

A moped chugged along Turkey Street, briefly throwing a shaft of light onto the Range Rover to reveal a thick handlebar moustache and an oily black wig. The kerb crawler jumped, slammed his foot on the gas and sped off towards the bus station, veiling Liam in a miasma of fumes. As he reached the gate on Sentry Lane and fumbled for his keys, Liam's booze-dulled brain fought hard to make sense of what had just happened.

I've seen that oily black wig before.

CHAPTER NINE

RAINDROPS ON ROSES

Humdrum Bodrum was as slow as pond water and it came as a relief when Mother Earth flicked the spring switch. We flung open the French doors and stepped into the garden to the sound of the *müezzin* calling at full volume from the sunken mosque on Halfway Square. It was quickly followed by the first row of the season between Beril and Vadim, a corker of a commotion with Beril's pipes used to Semtex effect as she squawked at her man like a circling gull. I feigned deafness, wiping down the patio furniture and shampooing cushion covers while Liam buffed the windows with scrunched up pages of *Woman's Realm*. That morning, almost as one, the entire population of Turkey Street escaped their winter confines to beat their kilims, sweep their yards and gossip over garden walls.

Just as we were nearing the end of our spring clean, the cacophony of a traditional Turkish band marched closer to the house and the voice of our landlady hollered over the garden wall.

'Come! I bring gift! Come!'

Liam whizzed along the path in his peach Marigolds.

'It was Hanife,' he said, returning to the house, clutching a Tupperware dish.

I took a seat at the patio table. 'I heard. What's all the fuss about?'

'Some kind of party. Circumcision, I think. Hard to tell. Something about a prince on a donkey.'

Liam placed Hanife's gift on the table and pulled up a seat.

'Cock-o-wretch,' he said, prising off the lid of the plastic container to reveal skewers of meat, tomatoes and peppers. 'I'm sure that's what she said. Cock-o-wretch.'

'They're just kebabs, Liam.'

Liam stepped into the kitchen and I sunk my teeth into a chunk of spiced meat.

'By the way,' said Liam, returning with a jug of water as I looked up from the table, eyes watering and hands clasped to my mouth. 'That isn't lamb. Well, not as we know it.'

He threw his *Secrets of the Turkish Kitchen* cookbook onto the table. 'You've just had a mouthful of Hanife's *Kokoreç*.'

'She's done it again, hasn't she?'

'Yep. Lamb intestines, Jack. You know, that bit just before the sheep's arse. *Bon appetit.*'

That evening, after a simple dinner of toasted *hellim* and orange squash, I lost Liam to a night at the Oscars. Sharing the sofa with his favourite Teletubby, he watched the entire back-slapping marathon online, from the glitzy red carpet entrée of fixed Hollywood smiles, borrowed designer frocks and asinine chatter right through to the tacky banquet of gushing acceptance speeches. *The King's Speech* won Best Picture and Colin Firth, who made his name from his magnificent britches and a stiff upper lip, got the gong for Best Actor. Liam was thrilled. Just days earlier, we had squinted through a snowy copy of the royal biopic courtesy of a very tall and badly dressed Dutchman, an enterprising emigrey who did a roaring trade in knock-off DVDs at the Bitez flea market. The next morning, I found Liam asleep on the settee, fully clothed, wrapped in a blanket and cuddling his Laa-Laa.

Mother Earth can be a deceitful old bag and after a full week of sunshine, she decided that spring could wait after all. Mini hurricanes whistled through the narrow streets and thunderclaps, unfettered flying objects and the constant banging of metal gates kept us on edge well into the small hours.

Liam turned on the bedside lamp.

'When will it stop? When will it stop!'

I sat up and clasped his hand. 'Raindrops on roses and whiskers on kittens...'

'Not being funny, Jack, but it doesn't have the same ring coming from a tone-deaf castrato.'

'Stupid lyrics anyway. Who the hell came up with *cream coloured ponies*?'

'The same person who came up with *schnitzel with noodles*. Listen, Jack. What do you hear?'

'Are we still doing Julie Andrews?'

'Listen!'

'What? I don't hear anything.'

'Exactly.'

The sinister winds had terrified the life out of all living things. The jackals were silenced, the cocks kept their own counsel and the temporary lull allowed us to drop off. For a while, at least.

The meteorological tantrum continued on and off for a week or so. In between squalls, we perched on the balcony in thick shawls, an ideal crow's nest for mocking optimistic tourists as they scurried along Turkey Street. Teutonic early birds in knee-length shorts, straw hats and sensible shoes were forced to take refuge from hailstones the size of golf balls. It was just as grim for the chain gang of navvies drafted in to finish off the new townscape before the Easter rush and working knee deep in foul-smelling mud.

Premature boarders weren't the only ones led down the garden path. We received word from our man in Bodrum that the rum punch was off. HMS Cumberland had weighed anchor and our canapés and quoits were sailing full steam ahead towards Benghazi. With the Libyan Civil War seriously out of hand, the Cumberland's captain and his jolly jack tars had been despatched to evacuate Western nationals. Not only was Gaddafi a toppling dictator with murderous intent, bad hair and Messianic tendencies, he was also a party pooper. Liam was inconsolable.

At last, after several false dawns, the race towards summer was finally on. The starting pistol was an earthquake beneath our bed, a 4.1 shock that woke Liam with a jolt. I slept like a fat dribbling baby through the whole thing. The tremors finally shook a languid Bodrum from its offseason torpor and soon, whole villages in the

East were being drained of young men as they followed the sun in search of casual employment and easy lays.

There was rapid-fire knocking on the salon window and Liam shook me from a post-nookie nap.

'She's back,' he said.

'Best go see what she wants, then.'

'You go.'

'Why me?'

'Because I got the wet patch, that's why.'

Sophia was back in town and our grandiose part-time neighbour knew just how to demand our attention. Our encounter on New Year's Eve had demonstrated as much and the rapping was a signal that the old girl was in need of urgent stroking. The previous summer, she had come laden with gifts – a trashy knick-knack from the local *pazar* or something sickly sweet from the Stone Oven – passing them through the ornamental grille of the window overlooking Sentry Lane. It was like feeding time at the zoo.

The knocking became more impatient. Liam leapt out of bed, pulled on a pair of shorts from his floordrobe, hotfooted down the stairs and flung open the wooden casement window.

'Sophia!'

'My dear boy! Am I interrupting something?'

'It's fine, we're done. Welcome back, Sophia. What can I do you for?'

Sophia flinched and stared awkwardly at Liam's bared chest.

'My, the exuberance of youth!'

'You flatter me, Sophia.'

'A gift,' she said, passing a box of candied fruits through the grille. *I frutti proibiti sono i più dolci.* And be sure to share with my darling Jack.'

'Of course. Your darling Jack. He's missed you terribly.'

'He is *such* a dear.'

'Isn't he just? Bye Sophia.'

Liam closed the window and waved goodbye.

'But darling!' she screamed, rapping on the window.

'Sorry,' said Liam, opening up the feeding hatch. 'I thought we were done.'

'My internet connection, dear, it has failed me. Could you possibly…?'

'Oh, I see. Give me a minute and I'll get dressed. Okay?'

'Yes… of course. I shall wait in the house and my maid will make tea. *À plus tard!*'

'Wonder if she knows about her man in the oily black wig?'

Liam sat on the bed and shoehorned himself into a pair of skinny jeans.

'Onur? Doubt it. Sophia never looks past herself. She's a one woman show, that one.'

'Then we should tell her.'

'That he's a bit hetero-flexible? No, Jack, we should keep out of it.'

'Maybe you're right. You sure you wanna wear those?'

'What's wrong with them?'

'Nothing. If you want to look like mutton dressed as. Anyway, I bet he went straight to the windmills that night.'

'What windmills?'

'On the way to Gümbet. It's where men go.'

'And how would you know that?'

'*Everyone* knows that, Liam.'

'It proves one thing, though. I've still got it.'

'Halitosis?'

Respectably topped and tailed, Liam flip-flopped along Sentry Lane, through Sophia's grand gate and into her oasis of avocado, pomegranate and lemon trees. A contending riot of efflorescent flowers tumbled over the borders, nudging for room.

'Welcome, welcome,' said Sophia, beckoning Liam through the sliding doors of the incongruous uPVC extension to her traditional Bodrum house. The busy conservatory was a this and that assortment of old and new furniture – mahogany, melamine and pine – jammed together like a Notting Hill bric-a-brac shop. Every surface was littered with a hodgepodge of wooden, silver and plastic photo frames, almost all of them featuring Sophia in her heyday. In the centre of the room, a cane three-piece suite was smothered in handmade throws, and on an armchair sat a dribbling walrus in an oily black wig.

'You remember my friend, Onur?'

Onur looked up and grinned at Liam, knees wide apart, his handlebar moustache dripping with *rakı*.

'How could I forget?'

'Onur has tried,' said Sophia, gesturing at her laptop,

'But, alas…'

'I'm sure Onur has other talents. Isn't that right, my friend?'

Judging by the panting and slurring, the bi-curious cruiser was on intimate terms with Sophia's drinks cabinet. As he shuffled in the creaking chair and reached for the bottle, Sophia's faithful retainer entered the extension with a tray of tea.

'Nuray!' said Liam. 'How are you? *Nasılsınız?*'

'*İyiyim, sağol…* good!'

'*Süper,*' said Liam warmly. '*Süper.*'

Nuray placed the tray next to Sophia's laptop, winked at Liam and returned to the kitchen. On the surface, Nuray was an old school Kurd, pious, compliant and covered. But attending to her unconventional mistress presented a host of decadent opportunities and she would grab them with both hands, any chance to forsake the headscarf and share tables with men at drunken carousels. One heady evening, Nuray had befriended two old poofs who had hired her for a fiftieth birthday bonanza. There were limits, of course; this was Turkey, after all. She had standards to uphold and preferred to think of me and Liam as 'cousins'. For Nuray's sake, we were happy to keep it in the family.

'Kaput!' said Onur as Liam fiddled with Sophia's internet connection. Onur was a Turkish man and, quite naturally, that made him a master of all trades. Liam sipped his tea and ignored the goading of the fat drunk but it was hopeless and after minutes of tweaking, running diagnostic tools and following audio instructions in Turkish, he finally admitted defeat.

'Looks like he's right, Sophia,' said Liam as he watched Onur slink out of the room *to do a bloody victory dance*.

'Never mind, darling. It seems to have expired. Help yourself to more tea.'

'Thank you, I will. It's delicious.'

'*Elma çay,*' said Sophia. 'It is medicine. It cleanses the body, it cleanses the soul. You must always drink apple tea. Promise me, Liam. It has magical powers.'

At that very moment Sophia's modem clicked into life. Its lights flickered and a flashing login message popped onto the screen.

'Maybe Onur should lay off the bottle,' said Liam, 'and try the magic tea.'

CHAPTER TEN

THE BEST OF TIMES

Our beefy *taksi* driver was everything Liam thought a Turkish man should be – five o'clock shadow, nicotine-rinsed teeth and aromatic pits. The boulevard was filled with rising columns of exhaust fumes and Jimmy seemed anxious. The streets of the anarchic city were in a permanent state of beeping paralysis. Turks were notoriously impatient motorists, kicking against the tide and playing nonstop with their angry horns – loudly and often. It was an exercise in utter futility. Our leathery cabbie found the logjam too much to bear and beads of sweat rolled down his forehead and bounced off his untrimmed unibrow.

'You'd think he'd be used to the gridlocks by now,' said Liam. 'This *is* Istanbul.'

The long samey days of an Aegean winter had taken their toll and with spring in bloom, we had jumped on a plane for a big city fix. We watched with growing alarm as Jimmy peered into the rear view mirror and rubbed his crotch in what appeared to be a combination of rapture and pain. As Constantinople's old city walls slowly advanced into sight, he dropped into overdrive, jiggling about like a tart with crabs and, without warning, leapt from the cab and hurdled off through the traffic.

'Now where's he gone?' said Liam. 'Heading for the border?'

Jimmy had abandoned his fare midway between two lanes, a hop, skip and a jump from one of the busiest intersections in Istanbul. Angry drivers blasted their horns as they manoeuvred around us and it wasn't long before a transit van pranged past, lifting Jimmy's left wing mirror with it.

'He's stopped at the city wall,' said Liam as a battered Renault weighed down by a stack of chairs tied to the roof squeezed by and scraped a layer of paint from Jimmy's right fender. Jimmy was at the massive Byzantine defences, leaning against the ancient masonry with one hand and grasping his peewee with the other.

'So he has,' I said. 'That wall will need repointing.'

Bladder discharged and family jewels faithfully shaken, Jimmy dashed through the traffic, bounced back into the driver's seat and continued the journey into town. Liam launched into a spontaneous ripple of applause and Jimmy grinned back in gratitude. *All in a day's work, my friend. All in a day's work.*

Our bedroom window at the proletarian Pera Majestik overlooked the infinitely more regal Pera Palace, an iconic Istanbul landmark and our digs three years earlier. The Palace was once the opulent end of the line for the Orient Express but had fallen on hard times, a piece of

Istanbul's neglected family silver in dire need of a damn good buffing.

Liam peered out between the budget curtains.

'Remember that room they stuck us in at the Palace?'

'The icebox.'

'Yeah. But that lift, that fabulous lift.'

'And the cute bell boys.'

'Camp cream teas.'

'Straight out of Poirot.'

'The huge antique bath.'

'And your big rubber dick.'

'Duck, Jack, duck. At the end of the day, you're just a grubby, chain-smoking dwarf, aren't you?' said Liam, moving away from the window and surveying the modest hotel room. 'God, the things you do for love.'

The chain-smoking dwarf left his husband fiddling with the settings on an antiquated TV set and ventured out for a pack of cigarettes. The city was in full swing, a writhing mass of noise, smells, people and traffic set against bright blue skies. I stepped out of the hotel foyer onto the main drag only to be accosted by a galaxy of freckles in the form of a young boy clinging to battered weighing scales and a shoe brush.

'You want weigh, mister?'

'Trust me, young man, I'd break your scales.'

'Shoe shine?'

I pointed down to my canvas trainers and shrugged. He was undeterred.

'Where you go, mister?'

'For cigarettes,' I said.

'*Sigara? Peki*. I take!'

I followed the boy a few metres and we both looked up at a small shop tucked behind the hotel.

'*Sigara!*' he announced triumphantly. '*Sigara!*'

'Well, well,' I said handing the enterprising ragamuffin a handful of coins. '*Teşekkürler*, thank you.'

The boy grinned, slipped the commission into his pocket and scampered off in search of his next punter. Despite Turkey's valiant economic growth and visceral devotion to family life, a miserable underclass still sniffed around the streets for a few scraps. Istanbul could be a brutal place and street children were at the bottom of the disenfranchised heap. I had seen it all before of course, but it never got any easier to stomach. Thousands of kids still lived wretched lives, some of them trapped within abusive families, rented out by the hour or thrown out into the cold to fend for themselves.

We spent the morning wandering along the well-rehearsed tourist trail of Sultanahmet and Liam was in his element, milling around the flower beds of Sultanahmet Parkı, taking arthouse snaps of Justinian's Aya Sofya and her upstart little sister, the curvaceous Blue Mosque. As he clicked his way through a zillion pretentious pictures, the amplified call to prayer came at us from all directions and washed over the gardens. God in surround sound.

The Topkapı Palace was our favourite distraction on the tourist circuit, an Ottoman theme park and, for four hundred years, the epicentre of the treacherous Imperial Court. The long line for the Harem stretched back to the middle of Divan Square and, as we queued, we killed time by hunting down badly-dressed tourists. After a dull start, Liam hit the bullseye with Prussian Eurotrash, awarding full marks to a tarty Fräulein and her suede micro skirt, thigh-high boots, mohair waistline jacket and a signature trout pout in slapper red.

Once inside the Harem, Liam snapped away at the antique tiles and we oohed and aahed at the exquisite arabesque designs as we followed the line snaking through the ornate corridors and grand rooms. We talked nonstop, as we always did, chattering about the undoubted claustrophobia and boredom of the gilded prison, the intrigue and pecking order, wild rumours of lights-out lettuce licking and the fate of the ball-less black boys who guarded the virtue of the Sultan's women. In the Courtyard of the Eunuchs, Liam found himself enveloped by a chattering stream of covered girls, a moving exhibit of sunny silk scarves shaped at the forehead into shallow peaks, painted faces and tailored maxi coats over kinky boots. Islamic chic at its coolest.

Close by the Harem, we stumbled upon a pavilion containing the Relics of the Prophet. Back in the day, the holy artefacts bestowed supreme religious authority, making Constantinople the spiritual centre of the Islamic world. Just like their Orthodox predecessors, the Sultans understood the sway of blind faith in a god-fearing world and the Prophet's bits and bobs served to underpin the political hegemony the Ottomans had acquired through conquest. We gawped incredulously at the remains of His beard, tooth, sword, bow and a clay impression of His foot – all allegedly genuine. Less credible were the rod of Moses, King David's skull, Abraham's chip pan and

Joseph's hat (though sadly, not his coat of many colours). In deference to the whirling Faithful, we remained silent throughout, even if we did sense most of them weren't that convinced either.

'About as plausible as splinters of the One True Cross found all over Christendom,' said Liam as we took our seats in the tea garden and gawped at the view across the Bosphorus. 'And where was the Ark of the Covenant?'

'In the British Museum,' I said. 'Next to the Burning Bush.'

Liam nibbled on a Dido and looked over to Asia.

'One city break, two continents and a chocolate finger to boot. Not bad, eh?'

We stared in silence at the never-ending convoy of oil tankers. From here, as the heirs to Rome, Europe's Muslim emperors had gazed out at a vast dominion stretching from the Great Hungarian Plain to the Persian Gulf, the Caucasus to the Sahara. I doubt they ever imagined that, one day, their stately pile would be trampled by plebs and infidels taking in the view.

That evening, we dined along İstiklâl Caddesi, the broad pedestrianised boulevard running through Beyoğlu like a spine. Sultanahmet may have been the heart of old Constantinople but Beyoğlu was the central nervous system, the fashionable, sophisticated and über-European district where bourgeois Istanbulers went to shop and where Turks from every walk of life went to protest and occasionally mutiny. There were no water cannons on the streets that night, just a riot of trendy young things out to party. We ate in a chic pastiche of a Parisian brasserie, all red leather banquettes, giant antique mirrors, terracotta tiled floors and aproned waiters. After paying the extravagant bill, we hit the bars. Unsurprisingly, the Istanbul gay scene was markedly superior to any other in Turkey. The vast and anonymous metropolis was a place where gay Turks could sow their wild oats away from the prying eyes of close-knit kin and the slow asphyxiation of family honour. We drank in a couple of minor-league clip joints before falling into Club Tek Yön, a large pulsating dance bar that could have been in London or New York, except the disco-tits grinding to the beat were attached to young musclebound Turks rather than over-waxed Yankees. The thumping music was a catholic mix of mainstream western dance and homespun Turkopop. Lady Gaga competed with Sezen Aksu and lost. Pushing through the sweaty gyration, we followed a spiral staircase to a first-floor balcony, a narrow gallery lined with seated alcoves where potential lovers could get better acquainted.

'I'm beginning to think there's no such thing as 'gay' in Turkey,' said Liam, ignoring the phone vibrating in his pocket. 'Does *everyone* play on both sides of the net?'

Liam had a point. I had visited the shores of Anatolia for fifteen years or more and still I couldn't work it out. After all, I hadn't been a public school fag or banged up with a lifer. Many Turks were happy to practice on the boy next door just as long as they were the ones doing the poking.

'And what's all this about pink exception slips?' continued Liam as a Hairy Mary in full camouflage paraded past. 'You couldn't make it up.'

A tasty scandal had erupted in the press and caused quite a brouhaha, even getting a mention on the BBC. Friends of Dorothy attempting to wriggle out of Turkish national service were obliged to prove their perversion with photographic evidence. Ahmed, get on your back and smile for the camera, there's a good boy.

'In a real war,' I said, 'nobody cares where you stick it. We're all bloody cannon fodder.'

Back at the hotel, Liam put his mobile on loudspeaker and played the message from his father for a second time. Things were about to change in the Brennan household. Liam's mother had dedicated thirty-eight years of her life to Sean, her youngest. She had washed him, dressed him, fed him, picked him up when he fell, carted him from doctor to doctor and slept by his side when one fit after another nearly carried him off. But now Cathleen was exhausted and would find herself daydreaming, her mind drifting off to a place where things could be forgotten, for a while at least. It wasn't real, she knew that, but it provided respite and for that she was grateful. Liam Senior had watched his wife struggle. He and Cathleen had become old and something once unthinkable had become inevitable. Sean would have to leave home, live in his own house, like Liam and his sister, Siobhan. He would be safe and expertly cared for. It would break hearts but there was no other way. The course was set. Siobhan had found the perfect place, a small care home close to the family house in North Finchley. Now it was up to Liam to explain to Sean. He would take it from him. Everyone knew the two brothers had a connection.

Liam joined me on the bed and we lay there in our disco kit, side by side, gazing up at the polystyrene tiles.

CHAPTER ELEVEN

THE WORST OF TIMES

Charlotte stared at the aeroplane window, studying her reflection in the blackness and fiddling unconsciously with the large buttons of her crumpled navy-blue power suit. Strands of wavy hair had broken free from a kirby grip and hung limply across her cheek. Annotated papers covered the fold-down tray; some had tumbled to the floor, concealing her plain court slip-ons. Charlotte had the look of an office temp down on her luck, but her reality was so much worse. Her husband was dozing in the seat next to her attempting to recover from endless days of sleepless nights, an unfamiliar Paisley tie slackened against his chest. In only a few months, Alan had aged visibly. The dapper silver fox had lost his lustre. Nancy occupied the aisle seat, flicking distractedly through the pretty pictures and lean articles of the shiny inflight magazine, taking little notice of either. Charlotte's perennial best friend fidgeted continuously. The bountiful bosom she always kept on display for the boys glistened in the reading light, ebbing and flowing as she sighed.

A year had passed since Adalet was snatched from Charlotte's grip by a posse of social workers flanked by an armed guard. Then came the inquisition, an investigation that turned their lives over and left the wreckage scattered about like so much dirty linen. Their phone was tapped, their movements tracked and their liberty put at stake. But then a corner was turned. They were cleared by the Turkish Prosecutor. The Judge dismissed the case. They did not buy Adalet. They were not child traffickers. The adoption was legal. It was official. Adalet would soon be home to torture Rogers, the dippy ginger cat, and torment poor old Plumb, the long-suffering garden tortoise. She would be changed, Charlotte understood that. But, with endless patience and attention, Adalet would heal and the family would mend. Then it came, the call they had been praying for, an invitation to put their case to the head honcho in Ankara. It was a cruel twist of the knife that saw them returning to Bodrum empty-handed.

Charlotte's plane landed at Bodrum Airport ten minutes before ours and we collided in arrivals.

'Jack? Is that you? How did you know?'

'Happy coincidence,' said Liam relieving Charlotte of her attaché case. 'We're just back from Istanbul. Christ, you look like I feel, come give your sister a hug.'

'It's good to see you, sweet pea.'

'So how was Ankara?'

'Horrid.'

Alan emerged through the mêlée with two small suitcases, a golf umbrella and a miserable Nancy.

'Need a lift, fellas? I'm sure we can squeeze you in.'

Charlotte stormed off towards the exit, dragging Liam with her. Alan followed on behind and I fell back to join Nancy, her silver Manolo Blahniks clacking away on the polished travertine.

'Well?' I said to Nancy as we wheeled our cases from the worn-out domestic terminal towards the corrugated car park. 'What happened?'

'Wot 'appened? A fuckin' disaster, mate, that's wot 'appened. Don't say anyfing to Charlotte, it'll set 'er off again. Tell me it ain't rainin'. It is. It's bleedin' rainin'. Just about tops off a perfik week, that does!'

'So? What happened in Ankara?'

'They went in all respectable, like. Charlotte looked a right pretty picture. I even gave 'er me lucky red knickers. I ain't done that before, I can tell yer.'

'I didn't know you had lucky red knickers.'

'Wotsa matter? I rinsed 'em frew first. Anyway, Alan told the guv'nor ee'd got it all wrong. Told 'im they'd been cleared by the beak.'

'The beak? I don't suppose Bill Sykes appeared as a star witness?'

'Don't get all cleva on me, Jack Scott, I ain't in the mood. Anyway, the bastards slammed the door in their faces. Said they stole a baby. Said judges could be bought, everyone could be bought. Called 'em criminals. Said they were lucky not to get done. Told 'em to piss off back to England.'

'But that's insane.'

'Ain't it though? Maybe if Charlotte 'ad worn an 'eadscarf she mighta stood a fightin' chance. Well, I've made me mind up, Jack. After this little episode, I'm movin' 'ere, permanent like. They need their Nancy.'

When she had first heard about the meeting in Ankara, Nancy had leapt on the first plane out of Heathrow to stand shoulder to shoulder with her oldest friend. She and Charlotte went back years, too many years to remember. Now, she would take up residence in Charlotte and Alan's spare room, and this time she was staying for the duration and maybe for good. But her decision wasn't entirely altruistic, and we both knew it. The austerity axe man was stalking the town hall corridors and social worker Nancy was happy to fall on her sword and take the bribe. There was little left for her in London other than long passionless nights in front of the box with a tray of Thornton's soft centres.

'What about the internet thing?'

'Bunch of bleedin' freaks, Jack. I ain't that flamin' desperate.'

Nancy's flirtation with *anyportinastorm.com* hadn't quite hit the spot. After being pursued by married deviants and pockmarked misfits who let their fingers do the talking, Nancy had come to the crashing conclusion that she had sunk to the bottom of the romantic food chain.

'I got chattin' to a cabbie online once,' she said. ''Ansome bugger, he was.'

'Nice.'

'I fought so too. Right perv. 'Ee only wanted me to play with me-self in the back of his taxi while 'ee watched in the mirra.'

'Wanker.'

'It's 'ard for a girl alone, yer know. Anyway, they offered me a deal and I took it. Look at the state those two are in.'

'And this has nothing to do with the randy old seadog?'

'Wot, Irfan?'

'Captain Hook, who else?'

Nancy groaned heavily and inflated her memory-foam mammaries.

'Maybe a bit. Gawd knows I could do with a little lovin' right now. Got cobwebs on me cat flap.'

For many years, Nancy had been conducting a holiday romance with a married boat captain from Yalıkavak, regularly returning to fill his net. In her absence, the randy paramour would fish in illegal waters and Nancy was determined that she should be the only one frigging in that particular rigging.

'What about the other woman?' I asked.

'That scrawny bitch, Marianna? Been packed off back to Dresden.'

'And that's the end of her, is it?'

'It better be. I'll cut 'is balls off if 'ee dips his wick again.'

'Just be careful, Nans.'

Nancy grinned. 'You know me, darlin', me 'art's got a mind of its own. Anyway, you goin' to the christenin'?'

'It's a three-line whip from Berni, of course we're going. What about Charlotte?'

'Not sure she's up to it after all this shit.'

Alan filled the boot of the Mini Cooper and sized up his human cargo. It would be a tight fit. Charlotte was already in the back. Liam and I crowded into the hard seats to join her and she grimaced as Liam's elbow dislodged the 'baby on board' sign attached to the back window. Nancy slumped awkwardly into the front passenger seat and when Alan wedged our overnight cases into the leg cavity, she was forced to lie back with her legs raised and parted, her high heels resting on the ledge above the glove compartment. I poked my head between the two front seats and smiled.

'Practising for later, Nans?'

CHAPTER TWELVE

IN THE NAME OF THE FATHER...

It was as a nice day for a christening. We climbed into our smart casuals, fought over the last lick of Beauty Flash Balm, wrapped up the silver eggcup and dolly-hopped to Yalıkavak. The baptism drew quite a flock. A multinational assembly of suited and booted, slapped and frocked parishioners milled around the balloon-covered terrace of Berni's Bar and Grill. At the centre of the scrum, the holy mother was showing off her newborn and an audience of winter hardened emigreys and curious Turks fussed around the baby boy. Joshua was wrapped in swaddling clothes and the cattle in the neighbouring field were lowing on cue.

'Well there's nothing wrong with his lungs,' said Liam as we approached the nativity scene. 'What happened to *no crying he makes*?'

Berni caught my eye and yelled over the crowd, struggling to be heard above the bawling.

'What about ye, lads?'

'We're grand!' I screamed back.

'Get yeselves a wee dram!'

Our hostess was something of an icon among the emigrey fraternity, the life and soul of one of the most popular hotspots on the Peninsula. Bernadette Kavanagh was famous for bagging herself a Turk who didn't cheat, beat or borrow. It would have taken a brave man to mess with Berni and her Gatling Gun Ulster accent. Not to mention her connections in the IRA. During the summer months, bottle blonde Berni and her team of punctilious waiters packed in the punters. Winter was an altogether different affair with Blackpool Bobbi's dire karaoke playing to an elderly lynch mob on a bargain bucket Saga break.

We lifted a glass of chilled and cheery and joined the peal of Belles huddled on the beach. Victoria, Jess and Doc were clanging with a double-dipped redhead, a short curvaceous thing with grey roots, straggly extensions and chandelier earrings. She was encased in denim – spray-on designer jeans cut short at the calf and a faded bolero jacket cradling her tangerine rack like a reinforced hammock.

'Vintage sex kitten,' said Liam, spotting the gold slave chain dangling from her ankle. 'A Seventies' original.'

The girls paused as we approached and after the obligatory round of pecks and lovely-to-see-yous, we took a pew. On one side the tarty apparition and her impossibly buoyant breasts and on the other, the ladies who lunched and their buttoned up christening gowns.

Liam jumped straight in.

'And *who* is this gorgeous thing? Don't believe we've had the pleasure?'

'Hiya,' said a pouting Cristal Cologne in her Brummie patois. Liam felt a flush of excitement. *My Dad had one of your calendars in his potting shed.*

'Actually, don't I know you?' *With the pages stuck together.*

'That depends, bab.'

'On?'

'Yow age, probably.'

'Let me see now,' teased Liam, 'British Embassy Garden party, Ankara, 2009. Lady Reddaway, wife to Her Britannic Majesty's Ambassador?'

Cristal stood up from the table and turned sideways to reveal a busty profile.

'That help?'

'My, my,' said Liam. 'That's a very distinctive décolletage you have there.'

'You seen it before then?'

Cristal pushed out her surgically enhanced puppies and cupped them in the palms of her hands.

'You're off the telly,' said Liam.

'Maybe, bab, maybe.'

'Actress?'

'Getting warm.'

'Got it!' shouted Liam, '*Celebrity Squares. Blankety Blank.* You're Cristal Cologne, the topless model.'

Cristal retook her seat at the table, crossed her legs and licked her thumb.

'Glamma, bab, glamma.'

Liam lowered his voice. 'My Dad—'

'Had one of my calendars in his potting shed. With

the pages stuck together. They all did, bab. Titillatin' the dads was a reet little earner.'

'As a matter of interest, do you call everyone bab?'

'Oh no, bab. Just the 'andsome ones.'

Berni's henpecked husband hovered nervously in the background, attending to the bar and overseeing the overheating kitchen. Alp was a fallen Muslim and found the whole concept of baptism completely unfathomable. Conversion to Islam was a simple affair. Recite the *Shahada* and that was that, slate wiped clean, good to go. Come to that, the Muslim Pillars of Faith seemed inordinately more straightforward than the Sacraments of the Roman Church, not to mention the guilt-laden rituals accompanying them. Still, Alp was content to give Joshua his day at the font, happy in the knowledge that the altar wine would soon be flowing into the glasses of all the Children of Abraham once the formalities were over.

Berni hollered across the din. 'Listen up people! We're about to start. Come watch the show.'

The congregation reformed into a rough semicircle around the makeshift font and Liam and I took up position in the front row.

'Christ, it's a fruit bowl,' Liam whispered with disappointment.

'We're in Berni's Bar and Grill, love. Not St Peter's. And no, the water hasn't been airlifted in from the River Jordan.'

Berni had hired a state licensed nondenominational, one size fits all preacher. The wrinkly reverend was drowning in an ill-fitting cassock run up on a Singer from a pair of old curtains. This was a discount version of the full Catholic production number Berni was used to, but it was the best she could do in the circumstances. Bells and smells Berni wanted a Holy show. That's what she paid for and that's what she was going to get. Once-a-Catholic-always-a-Catholic indoctrination ran through her bones like a chronic case of osteoporosis and Joshua's path to salvation was more important to her than she cared to admit. Key to Berni's grand plan was the guest appearance of a fairy godfather, someone who was certain to raise the level of camp to maximum thrust. Blackpool Bobbi glided to the font like a pantomime dame on ice, decked out in his customary Omo whiteness and glowing like the Ready Brek kid. Not only was Bobbi a superannuated female impersonator – his Liza Minnelli was the stuff of legend on the Lancashire drag circuit – he was also Yalıkavak's only gay in the village. Even in his sleep, Blackpool Bobbi could give Zeki Müren, Turkey's late lamented answer to Liberace, a marathon for his money.

Liam pinched my arm and gestured to the back of the gathering. Charlotte and Nancy had slipped in at the rear. There was no sign of Alan. We hadn't seen any of them since our chance meeting at the airport but we knew Nancy had taken up permanent roost in the basement of Charlotte's Yalıkavak home. When she wasn't filling the captain's quota, she was doing her best to provide an emotional safety net. Her best wasn't working. Charlotte was going under while Nancy was going down. As Nancy fanned herself with the order of ceremony, smouldering in the sunshine like a dog in heat, Charlotte peered over the heads of the row in front, staring at the font and clasping a large silver crucifix hanging from her neck.

'She's a sucker for all this Voodoo,' I said dismissively.

'That's *my* God you're talking about.'

'Don't give me that, Liam Brennan. The last time you stepped inside a church was that holiday in Sitges. And that was only to get directions to the gay beach.'

The preacher went about his business with suitable reverence.

'What name do you both give this child?'

'Joshua,' said Berni assuredly.

She looked at her man. 'Alp?'

Alp looked back at his wife in terror.

'It's not a trick question, you eejit. Answer the man. What name do we give this child?'

'Joshua,' said Alp. 'Joshua.'

'Praise the Lord,' snorted Berni.

'And what do you ask of God's Church for Joshua?'

'Baptism,' said Berni. 'We ask for baptism.'

The parson turned to Alp.

'Look, Father,' said Berni, 'I answer for both of us, right? We both ask for baptism.'

The reverend looked to Joshua's iridescent godfather. Blackpool Bobbi was already blubbing.

'Are you ready to help the parents of this child in their duty as Christians?'

'Oh yes!' said Bobbi, dabbing his eyes with a Postman Pat serviette. 'I'm *so* ready.'

'The correct response is *I am*,' said the parson. 'Just *I am*.'

'I'm sorry. I am. I *really* am.'

By the time Bobbi was asked to renounce the Devil, he was inconsolable. Berni took to answering for everyone, her husband, the godfather and the congregation. The parson was happy to oblige the force of nature that was Bernadette Kavanagh and after a little sprinkling, anointing and naming, he welcomed the baby into the body of the kirk. Joshua was signed up as a bona fide Christian and the enthusiastic flock responded with an enthusiastic hand. As the crowd gushed and the baby bawled, I looked to the back of the class. Charlotte and Nancy had vanished.

After Christ came the craic and Berni was the best craic dealer on the Peninsula. Reverence was tossed aside for revelry, water for wine. In the best Irish tradition, we settled down for an afternoon of drunken debauchery with Bobbi doubling up as DJ and spinning his cheesy tunes with religious alacrity. A small procession of waiters filed out from the kitchen carrying trays of fodder, and the feeding of the five thousand began in earnest. Each table was serviced with a hybrid of hearty Derry fare and run-of-the-mill mezes, fusion finger food to line the bellies of the merrymakers. With newly saved Josh safely tucked up in his crib, Alp kept watch, leaving Berni to do what Berni did best: let down her hair, drink the profits and play the tables with infectious barmaid bonhomie. She finished her rounds by dropping into the chair next to us.

'Ach, grand to see ya boys.'

She gazed over to the neighbouring table where a loaded Cristal was holding court.

'Youz know Cristal?'

'Not really,' I said. 'Just met.'

'A handful, so she is. And troubled. Poor cow. He doesn't let her out much.'

'Her man?'

'He's no man. He's just the bastard she's married on.'

Twinkle Toes Bobbi, cha-cha-cha'd across the terrace like Louie Spence's grandma and pulled Berni to her feet for a fast waltz around the dance floor.

'Come on, Berni, time to shake that tush.'

A pair of wide-eyed emigreys approached Cristal. Mr and Mrs Nondescript were a riot of beige – beige hats, beige slacks and beige slip-ons.

'Sorry, but are you…?'

'Yes,' said Cristal. 'I am.'

'I knew it. I said to Iris, didn't I, Iris?'

'Yes, Harold, you did.'

'That's Cristal Colon, I said.'

'Cologne.'

'We've always been huge fans of yours, Miss Colon.'

'It's Cologne.'

Harold grabbed a serviette from the table.

'A pen, Iris, a pen!'

Iris scrambled inside her beige handbag and fished out a betting shop biro.

'Would you?' he asked.

'Of course,' said Cristal. 'Delighted.'

Cristal took the serviette and pen and scribbled '*With love from Cristal COLOGNE.*'

The giddy fans snatched their prize and hobbled off down the beach.

'She looked a bit rough if you ask me,' said Iris disparagingly.

'Never much liked her, anyway,' replied Harold. 'I knew she'd turn to fat.'

'Don't give me that, Harold Grimthorpe, I saw you gawping at her tits.'

Cristal Cologne was feeling frisky and the more she drank, the friskier she became. As the afternoon turned to evening and the Malibu and Cokes hit their mark, it was Liam she became frisky with.

'Don't you mind, Jack?' asked Jess, leaning in for a gossip as Cristal wrapped herself around Liam's waist.

'Many have tried and many have failed. It doesn't matter how many times she thrusts those artificial cupcakes in his face, it's a lost cause. She's got all the wrong equipment. And I must say, that damsel doesn't look too distressed from where I'm sitting.'

Cristal stretched across the table to grab a jumbo saveloy. As the back of her jacket and jeans parted company, the waistband of a pink thong came into view, a lacy number the width of dental floss. A cluster of black and purple marks was spread across the small of Cristal's back, thinly disguised with smudges of powdered foundation.

Jess welled up.

'I told you, Jack, she needs help.'

'What she needs is a good talking to.'

Cristal licked Liam's chin and puckered up for a kiss.

'She's not normally like this,' said Jess. 'She's just craving attention.'

'Well, I think she's had enough attention for one day, don't you?'

Liam picked up a napkin and signalled for help.

'We've all told her,' said Jess. 'To get out before he kills her.'

'I'll kill her if she doesn't keep her fake nails to herself.'

I leant over and put the brake on her embrace.

'Cristal, honey, Cristal Cologne isn't your real name, surely?'

'Actually, bab, no, it isn't.'

'Care to share?'

'It's bin so long, I can't remember.'

'Come on, spill the beans darling. No one forgets their real name. Not even Ilyena Lydia Vasilievna Mironoff.'

'Helen Mirren,' said Liam helpfully.

'So what's on your passport?' asked Doc.

'You know what's on my passport: Cristal Cologne.'

'The *other* name.'

'Ooroyt, okay, it's…'

With Cristal on pause, the coven stiffened in collective anticipation.

'Well?' we said in unison.

'Beverley… Beverley Slack.'

Four incredulous faces waited for my inevitable question.

'And, my dear? Are you?'

As we teased our Z-list diva, a heavyset silhouette crunched slowly across the gritty beach. The spectre at the feast crouched behind a stack of plastic sunbeds and glowered at the inebriated Beverly Slack as she slithered further down her chair.

CHAPTER THIRTEEN

BLESSÉD ARE THE MEEK

Siobhan Brennan was the first to admit she was more Marks and Spencer than make do and mend. Her novice fingers ached from hours of sewing name tags into a closet full of clothes – shirts, underwear, trousers, pullovers and jackets – everything needed for the long haul. She stitched slowly and deliberately. The production line was stacked to each side – tagged to the left, still to be tagged to the right – and the haberdashery box she had bought for the exercise lay open on the floor. She fretted as she sewed, tears contained and emotions checked by *The World at One* on Radio 4.

Sean grinned at my time-lapsed greeting and stared at my stuttering image. He clapped his hands and beamed at Liam. 'N-n-n-nice!'

'Bloody hell, Sean, you're naked. What's that brother of yours done to you?' I asked.

'He's only half-naked,' Liam barked into the screen. 'It's hot, isn't it bruv?'

'H-h-h-hot!'

They were sat in semi-shade at a long wooden bench table. Liam panned the laptop camera so I could see the bowling-green lawn. It was edged in regimental planting and the bungalow beyond was bordered by a white picket fence. Summer was in full swing and a warming breeze washed across the Norfolk flatlands. It was a perfect afternoon for Sean to tackle his jigsaw puzzles and he dispatched them with the self-assurance of a grand master.

The bond between the two brothers had always been strong. On the day he was born, Sean struggled to breathe and as one diagnosis after another was scribbled onto his bedside chart, Liam had made an unconscious decision to look out for his little brother.

'Well, it wasn't just me, everyone did. But it was like I could read his mind or something. It freaked me out. I was only ten.'

Every summer the Brennans would spend a week on the Norfolk coast, crammed into a two berth caravan by the side of the beach. On the afternoon of his seventh birthday, Sean flew a sparrowhawk kite on Cromer Sands and gasped at the strength of the North Sea wind as it snatched his kite and forced his spindly legs to give way beneath him. Liam's eyes were fixed hard on Sean's hands, willing them to cling on but they both anticipated the inevitable slow-motion outcome. Sean's white-knuckled fingers curled open and as the kite disappeared over the cliff, he dropped to the sand, head in hands and weak with embarrassment. Liam swept him up and said he'd buy him another kite. They were two a penny and anyway, he was his special brother. But even then, they both knew Sean didn't want to be special. He just wanted to be like everyone else. And now, thirty years on, the two brothers were back on the Norfolk coast. It was Liam's big idea. The perfect place to explain the unexplainable.

'So what's on the agenda for tomorrow?' I asked as Sean returned to his jigsaw.

'Norwich,' said Liam. 'Retail therapy.'

'Never been.'

'Me neither. Full of inbreds and fiddling siblings, I hear.'

'Nothing else to do on a Saturday night, I imagine.'

Liam stared into the laptop camera.

'So, what's new your end?'

'Oh, Beril's feeding me up and I'm gonna be in the papers.'

'The papers? What have you done this time?'

'A journalist's doing a feature. About me. Well, about expat bloggers… in the Turkish Daily News.'

'The nationals?'

The blogging malarkey had opened doors in wholly unexpected ways and hits to my irreverent site had risen exponentially. My gay couple in a Muslim land angle had caught the imagination of the blogosphere. Buoyed by the unexpected kerfuffle, I was experimenting with social networking, anything to extend my fifteen minutes of infamy.

'Apparently, I need to court Faceache and the Tweety thing,' I told Liam. 'The gruesome twosome of social media. Just like I courted you.'

'I feel sorry for both of them, if that's the case,' said Liam. 'You were a crap first date.'

For reasons I didn't understand, I had become popular with tweeting Turks. I would follow back of course; it was the polite thing to do. Not that I had the faintest idea what they were tweeting about. My new Turkish friendships were often short-lived. Once they realised I was a raving gay, most of them unfollowed in an instant. *Not* the polite thing to do. They didn't want to be tarred with the same brush, I supposed. I would spend my days unfollowing in revenge, clicking furiously with a savage mouse. *Take that! Go back to your futbol, misogyny, and wanking off the boy next door.*

I smiled at the screen as Liam helped Sean with the final piece of the jigsaw.

'Have you said anything?'

'Not yet.'

Sean put his arm around his brother and sighed. 'H-h-h-hot!'

'Time for a swim,' said Liam. 'Be good, Jack. And for God's sake go light on the gay thing. Tell 'em we just hold hands and talk about ballet. We don't want a *Midnight Express* moment. Bye, love.'

Left to my own devices, coffee excursions became a daily ritual. A smart café at the heart of the fancy marina became my venue of choice with its superior brew, complimentary chocolate spoons and the flakiest croissants in Bodrum. It was virtually impossible to attract the attention of the waiters at Kahve Dünyası and when I did manage to place an order, I would do it in English. Liam had implored me to try some Turkish ('what's the worst that can happen? Don't be such a pansy!') but whenever I did, the lofty lads feigned selective deafness. So, I played the Englishman abroad.

The marina side of town was almost exclusively populated by well-to-do Turks and those who serviced them, the perfect place to people watch and study the steady stream of mixed-bag strollers. As I surveyed the passing footfall, I realised there was no such thing as a typical Turkish type, certainly nothing akin to the cliché of an English rose, a Celtic redhead or a blonde Swede. This was a patchwork of Turks, a veritable United Nations of a people, from ginger to dusky and European to Asiatic. I shouldn't have been surprised. Anatolia had been a battleground for millennia, settled, won and lost countless times. Each phase of Anatolian history had left its DNA on the population, from the twelve thousand-year-old settlement at Göbekli Tepe in the East, to the British *yabancı* marrying into the fold, and everything else in between. Conquests of antiquity rarely replaced whole populations entirely. Invaders would kill a few, displace some others and breed with the rest. Turkey, it seemed, was the perfect example of a genetic melting pot bubbling down the centuries.

As for the Turks, they didn't think of themselves as Middle Easterners and were certainly not Arabs (though many had the swarthy look that made Liam's knees tremble). And Istanbul may have been a city straddling two continents but its heart was in Europe. In the end, who could tell the difference between a grandma riding a donkey in Greece, Bulgaria or trotting through a Turkish village? So, the Islamic world was no more homogeneous than Christendom and to be Turkish was more of a state of mind than a state of body. We were all mongrels really.

A pool of sticky brown mess had filled my saucer and covered the base of my coffee cup. As I licked my fingers, two mongrel waiters rushed over with a theatrical flourish, extra serviettes and concerned faces. That's what happens when you daydream. Your chocolate spoon melts. Maybe the waiters at Kahve Dünyası weren't so useless after all.

I paid my bill and dawdled along Marina Boulevard. The first phase of Bodrum's radical and expensive new livery was complete save for a few rough edges to be rounded off the following year. Crazy paving had given way to smooth marble slabs and uneven cobbles to a thick layer of coal-black tarmac. Plastic bollards and newly planted saplings polished off the corporate look and a mixed economy of cars – from Chelsea tractors to clapped out Fiats – cruised along the newly planted avenue.

I paused outside Helva, one of Bodrum's most popular fleshpots. Inside, big-haired, bare-chested skinny boys scrubbed down the floors. The bar was being washed and dressed for another profitable night courtesy of the urban elite and the Ukrainian prostitutes who plied their trade among them. Strutting young peacocks passed me by in twos and threes, splashing through the soapy water that had flooded the newly laid pavement, stopping now and again to check their handcrafted reflections in the porthole mirrors lining the external wall of the bar. A sink estate of tattooed, pot-bellied Brits wobbled along the prom looking lost, disoriented and thoroughly hacked off, adding a little Croydon to my panorama. Mummy monster cursed Daddy monster, Daddy monster cursed Mummy monster and Kylie and Riley shuffled behind fingering their smartphones. A deep-fried grandma with a face that launched a thousand chips brought up the rear, cursing the day she'd ever set foot in Asia and wishing she'd gone to Fuengirola instead. When Bodrum's resident drunk began his late afternoon cabaret, toying with the traffic, frothing at the mouth, haranguing passers-by and chatting to the street animals like Dr Doolittle on ketamine, I knew it was time to scuttle home.

Liam pushed his brother along Gentlemen's Walk, passing a neat row of multi-coloured market stalls lined up like beach huts marooned at low tide. Sean's head bobbed about as the wheelchair bumped over the irregular cobblestones of Norwich's busy thoroughfare. Market Square was heaving with a fruity cocktail of Saturday morning grazers: Vicky Pollards pushing fake Burberry buggies, leathered bikers, scruffy students, smart-tailored Henrys, well-appointed pensioners and farmers' wives in waxed jackets. When the rubber wheels wedged into a crevice for the umpteenth time, Liam parked Sean at a table outside Caffè Nero and went in for drinks. He kept his eye on his charge through the plate-glass window as he queued; Sean was an outrageous social flirt and in Liam's eyes, that made him vulnerable.

'F-f-fwend,' said Sean, holding out his hand to an ageing skinhead with a trio of studs in one ear and a spider tattoo crawling up the side of his neck.

'Can't leave you anywhere,' said Liam, returning with the drinks. 'Who's your friend?'

The skinhead smiled and grabbed Sean's hand. 'Been good talking to yer, fella.'

'N-n-nice,' said Sean.

'He's over friendly, my brother, sorry.'

'He's a nice kid. Look after 'im.'

'Oh, I will.'

'See yer later, fella. Be good now.'

While Liam was away on family duty, election fever gripped the nation. Democracy could be a serious and sometimes deadly business in Turkey and I witnessed the drama unfold with some apprehension. Our Sentry Lane watchtower provided the perfect view of the electioneering travelling vans wrapped in patriotism, blazoned with party political slogans and crowned with giant loudspeakers. The political temperature was raised by marching tunes and cavalcades of campaigners honking their car horns with religious zeal; tension swept along Turkey Street like a tsunami. With the governing AK Party riding high in the polls, the question was not if they would win but by what margin. The unequivocal answer came when the AKP swept to victory with sixty percent of the parliamentary seats, but the polarised distribution of those seats revealed the deep divisions within Turkish society. The main opposition CH Party dominated the Aegean coastal provinces and Thrace outside Istanbul. Beyond the Kurdish majority regions, the rest of the country was bathed in AKP yellow. I began to wonder if Turkey really was the crossroad between East and West or simply the deepening fault line.

Liam lifted the glass to Sean's mouth. Milk dribbled down his chin and Liam wiped away the trickle with a napkin.

'Enough?'

'N-n-n-no.' No meant yes.

Liam nudged his seat closer to Sean's wheelchair.

'Sean. You know I live in my house?'

Sean raised his eyes.

'P-p-plane.'

'Yeah. It's a long way. On an aeroplane.'

Sean grinned. Despite the pills and potions, he wasn't daft, whatever people thought. He knew Liam lived with Jack, somewhere hot. He'd seen the photos and got the postcards. He loved looking at the postcards.

'Siobhan lives in *her* house,' continued Liam.

More eye movement.

'And Mum and Dad live in *their* house?'

'M-m-m-mamy!'

'Yes, Mammy.'

At the age of thirty-eight, Sean was still so close to his mother, the very mention of her name made him homesick.

Liam put his hand in his brother's.

'Sean?'

'Huh?'

'How about having your own house? Just like me and Jack?'

Sean snatched back his hand and stared at Liam in disbelief.

'N-n-n-no,' he said in a whisper, his voice cracking. 'N-n-n-no.'

This time, no meant no.

Muzak filled the corridors of the care home as Siobhan struggled into a small ground-floor bedroom. She pushed the door shut with her foot, dropped the bulging IKEA bags to the floor and sat on an unmade single bed. The room was quiet save for the cracking of the plastic sheet beneath her. She looked around the Spartan room and set to work.

That night, another without Liam, the electricity pylon on Turkey Street exploded like a Roman candle, shorting the street lamp. The spectacular light and sound show shook me from my sleep and I dashed outside to greet blurry-eyed Beril and Vadim. Bonfire Night had come early. All that was missing were the sparklers, hot dogs and a punch bowl of mulled wine.

Vadim lit a cigarette and took a seat at the base of the old olive tree.

'Is bad. Is very bad. Tonight we die.'

I could see his point. High above the head of my harbinger of doom, arcs of lightning pirouetted magically along a cable to a neighbouring building and our house lights flicked on and off like a discotheque. As sparks bounced across the roofs, I wondered what Liam might say if he returned to find our home razed to the ground like Tara in *Gone with the Wind* and his husband lying in the morgue with a name tag swinging from his toe.

The morning after our dice with death, Beril yelled from the garden and I stuck my head through the French doors, can of Pledge in one hand and a duster in the other.

'Jack, Jack! *Kahve*? Come. We talk!'

She pointed at two freshly filled espresso cups steaming away on her patio table and I pulled up a chair to face another grin-and-bear-the-grit-at-the-bottom-of-the-cup moment.

'Vadim,' she said as soon as I took my first sip. 'Vadim gone.'

Since they hadn't quarrelled for days, I took this to mean he had popped out on an errand rather than walked out on her completely. She leaned towards me and whispered.

'Liam, *kardeş*. Problem?'

'Liam's brother? Yes... there's a problem, Beril. *Problem var.*'

'Ahh!'

She signed.

'Sorry. Is sad?'

'Yes,' I said. 'Is sad.'

Beril studied my eyes to measure the scale of the sadness.

'Oh, is big sad.'

'Yes,' I said. 'Big sad.'

I sipped my coffee and she sipped hers.

'Jack?' she asked after several minute's silence.

'Yes, Beril?'

'Look.'

Beril presented me with a large luxuriously bound brochure. It was printed in Turkish and stuffed full of vulgar reproduction furniture, backlit for dramatic effect and priced to appeal to the loaded. I thumbed through and thought footballers' wives. I thought nouveau riche.

I thought why the hell would I be interested in gilded swirls, silver tassels and flock wallpaper?

'*Kardeş*,' said Beril, stabbing her index finger at the catalogue. 'Brudder!'

'Your brother?'

'Yessss! *Dizayn, restorasyon, dekorasyon.*'

'Your brother is a designer?'

'Yessss!'

'Ankara?'

'*Yok*, Istanbul.'

Beril snatched the brochure and opened it out at the centrefold, a replica Queen Anne chaise longue topped in crimson silk and edged in gold. It screamed Blackpool Bobbi.

'*Süper*,' I lied. '*Süper.*'

'No!' said Beril, grabbing my hand. 'Brudder. No *eş!*'

'Sorry, not a clue. Where's Liam when you need him?'

Beril was insistent. 'No *eş!* No *eş!*'

'I'm sure it's important, Beril, but repeating it doesn't really help.'

Beril rummaged in the pocket of her house coat, pulled out her little electronic translator and typed *eş* into the micro keyboard.

'Wiffy,' she said in triumph. 'No wiffy.'

'Makes a change for a Turkish man to use a bit of deodorant, I can tell you.'

Beril screamed and tossed the machine across the table.

'*Yok!* No *eş!*'

When Beril grasped my wrist and her eyes bore into mine, all my pennies dropped at once. Beril was sharing a secret. She was shaking out a family skeleton. Beril's brother had no wife. Beril's brother was just like me.

The moment was shattered by the clatter of the gate and Vadim's return.

It was time. Liam wheeled Sean into his new bedroom. There was a smell of fresh paint. Newly framed family photographs hung on the walls, a stack of jigsaw puzzles was heaped up on the small coffee table and well-ordered piles of labelled clothes were layered into open shelves. Sean looked around the small room. Everything was strangely familiar: the single bed with his Disney print cover, the crayon drawings he had brought home from the day centre for Mammy and the old biscuit tin full of familiar photographs and postcards. He knew what this meant. Mammy was tired and his life was about to change forever.

'Well, bruv. Will this do?'

Liam helped Sean from his wheelchair and the two brothers sat side by side on the small bed, hands held, sensing the overwhelming inevitability of a situation neither of them could change.

CHAPTER FOURTEEN

A NEW BEGINNING

Dreams come at a price and our Turkish variety was calling in the debt. Interest rates got slimmer by the month, electricity and meat prices soared and when Liam returned home, he was forced to double our wine budget when the puritan Government hiked up taxes on the Devil's brew. Legitimate employment was all but outlawed for Johnny Foreigner and with no way of fattening the pay packet, we resolved to cut our threadbare cloth even further. Things hit rock bottom when the home delivery of alcohol was banned and we were forced out to Tansaş, risking life, limb and libation on the blind bends of Turkey Street. With more restrictions in the pipeline, Liam considered preparing a vat of fermented spuds at the back of the courtyard.

With the Scott-Brennan economy plunging faster than Greece's, Liam consulted the financial oracle. Bill, his all singing, all dancing, multicoloured spreadsheet, crunched the numbers and delivered an unambiguous bottom line: do something and do it quickly. We decided to shift our dwindling shillings to a bank offering a higher savings rate. Our friendly bank manager was having none of it, doing everything short of outright refusal to scupper our treacherous plot.

'We don't permit withdrawals on Mondays... I need permission from Istanbul... I failed to get permission from Istanbul... Even if I do get permission from Istanbul, it will take months... The other bank is full of crooks... Have some tea... How could you do this to me, after all we've been through?'

As the list of excuses grew more absurd, Liam finally lost his rag and one Friday morning in downtown Bodrum, an angry Brit banged his fists on the desk of a shiny-seated banker. Liam's shock and awe strategy loosened the till drawer and minutes later we were at the counter watching a tutting teller with a face like a slapped arse pile up the wads. The Bonnie and Clyde of Bodrum stuffed the filthy lucre into their man bags and emerged from the bank clinging to their entire worth like limp-wristed limpets.

'We're being watched,' said Liam, staring at passers-by with daggered eyes.

'Don't be ridiculous.'

'So they can't tell we're carrying a squillion lira in cash?'

'It's not like your white knuckles aren't giving the game away.'

Liam relaxed his grip.

'Tell me again why we didn't do the electronic transfer thing?'

'Because the money grabbing bankers would have charged us a fortune, Liam, that's why.'

'And what if someone follows us?'

'We're fucked.'

We survived the five metre journey without being mugged, deposited our swag into the vaults of the bank next door and plodded down to the harbour.

'I don't care what Bill thinks,' I said. 'I'm not doing that again.'

Liam wasn't listening. He had spotted a familiar figure waiting by the roadside, holding onto the handle of a large suitcase. We crept up behind her.

'Susan!'

'Wicked boys, you made me jump!'

We exchanged double air kisses – the stripped down, sanitised version of the traditional Turkish greeting that all emigreys had mastered – and caught up on the news.

'Off somewhere nice?' I asked.

'Just got back from Kos,' said Susan in her best Mid-Atlantic drawl. Twenty years as a Long Beach barista had stretched Susan's clipped Fulham vowels to the point where she sounded neither English nor American. 'Just a day trip.'

'With luggage?' I asked.

'For the products.'

'Products?'

'Pig mainly. And a hundredweight of cheddar.'

'And you're standing here because?'

'I'm waiting to be picked up.'

'By Customs?'

'Very droll, Jack. By Chuck. He's gone to fetch the car. Look boys, I'm glad I bumped into you. We're having a 4th of July party at the weekend. Chuck's feeling homesick.'

We first met Susan and her Yankee husband at a cheese and wine bash in Yalıkavak. They were members of a select group of foreigners who considered themselves a cut above the rest. With a few notable exceptions (Susan and Chuck among them), they weren't and we binned most of the detritus when we legged it to Bodrum. That first year taught us a valuable lesson. Apart from obligatory visits to the Motherland and the occasional cultural field trip, we rarely ventured from Bodrum's warm bosom anymore. We loved Susan's gossipy titbits and Chuck's racy tales about his days as a Hollywood extra. But a party full of golf club bores with their Attila the Hun liberalism and bumper-sticker wisdom was a dolly hop too far.

Susan sensed our reticence.

'Please come, boys. Can I tempt you with my all-American apple pie?'

'What about the pork?' asked Liam. 'Will there be pork?'

'Oh yes,' said Susan. 'A suitcase full.'

'Sean?'

'Huh?'

'Sean, is that you? It's Liam.'

'He's smiling,' said Sean's carer, putting the phone on loudspeaker. 'Ear to ear.'

'He is?'

'He talks about you all of the time. In his way.'

'Sean? It's Liam.'

Sean grunted as if to say *I gathered that much. Don't embarrass me.*

'P-p-p-plane.'

'Yeah, I'm in Turkey. With Jack. It doesn't matter how far away I am, I'll always be your big brother, Sean. You okay? How's your new home?'

'S-s-s-sad. N-n-n-nice!'

Liam took this to mean he missed Mammy and Daddy, but the home was fine.

'He's about to watch *The Simpsons*,' said the carer, 'aren't you, Sean?'

'He is? He loves Bart. It's just... I think about him all the time.'

'I know, you told me yesterday. And the day before that. He's fine. Your brother's just fine.'

Liam would remind everyone about *The Quick Guide to Sean Brennan* pinned to a noticeboard on Sean's bedroom door.

'It's all there,' he would say. 'Everything you need to know. Have you read it?'

'Aha,' they would say. 'Every word.'

THE QUICK GUIDE TO SEAN BRENNAN

Please DON'T:
Leave him alone.
Mislay his tin of photographs.
Tell him off. Whatever he's done, he can't help it.

Please DO:

Let him choose his own clothes, however bizarre the choice. He likes to be different.
Be patient when he asks the same questions on a loop. He forgets.
Tell him he's loved. He forgets that too.

CHAPTER FIFTEEN

HAPPY BIRTHDAY, UNCLE SAM

It seems to me that the only purpose of a baby during waking hours is to eat, pee and poo, using its tiny but powerful lungs to proclaim each preoccupation. When we rode the dolly to Uncle Sam's birthday bash, we were unfortunate enough to witness a particularly pungent stage three. The minibus was stuffed with orange-faced day trippers returning to their swimming-pooled compounds, most of them in the semi buff and reeking of Ambre Solaire and one or two on the turn like week old milk. A young Turkish couple sat in the row immediately behind us, laden with shopping bags and kissing and canoodling like high school prommers. They were also armed with a screaming infant, a high-pitched bundle of joy who asserted its discomfort in the only way it knew how. The doting parents dutifully obliged with a full service. As the stench of the runny evacuation churned around us, fan assisted by the speeding bus, the retching spectators parted like the proverbial. Noses were held and mouths covered for the remainder of the journey. When we stepped off the bus just before it descended into Yalıkavak, the crappy bouquet was still dispersing into the brittle hills.

Chuck and Susan lived in Gökcebel, a sprawling suburb in the foothills above the town. Their impressive detached pile was surrounded on all sides by a well-manicured walled garden and patrolled by a trio of cats Susan had brought in from the bins. Just like its owners, the house was elegant and unpretentious.

I stopped at the entrance and sighed.

'Just the thought of it brings me out in hives.'

'We can do this,' said Liam. 'For Susan's sake. You like Susan...'

'Yes and Chuck too. It's the hangers on I can't abide.'

Loins girded and grins fixed, we passed through the open gate towards the sound of tranquillising chatter and Bruce Springsteen. A Stars and Stripes banner hanging over the path welcomed guests with *Happy Independence Day.* Susan was jiggling a cocktail shaker in time to *Born in the USA* beneath patriotic bunting. Chuck, her handsome sidekick, was lancing a large brick barbecue with a fireside poker. Susan had dressed her cowboy in a Stetson, rhinestone shirt and shoelace tie.

'Boys!' Susan whooped. 'Welcome to Dallas!'

We air kissed and our hostess handed us each a glass of her freshly infused concoction. Susan Richmond was famed across the entire Peninsula for three things – her fine figure, her non-stick liver and her ability to mix a mean Manhattan. I took a sip and gasped.

'You trying to kill me, darling?'

'We aim to please, honey... there's plenty more where that came from.'

'You're a dangerous woman, Susan Richmond, and looking good. Lurve the outfit.'

She was dressed to impress in close-fitting powder blue *churidar* pants and a white *kameez* tunic, a gift to herself from a spring pilgrimage to India.

Susan curtseyed. 'Why thank you, kind sir, I picked it up in Jaipur. It's my Bollywood meets Hollywood thang.'

'We were kind of expecting *Glee* cheerleader meets Doris Day.'

'That's Chuck's department, honey. He's the only real Yankee Doodle Dandy round these parts.'

'Not sure I can see Chuck flouncing around in a micro skirt and shaking his pom-poms. So, how was the Indian trip?'

'Enlightening. If the brochure had come with a scratch and smell card, I'm not sure I'd have bothered.'

'And Chuck?'

'Chuck! There's no way he would have gone.'

'Hell, no,' said Chuck, wandering over from the barbecue. 'They shit in the street out there.'

'That's the elephants, honey, not the people.'

'So you say, darlin', so you say.'

I handed the all American guy a CD of *The Boston Tea Party,* the seminal one hit wonder by the Sensational Alex Harvey Band.

'It's a gift, Chuck, a topical gift,' I said. 'I guess you'd call it a commemoration…'

'Um, thanks, bud.'

'...of the day you lot dumped a ton of British tea into Boston Harbor. Not that we're bitter.'

Susan hugged her man. 'I think Jack's playing with you, honey.'

'Today of all days,' said Liam, returning for a second cocktail. 'Ignore him, Chuck. I do most of the time.'

'I'm off to Thailand next,' continued Susan. 'Chuck's not keen on that either.'

'Too right, Chuck's not keen,' said Chuck. 'Those Siamese are obsessed with sex.'

'Oh hon, don't exaggerate.'

'They all live in 'Bang-cock,' don't they? They go down to 'Fuck-it' at weekends, don't they? Who's exaggerating?'

'It's *Pookette*,' said Susan.

'Puck-it, fuck-it, whatever. And what's with the chicks with dicks?'

'Don't know which way to turn, Chuck?' asked Liam.

'Tell me about it, bud. It ain't right!'

Chuck rescued a blackening corn on the cob from the back of the barbeque and looked around the garden at the emigrey rat pack. 'Look at 'em. Bunch of assholes.'

'Honey, they're our guests,' sighed Susan. 'And watch the beer butt chicken, it's about to burn.'

'Nothing worse than a burning butt,' said Liam camply. 'Who's in?'

'The usual suspects,' said Chuck. 'We sure are fishin' in a pothole.'

'Just go socialise, boys,' said Susan, loading up her cocktail shaker. 'This lot could do with a kickstart. But play nice, Jack, you hear?'

Liam laughed. 'Jack doesn't do nice. Jack does wasp at a picnic.'

We edged around the pick and mingle zone and crept into the kitchen to hunt for Susan's fat sausage rolls. There they were, stacked high on the table, artery-hardening cylinders of flaky butteriness, crammed with the pork Susan had foraged from Kos. We took a fistful each and ambled into the salon, hunting for a comfy corner to hide, munch and blather. The hiding bit proved impossible and it didn't take long for the vipers in paradise to emerge from the undergrowth.

'What's that smell, Liam?'

'What smell?'

'Like a toilet block, and it's getting stronger.'

'Whatever it is, it's attached to that ginger shipwreck drifting our way. Remember, Jack. Be nice. Refill?'

'You're not leaving me with *that*?'

'Watch me.'

A partridge shaped vision in an orange curly perm and lime-green halter top sidled up to me, fingering a sausage roll and grinning ominously. She licked her lips and stretched out a greasy trotter.

'I'm Deborah!'

'As in Kerr?' I asked, eyeballing the slick of lard on her painted nails.

'As in Deborah.'

'Well hello there, Deborah as in Deborah.'

'I've heard all about you two.'

'All bad I hope.'

Deborah brayed like a donkey.

'It's wonderful to meet you at last,' she said, offering her hand for the second time. 'I think it's marvellous.'

'Marvellous?' I asked, taking another look at the hand and resolving not to go anywhere near it.

'The man on man thing,' said Deborah. 'I do *so* love the gays.'

My heart sank.

'That's a very distinctive scent you're wearing, Deborah.'

'Isn't it? You'll never guess what it is!'

'Febreze?'

Deborah threw back her head and hee-hawed.

'You gays are *so* witty,' she said. 'It's like meeting Colin and Justin in the flesh. It really is. You know…'

I knew very well, a pair of weak-wristed makeover maestros who ravaged suburban homes with cheap and nasty kitsch every weekday at two p.m. Realising that so-so Deborah was incurably stupid rather than malicious, I let it pass.

Deborah nibbled away on her piece of pig, her sharp incisors pressing through the pastry like a hole punch as flakes of filo dropped from her mouth.

'On your own, Deborah?'

'Yes,' she replied vaguely. 'I lost my husband.'

'Probably at the bar with all the others,' I said. 'Susan's cocktails are a big draw.'

'Lost as in dead.'

'Oh. Shit! I'm sorry... I…'

'Oh, don't be, I'm not.'

'You're not sorry your husband's dead?'

'Not really, no. We ran a bistro in Eton Wick and I found him in flagrante with the sous chef.'

Now that got my attention.

'A massive heart attack according to the coroner. Presumably at the shock of clocking me at the pantry door.'

I choked on a supressed laugh. 'How awful.'

'And let me tell you, if he hadn't croaked it, I would have *so* murdered the bastard.'

'It must have been a terrible shock,' I said, grabbing a handful of Susan's cheesy balls.

'It was Gavin I felt sorry for.'

'Your husband?'

'The sous chef.'

Deborah's bonking bronco had been riding our dolly for years – cottages, saunas, Windsor Great Park, anywhere for a hand shandy, a bit of bumming or a date in the mouth. Deborah had never suspected. Even his collection of vintage Judy Garland vinyls hadn't spoiled the surprise.

'Of course, I should have guessed,' said Deborah, fiddling with her frou-frou earrings. 'The last time he lifted my nightie was on Millennium night and that was only because he'd been on the Sambuca. Quite frankly, Jack, after twenty years of five minute fumbles in the dark with him poking round the wrong hole, I was rather relieved when he stopped trying.'

The final insult came when she discovered a frayed appointment card for a Slough clap clinic in a Burberry continental purse.

'I didn't even know he liked Burberry, for pity's sake.'

'So what did you do?'

'Do? I burned the card, pocketed the cash and cremated the cheating little shit on the cheap. What would *you* do?'

As we sipped our cocktails and nibbled the cheesy balls, the tragedy of Deborah's tale was concluded in all its tawdry detail. With her husband scattered over the playing fields of Eton, Deborah sold the bistro, moved to Turkey and drowned her sorrows by jumping on top of any would-be gigolo who sailed past her patio. The boys got younger as she got older and she clung to the VOMIT lifeboat until her nails bled. Despite the predictable pattern of broken heart and emptied purse, Deborah remained irrepressibly upbeat about her lot. Given her husband's predilection for male cooks and dogging in the woods, her fondness for 'the gays' was admirably magnanimous.

Nancy appeared through the mob with a grin as broad as her cleavage.

Saved by the cavalry.

'Drink, Nans?'

'No need, darlin'. Liam's sortin' me aart.'

'You look sensational.'

Nancy had slipped into her Ava Gardner in *Bhowani Junction* number, a vermilion wraparound frock that accentuated her bouncing baps and trimmed her waist.

'You old flatterer, Jack Scott. This ol' fing? Just frew it on.'

'Well, it fell on in all the right places.'

Nancy beamed and pressed out her famous rack.

She had the juiciest mandarins on the Peninsula and she knew it.

'Don't 'alf chafe, though' she said pulling at her bra strap. 'Got awful nipple burn.'

'You two know each other?'

'Course we do,' said Nancy. ''Ow's it 'angin', Debs?'

'Sorry, I left my Cockney slag phrasebook at home.'

'Well pardon me for breavin', Debs.'

Deborah twitched. 'It's Deborah, as in DE-BO-RAH. How many more bloody times!'

De-bo-rah stomped off through the French doors and Nancy curtseyed.

'Get the bleedin' madam.'

'You two got history?'

'She finks I'm common.'

'Well she's the one humping the pool boy.'

'Tell me about it. We all call 'er Debbie dog.'

'Poodle perm?'

'Always on all fours.'

We screamed, startling the chattering classes with their clattering glasses.

'So?' I asked, lowering my voice. 'No Charlotte?'

'No. She 'ad a barney with Susan.'

'Oh?'

'Susan told 'er to give up Adalet.'

'You know, and it pains me to say this, but maybe she's right.'

'No way, Jack. It ain't over 'til the fat lady sings.'

'Even if she's singing to empty seats? Think about it, Nans. Just think about it.'

Liam discarded his cocktail glass and rummaged at the bottom of the fridge for a fresh bottle of white.

'While you're down there, young man...'

Liam turned around. A lanky six footer stood over him with an outstretched arm wriggling an empty Paris goblet. A greased-down comb over stretched in a large arc from sideburn to sideburn, a psychedelic Hawaiian shirt hung over a sunken chest and loose khaki shorts flapped above two knobbly knees.

'I'm Gordon,' announced Gordon. 'And you're Liam.'

'That's a relief. For a minute there I thought I'd turned into Googie Withers.'

'I saw you come with your 'friend'.'

'Bit of a peeping Tom, are you, Gordon?'

Gordon's lantern jaw hung beneath hollow cheeks and an angular nose was crisscrossed with a network of thread veins: Bruce Forsyth without the easy charm or dodgy rug.

'So... you know who I am?' asked Liam, pouring wine into Gordon's empty glass.

'Of course. Who doesn't?'

'For all the wrong reasons, I'm sure.'

Gordon smiled. 'There's no shame in infamy, young man. I should know.'

Gordon's statement was the opening volley of an uninvited exposé of his life, prejudices and opinions and, not for the first time, Liam found himself trapped in a conversation of catatonic mediocrity. Gorders had recently retired following an unrequited love affair with Margaret Thatcher, and a lucrative career in slum rentals.

'That woman had balls,' boomed Gordon. 'Sorted out all the lefties and skivers.'

'Let me get this straight,' said Liam. 'You made a fortune ripping off the poor?'

'It was easy money, why wouldn't I?'

'Dunno. Principles?'

'I'm a naked capitalist. No point pretending I'm a soft-brained liberal.'

The naked capitalist was unhappily married to Wanita, a woman a third of his age.

'She doesn't get out much. Too fond of the bottle, if you get my drift,' he explained, wiggling a re-emptied glass. Liam poured the last of the wine, not in the least bit surprised Wanita was blotting out life with Gordon by self medicating with the hard stuff.

'I leave her to it and play a round.'

'And she doesn't mind?

'It's only golf. Where's the harm?'

'Oh, I see.'

'Anyway, Lee, as I was saying, I'm very broad-minded. No flies on me. No siree.'

'No one's ever called me Lee before.'

'As long as you don't rub my nose in it, I don't care what you people get up to.'

Hell would have frozen over before Liam rubbed anything attached to Gordon.

'Still,' continued Gordon, 'I don't suppose the natives like it much.'

'The natives?'

'Look son, we're both men of the world. I was in the merchant navy and I saw some sights, I can tell you.'

'I'm sure you did, Gordon.'

'I had this mate, my old mucker, Archie. One time we were on shore leave in Singapore. Summer of '66... Archie got himself a ladyboy. Not that he knew it at the time.'

'Okay...'

'Pearl. A right looker he was.' Gordon's eyes narrowed. 'Turns out Pearl was the bigger man.'

'I'm not sure I like where this is going, Gordon.'

'Put it this way. Archie thought he was getting an all you can eat buffet but ended up with a spring roll.'

'Yes, I thought that's where we were going.'

'He couldn't sit down for week.'

'Well, it's been lovely meeting you, Gordon.'

'And then he started using my Brylcreem as—'

'Okay, I get the picture. So where is he now, this Archie?'

'Shacked up on the Isle of Wight. With Pearl. The point is, my friend, I've seen it all. I don't care what tosses your salad.'

Gordon put his arm around Liam and turned him to face the other guests.

'Look at 'em, Lee, the moral majority. This lot don't get it like me and you. Two men living together as husband and wife? As far as they're concerned, it's not on.'

'Husband and husband.'

'That's what I'm saying, Lee. Mark my words. They don't get it. And like I said, let's not even go there with the natives.'

Liam had one of his *what the fuck am I doing here talking to this total knob* moments and decided on a strategic withdrawal.

'Thanks ever so much for the pep talk, Gorders. It's been a real education. How very nice to meet you. To meet you, nice.'

He passed Gordon the empty wine bottle. 'I'm sure you can find something to do with that. Maybe try a dash of Brylcreem.'

Liam disappeared through the French doors like an extra from *Hay Fever* and Nancy cantered into the front garden after him, dragging me behind. We found Liam resting under a fig tree, puffing on a palliative fag.

'Where's my bleedin' drink?' asked Nancy.

'Oh God, sorry. Got caught with an old windbag. You have no idea.'

'Bruce Forsyth lookalike?'

'That's him.'

'Flesh Gordon. Right letch. Always tryin' to get into me knickers. And his poor wife…'

'Wanita?'

'Yeah. The Filipino virgin.'

'Filipino? How terribly exotic,' I said.

'Not really, 'ee picked her out of a catalogue. She came with a bar code.'

'Poor cow,' said Liam. 'Imagine living with *that*. No wonder she turned to drink.'

'She's not the only one turning to drink,' said Nancy. 'Abracadabra…'

Nancy whipped out a bottle of red from behind her back, quickly followed by a stack of beakers.

'Ta Dah!'

We huddled under the fig tree like a gang of naughty schoolchildren sharing their first flagon of Strongbow and Nancy raised a toast to her best friend. Ever since the christening, Charlotte had gone into self-imposed seclusion, rarely leaving the house and even struggling to crawl out of bed some days. The court battle to get Adalet back dragged on with one adjournment after another and Charlotte had convinced herself that she and Alan were the talk of the town. They probably were. Charlotte's husband was a broken man, frozen into inaction by the trauma and worried about losing his wife on top of losing his daughter. Liam suggested a pick me up dinner at Sentry Lane and despite Nancy's reticence, she promised to persuade Charlotte and Alan to come. It could hardly make things any worse.

'Well, boys,' said Nancy tidying her bust and straightening her skirt. 'Time for this glamour puss to circulate before she leaves the party. I got plans. Big plans.'

'Hot date?' asked Liam.

'Steamin', darlin'. Absolutely steamin'.'

The party reached its drunken climax and swung further and further to the Right. Idle chatter gave way to hard-boiled arguments about the evils of smoking and a woman's place in the home with the pros and antis lobbing grenades at each other from the trenches. Leaving Liam hidden in the bush, I ventured into no man's land and found Susan clearing up the wreckage.

'Top up, Jack? Try the punch on the trestle table. It's lethal.'

She pointed towards a slender brunette clasping a drink with one hand and drawing on a cigarette with the other. 'You'll have to share with Muffy.'

Susan's Muffy had an unmistakable look: runway chest, fat round bob, bush baby eyes and a grey face. A shapeless flapper-style frock accentuated her androgynous figure giving her the look of an upturned exclamation mark.

'Hi,' I said, ladling some punch into a couple of tumblers. 'Great minds.'

Muffy leapt into conversation and rammed her entire uninteresting life story down my disinterested throat. She was a hoity-toity Old Roedeanian with a grand Victorian pile overlooking the Thames on Putney Towpath and had a farthing or two stashed away offshore. Muffy was in Turkey on the hunt for something with 'big' stamped all over it – big place, big views, big pool and big lira, anything to match her big ego.

'Putney?' I said. 'Lovely. I misspent my fumbling years in Putney.'

'I'm not surprised you got out,' she said with the gravelly voice of a forty a day habit. 'The only good thing about Putney these days is the low council tax. Just a few streets away, it's double. Double!'

'And you know why that is, don't you?'

'I'm not sure I do, no.'

'Well, in Putney, don't be old, don't be young and don't be disabled.'

Muffy pondered, picked up a carrot crudité and snapped it in her mouth.

'Oh, I don't care about people like that.'

'Well, my dear Muffy, I hope *you* don't end up in a wheelchair.'

I left Muffy to her crudités and went to fetch Liam. I'd finally had my fill of *Tenko* without the guards, guns and barbed wire.

Nancy wobbled across the shingle, stopping to shake out a sharp stone caught in the arch of her foot. She jumped into Charlotte and Alan's Mini Cooper, threw off her Manolo Blahniks and sped off down the dusty street.

'I wish she'd stop screwing that odious village man,' said Susan, waving Nancy off at the gate.

'Village idiot, more like,' said Chuck. 'Freakin' dumb ass.'

Susan was worried. 'She'll be out on her ear if Marianna pitches up.'

'And what's Marianna got that Nancy hasn't?' asked Liam.

'Euros.'

To avoid the unwanted attention of evening revellers, Nancy held her silver Manolo Blahniks in her right hand as she crept through the backstreets of Yalıkavak towards the sleepy harbour. Her pneumatic chest heaved expectantly and her heart pounded like a virgin on her wedding night. Irfan's love boat was squeezed into its usual tight berth. The deck was sheathed in blackness save for a glowing spot of light darting about like an orange firefly from inside the cabin. Irfan was reeling in the catch of the day with all the confidence of a champion angler. Nancy reached the stern and tiptoed gingerly across the wobbly gang plank. Feeling her way along the side rope in the dark, she lost her footing and almost tipped chest first into the diesel-filmed waters. With sea legs regained, she slipped out of her damp panties, sneaked across the deck and without a word, greeted Irfan with a royal curtsy on the old seadog's face. Moments later, Nancy's trick hips slammed into top gear and Irfan's little boat started to rock, breaking the glassy water and producing a wash that lapped up against the quay. The gulets either side swayed in rhythmic concert. Captain Irfan had moored his vessel in more ways than one, and though she didn't know it, Nancy was going down like the Titanic.

CHAPTER SIXTEEN

LITTLE DRUMMER BOY

We woke with a jolt. Liam leapt out of bed, lurched over to the window and pulled back the curtains. It was a steamy four a.m. and the sleepy street echoed to the sound of a lone drum beating out a persistent monotonic thump.

'For Christ's sake!' I moaned, wrapping a pillow around my head to muffle the racket. 'Make it stop.'

'It's just the *Ramazan* drummer boy,' said Liam. 'It's tradition. He's waking the Faithful. Like last year.'

'Waking the dead, more like. Tell him to pack it in.'

'Don't be such an old grump,' said Liam as the thumping became more complex and irregular. 'He's mixing up the rhythm. Listen.'

'Unless it's Harry Judd in a studded jock strap, I'm not interested.'

One by one, the houses along Turkey Street sparked into life. Light switches flicked on, doors slammed, babies cried, dogs barked and cocks crowed. The pious and the agnostic both suffered the same fate.

Liam turned on the bedside lamp.

'Let's go native and eat before sunrise. I'll do breakfast.'

'Then what? Pop to the mosque and pray for rain?'

Liam opened the bedroom door and quickly closed it behind him to keep the heat at bay. I whacked up the air conditioning, buried myself under the top sheet and tried to doze off. Minutes later, Liam returned with a pot of Earl Grey and a plate of jammy dodgers.

'It's hardly an Ottoman feast, is it Liam?' I said, sitting up and rubbing the sleep from my eyes.

'It's all we've got. Unless you fancy pomegranate ice cream?'

Liam sat on the side of the bed and licked the jam from a dodger.

'Jack?'

'What?'

'You happy?'

'Of course I'm happy.'

'So you still like it here?'

'Of course I still like it here, Liam.'

'Despite the drummer?'

'Yes. Despite the drummer, the barking dogs, the searing heat, the whinging emigreys, financial ruin, the slow slide to Sharia Law and a husband who serves up jammy dodgers for breakfast.'

Liam nestled into me and closed his eyes.

'Me too.'

He sighed.

'You missing Sean?'

'Yeah.'

'He's happy isn't he? In the home, I mean?'

'Loves it.'

'So, panic over. We'll stay, then. In this crazy country?'

'We'll stay.'

I stroked his forehead.

'Liam?'

'What?'

'It's not just food that's forbidden after daybreak.'

'Is that all you ever think about?'

'More or less. That and full fat croissants.'

'But what would Allah say?'

'I'm sure he loves a nice continental.'

Vadim dragged two large suitcases across the courtyard, quickly followed by Beril carrying an angry cat in a box. In twelve short months, their child substitute had grown from a ball of fluffy white fur into a feisty minx with balls. Literally. Bianca was, in fact, Bianco and as he yowled from the inside of his plastic carrier, Beril whispered sweet nothings in an attempt to placate her little boy. The embarrassing gender confusion had thrown Beril into a complete tailspin and I had been asked on more than one occasion to re-examine the evidence with a spot of tummy rubbing.

'Yes, Beril,' I would say. 'There's absolutely no doubt. Look at those. What do you think they are? Liam, what's Turkish for testicles?'

The newly empowered tom tolerated no incursions and patrolled the garden wall with uncompromising fortitude. Beril would also keep vigil, fretting that Bianco might venture out into the speed junkie world of Turkey

Street. The thought of Bianco ending up as road kill was bad enough, but worse, much worse, was the thought of him being tortured by the clowder of streetwise moggies strutting their stuff by the communal bins.

Bianco was on his inaugural holy month trip to Ankara and as head gardener, Vadim left strict instructions that I should soak the bedding twice a day while they were away. Ramazan was sizzling. Varnish peeled off window sills, tourists wilted and daytime Bodrum had descended into terminal inertia.

'Water, Jack!' insisted Vadim, picking up a hose and demonstrating the advanced workings of a tap to hose operation. I played inner city idiot and gasped when water trickled out onto the lavender patch.

'Incredible, Vadim. Run that by me again. This time, I'll take notes.'

'Don't be a twat,' said Liam. 'He's only trying to be helpful. Very good Vadim, I'm sure Jack will master it.'

'He hasn't a clue what you're saying, Liam. You might as well tell him you've got a lovely bunch of coconuts. Which, of course, you haven't.'

Vadim muttered to Beril in Turkish – probably something along the lines of *no wonder the English lost India* – and returned the hose to its resting place. Beril rushed towards me and flung her arms around my neck.

'Bye bye, Jack.'

'*Güle güle,* Beril. Don't be a stranger, now.'

Despite our fondness for our neighbours, we were glad to see the back of them for a few weeks. It was like the 1918 Armistice and we could potter about in the poppy fields without getting caught in the crossfire. As soon as the garden gate clattered behind them, I clipped Liam's head and threw myself into my new role as Capability Brown's new apprentice. According to Liam, I showed great enthusiasm but remarkably little skill and as I snipped and pruned, shaped and twined, he pointed to a mandarin sapling wilting in a large planter outside Beril's French doors. The cracked soil was as dry as a Saturday night in Tehran and I drenched the tree using Vadim's magic hose. Seconds later, thousands of panic-stricken ants swarmed through the rising tide, scrambling up the inside of the terracotta formicary holding their grubs aloft with their forelegs. Liam was aghast and accused me of wiping out an entire subspecies of Turkish hymenoptera. As I watched the unfolding genocide, I could almost hear the worker ants scream 'Save the babies! Save the babies!' and realised my cosmological journey to Buddhist enlightenment had suffered a bit of a setback.

As it turned out, my amateurish horticultural efforts were pretty much in vain. One hot morning, we awoke to the sound of grunting and threshing. Hanife, our slash-and-burn landlady, was barking orders at a scythe-wielding gardener. The florid stranger decimated the shrubs, hacked back the bougainvillea and shaved the bedding to within an inch of the ground. By midday, our garden had been well and truly scalped and that was that. Vadim would be livid and guess who would get the blame?

One of the more exciting aspects of living on Sentry Lane, for Liam at least, was the daily appearance of a water seller, heralding his arrival by ringing a small antique bell.

Waterman was a giant of a beast who effortlessly lugged nineteen-litre bottles about like Aquarius on steroids. When Liam first encountered Waterman, he announced that he was in love for *the very first time* and that it was enough to *make a batty boy faint*. The ensuing romance cooled when Waterman's familiar ding-a-ling stopped ding-a-linging during the heatwave. At the expected time, Liam would hover at the garden gate waiting, but he didn't come. Even when we were seriously low on drinking water, Liam refused to betray Waterman by purchasing 'inferior' bottles from Marketman on Halfway Square.

'What if he's ill?' Liam speculated. 'Or dead? How would we know?'

Just when Liam had given up all hope, Waterman pulled up at the end of Sentry Lane.

'Your lover's back,' I shouted down from the balcony as I was hanging out the washing.

Liam raced out, empty bottle in hand and swung open the gate.

'*Merhaba!*' said Liam. 'But where's your little bell?'

'Finish.'

'Finished?'

'*Evet*. Finish. Many complain of noise.'

'But I like your little bell.'

Waterman smiled and shook Liam's hand with the slippery grip of a Turkish wrestler.

'Not so little, my friend.'

A victorious Liam rolled his prize through the courtyard as I whistled disapprovingly.

'You're only jealous,' Liam shouted up. 'Get back to your guard duties.'

For several sticky days, I had been keeping an eye on our Dolce & Gabbanas. There was a knickers nicker about. The thief had been skulking around the ward pilfering underwear from unsupervised washing lines and only the night before had snatched a pair of granny pants. Theories about the tea leaf's motive had tongues wagging from Old Hamam Street all the way down to Ali Berber's. As it happened, there wasn't much for me to stake out anyway. During the height of summer, we went commando in loose cotton shorts, anything to keep our nether regions daisy fresh. Together with judicious pruning of our prickly pairs, it helped stave off the prickly heat.

Liam appeared on the balcony with two glasses of iced tea as I was pulling open the top of my shorts and peering into the abyss.

'You know, Liam. When your balls drop nobody tells you they just keep on going.'

'Put 'em away, Jack.'

'Look. I could run a grandfather clock with 'em.'

'I'm not interested.'

'That's because there's someone else, isn't there? You made that tea with *his* water, didn't you?'

'What if I did?'

'Well, I'm not drinking it.'

'Fine with me.'

'I *saw* you. In broad daylight. It's holy month. Have you no shame? People have been stoned for less.'

'He's a good Turkish boy,' said Liam looking down to the street below. 'He's only got eyes for the girls.'

A pair of scanty teenagers tottered along Turkey Street in single file, squeezed into Barbie-sized bikinis and vertiginous heels. As their buttocks wobbled, cars broke, horns blared, and curtains twitched. The leading lady swigged a large bottle of Efes while her dumpy companion stooped behind, arms folded, shielding her Cherry Bakewells from the boys in heat. It was an unrelenting embarrassment. Brits airlifted into Asia for Turkey's low-cost delights hadn't the slightest notion where they were. Bikini babes and speedo'd boys wandered round with impunity, neither understanding nor caring what was acceptable on the beach might not go down so well on the streets. It was a small wonder some Turkish men, particularly nomads from the East who rarely saw more than a flash of an ankle from their covered kin, thought western women were the Whores of Babylon. As if to ram the point home, there he was, Liam's Waterman, glued to the spot, transfixed by the bouncing buns of the passing trade, his jaw dropped like a limp JCB. Liam was right. Waterman was as straight as a Roman road.

CHAPTER SEVENTEEN

THE LAST SUPPER

As the sun started to set and temperatures fell to the low thirties, Liam went to work in the kitchen and I put finishing touches to the large dining table we had hauled out to the centre of the courtyard. It was a state banquet vision in white, topped off with a centrepiece of candles encased in glass to protect the flames from the supercharged breeze.

Liam came out to admire my handiwork.

'Sweet Lord of mercy, who's died?'

'Too much?'

'Too much? It's like Donatella Versace's dressed the altar for her own funeral. Where's the coffin?'

'I was going for high camp.'

'Well you've got high church. Grab a crucifix and we'll re-enact the Passion.'

'So, Liam, what culinary disaster have you planned for tonight?'

'Chicken Kiev. Charlotte's favourite.'

'Chicken? It's always chicken. Why is it always chicken?'

'Because it's cheap. Like you.'

Red meat was off menu at No. 2. The price of beef and mutton had soared to stratospheric levels and on a lean budget, chicken had become our staple source of protein. We weren't the only ones feeling the pinch either, judging by reports in the national press and the growing chorus of early morning cocks. In every other backyard along Turkey Street, harems of hens were corralled by twisted chicken wire and regularly mounted by a bad-tempered rooster with dandy plumage and a cock-of-the-coop demeanour. To my eternal shame, before the move to Bodrum, I had never seen a live chicken in the flesh. My chickens came ready plucked, hung, drawn and often quartered and I had no intention of changing that particular custom. Liam and I plucked our breasts from the chiller cabinet at Tansaş.

With preparations complete and Liam's tealights flickering away in the olive tree, we sat at the altar and sipped the wine.

'This could be a disaster,' said Liam.

'I know.'

'It was your idea.'

'I know that, too.'

The theme from *Titanic* seeped through the open salon windows and Liam hummed along.

'We have to be honest with her, Liam.'

'Some people can't take that much honesty.'

'Some people can't take that much Celine Dion.'

As the final note of Ms Dion's warbling faded to nothing, things went tits up in a rather unexpected fashion. A luckless sparrow flew into an electricity cable strung high above the courtyard. Tweetie Pie exploded like a clay pigeon and a flurry of toasted feathers floated gently to the ground. The impact tripped the lights, plunged the neighbourhood into darkness and Liam's undercooked chicken continued to undercook in the cooling oven.

'What were you saying about disasters?'

'All's not lost, Jack. We just need to pray.'

'Who to?'

'Saint Martha. The patron saint of fine dining.'

'I see. And what if old Martha's busy with her vol-au-vents?'

'We'll try St Jude. He does lost causes.'

An hour later, our guests were greeted by a candlelit house, a hastily prepared salad and an inebriated cook. As they took their seats and I dragged Liam into the kitchen to funnel water down his throat, the saints in heaven restored power and the night of reckoning was back on track.

Liam cleared away the plates.

'That was lovely, sweet pea,' said Charlotte. 'Really, it was.'

'Those breasts were enormous,' said Alan.

'Yes,' I said. 'Liam's chumbawumbas are the talk of Turkey Street.'

Charlotte laughed for the first time that evening, probably for a hundred evenings. Jack and Liam's campfest made a change from picking over the dry bones of the never ending adoption case.

'It must be lovely having the garden to yourselves?' she said.

'Yes,' I replied. 'We haven't missed an opportunity.'

'Opportunity for wot?' asked Nancy.

Liam sighed and retreated to the kitchen.

'You know... a touch of al fresco frottage. Reprising the roles of our Hampstead Heath years. Thank Allah the courtyard's secluded. Wouldn't want to frighten the donkeys.'

Charlotte collapsed into giggles. 'Sometimes, Jack, I don't believe you.'

'Oh believe it,' said Liam returning to the garden with a platter of French fancies. 'Jack's held together by innuendo, clichés and sticky-back plastic.'

'Picture it,' I said, 'a West End revival. Rave reviews and quite a few encores.'

Liam took his seat and kicked me under the table.

'What have I said now?'

'A rat the size of a beaver just ran across the salon floor.'

Nancy let out a piercing scream.

'It's a rat, Nans,' said Liam, 'not the Grim Reaper. Get a grip.'

Liam and I found the wayward rodent panting behind the sofa and when it saw four eyes peering into the darkness, it darted out across the tiled floor and took refuge behind the Chinoiserie cocktail bar, defecating wildly en route.

'They make 'em big in Turkey,' said Liam. 'Like the chicken breasts. He's a monster.'

Nancy bolted upstairs and fell off her Manolo Blahniks. 'You gotta be fuckin' jokin'. And now I've broke my bleedin' ankles! Kill it! Kill it!'

Charlotte and Alan came to help the last of the great white hunters, and together we chased the rat around the perimeter of the room as it sought sanctuary in various dark nooks. Agile, cunning and resourceful, the clever creature ran us ragged, eventually vaulting onto the top of a tall speaker. Liam grabbed a broom, Alan collected up a pile of scatter cushions and we lined them up across one half of the room like a hoplite phalanx. We took our positions, Alan, Charlotte and me crouching behind the barricade, Liam and broom at the front and Nancy safely locked away behind the upper balcony door.

Liam approached the enemy to discuss terms.

'Look Roland. Give it up. Unless you wanna meet your maker?'

Roland twitched his long whiskers. *You and whose army, baldy? Do your worst.*

Liam jabbed the broom at the creature, forcing it to leap down from the speaker and run towards the wall of cushions. Shields of soft furnishings were advanced with Spartan precision and Roland slammed on the brakes, skidding to a stop, inches from the barrier. The game was up and he knew it. The cornered rat reared up on his hind legs, rubbed his snout with his claws and sped off through the open front door leaving a trail of droppings in his wake. A final parting gift.

I shouted up to the balcony. 'It's gone, Nans. You can come down now.'

'If you're 'aving me on, I'll 'ave yer, Jack Scott. I will. I'll 'ave yer.'

With rat ousted, Nancy back at ground level, dessert eaten and the olive tree tealights about to expire, Charlotte released her hair from its ivory clip.

'Nice to see you relaxing,' I said. 'We've been worried about you.'

Charlotte smiled and looked over at Alan.

'It's been a difficult time, Jack.'

'And we'd like to help,' said Liam.

Tears formed in Charlotte's eyes. 'You can't help. No one can.'

Alan filled us in on the depressing news. An unknown UK source had rung the child trafficking bell and the UK authorities had alerted their Turkish counterparts. It was nonsense, malicious nonsense, but Turkish Social Services were duty bound to remove Adalet.

'Fair enough, I suppose,' said Alan. 'But what they did next was unforgiveable.'

It was what our Yankee cousins call 'cruel and unusual punishment.' A brick wall spanning two continents was constructed as the British authorities washed their hands and Turkish Social Services refused to give an inch. Charlotte and Alan became hopelessly gripped in the vice of a judicial system pressing down on them like a dead weight. The powers that be opposed at every turn.

'They called us baby buyers, child traffickers, criminals,' said Charlotte. 'Us! How could they? I loved that child. I *love* that child.'

'And where's Adalet now?' I asked.

'That's the problem,' said Charlotte sniffing into a tissue. 'We don't know.'

'Not at the orphanage,' said Alan. 'We checked.'

Nancy smiled at Charlotte. 'We think she's wiv a nice Turkish couple, don't we Charlotte?'

'How can she be? She's *my* daughter!'

For only six short months Charlotte had been the perfect mother, a mother who planned to raise her daughter as a proud but independent Turkish woman, albeit within a Christian family. As the conversation turned and the tears rolled, I wondered if that was the real root of the problem, the hidden agenda pulling the levers in Ankara: the unpalatable prospect of foreign Christians adopting a Muslim child. A Turkish child. Had their anonymous accuser not blown the whistle from the shadows, Charlotte and Alan might have kept their private adoption under the radar. But once the bomb had gone off, national politics and religious pride took centre stage and there was no justice to be had.

'I know this isn't what you want to hear, Charlotte,' I said, 'but…'

Charlotte stared at me with wide eyes, tears streaming down her cheeks.

'…maybe it's time,' I said. 'To let go. For Adalet's sake and for yours. You can't take on the entire Turkish State.'

'She's my baby! How could you even think that!'

'Adalet's not a baby anymore, my love,' said Liam. 'Maybe it's time to think of *her* too.'

Charlotte let go of Liam's hand and threw down her tissue.

'*Think* of her? I live and breathe my little girl, twenty four hours a day. I wake up and the first thing I think about is Adalet, her eyes, her little hands, her fingers, her sweet-smelling skin. *Think* of her? I don't do anything *but* think of her! How could you!'

'I only—'

'No Liam! You're just like Susan. I'll never give her up, never! No matter who tells me to, not even you. Do you hear!'

Alan slumped into the back of his chair. Charlotte's heart was broken into too many pieces and it would take more than one night at No. 2 to put it back together again. The fat lady had finally left the stage and there was nothing we could do but leave Charlotte alone in the stalls.

CHAPTER EIGHTEEN

IRFAN THE SLUT

Liam ran his fingers up and down the inside of my thigh. We were stretched out on Chuck's shady rear deck in the company of three soporific cats and two empty bottles of Misli white. Like the British Raj of old, we had headed for the hills to escape the oppressive heat of Bodrum, supposedly to cat sit while Susan and Chuck were back on Kos restocking the bacon and cheddar. Liam was in a frisky, horizontal mood.

'I'm ready for my blow job, Mr DeMille.'

'Well ain't that a shame, Miss Desmond?' I sighed. 'Mr DeMille's out to lunch.'

Liam's amorous advances were curtailed by the municipal PA system, a cross between *1984* and *Hi-de-Hi*, a comical if slightly sinister way of making official announcements about local events, planned power cuts and the state of the Mayor's lumbago.

'*Bugün,* today,' Liam translated, 'many services will close.'

'There you go,' I said. 'No servicing for you today.'

'*Yarın*,' he continued, 'tomorrow, many roads will close.'

'We're stuck in the sticks forever.'

'And *yarın*, also tomorrow… many shops will close.'

'We'll starve.'

Liam strained to understand the next crackling announcement.

'What the hell is *Zafer Bayramı?*'

'I'm not convinced you understood one word of that babble, Liam. For all we know, Turkey's just declared war on Germany. And with Merkel hellbent on scuppering Turkey's EU aspirations, I wouldn't be at all surprised.'

'Turkey's not ready for Europe,' said Liam. 'And why should it be? All those hoops to jump through like a performing dolphin. Turkey's different. That's why we're here.'

'I'm not sure Mutti Merkel sees it that way.'

'What does she know? Never trust a politician with thick ankles and a *Cadfael* hairdo.'

After an emergency call to Doc, Liam discovered that the Turkish defeat of Greek forces in the War of Independence was about to be celebrated throughout the land. Victory Day was one of several national and intensely nationalistic public holidays punctuating the year. With the patriotic masses planning a day of pomp and partying, things were looking less rosy along the corridors of power. As Commander-in-Chief of the Turkish armed forces, President Gül was about to host a top-notch reception for the top tier. The First Lady, though, had not been invited, and her omission had caused a furore in the national press.

Like many spouses at the heart of the Islamic-leaning governing AK Party, Hayrünnisa Gül was in the habit of slipping on a headscarf. And very fetching she looked in it too. In the eyes of the Turkish military, this was a clear violation of the secularist principles established by Atatürk, founding father of the republic and hammer of the Greeks. To the casual observer, the spat appeared rather trivial. After all, we were talking a simple head covering not an Afghan letterbox onesie. Back in the day, my own mother would throw on a headscarf when she popped out for a sliced loaf and ten No. 6 and I don't remember the checkout girl at the Spar accusing her of religious fundamentalism. Anyway, scarves were de rigueur for the post-war factory classes and good for keeping a bad hair day under wraps. But in twenty-first century Turkey, the question was at the very core of the widening chasm between secularists and traditionalists. The headscarf ban in higher education, public buildings and public life was something the Government was determined to repeal and the opposition was equally determined to preserve. Things were beginning to rot in the State of Turkey.

As we fried in the midday shade, I was more concerned about the rotten state of Susan's wine cellar. It was one thing her thinking we were a pair of old lushes but quite another having it confirmed by row after row of missing bottles. We would replace them all, I decided. Susan would be none the wiser and our reputation, such as it was, would remain intact.

The cool of the Migros supermarket was a welcome break from the paint-stripping heat of Gökçebel. The aisles were full of pallid-skinned holidaymakers in floppy hats and strappy sandals looking for familiar brands and home comforts. Fortunately for them, Migros had cornered the market in overpriced imports, from Cheesy Wotsits to Weetabix, Milk Tray to Marmite, all to satisfy the cravings of the foreign infidels. Liam wheeled a wobbly trolley past the red-shouldered scrum. It didn't so much squeak as screech, and we were getting pained looks.

'Don't raise your eyebrows at me, dwarfy,' said Liam. 'It was the only one left. Okay?'

We screeched past the confectionary aisle towards the wine racks at the rear of the store. Liam did a sudden double take.

'Move it, Jack!'

'What's the matter? What are you hissing at?'

'I'm hissing at you. Shift those stumpy legs.'

The trolley picked up speed and the screeching of the wheels jumped two octaves. Street dogs basking in the sun began to howl, and Liam bundled me behind a square pillar plastered in special offer posters.

'Two for one *bulgur*?' I said. 'That's it?'

'I've just seen Nancy. At the chocolate display.'

'She likes a finger or two of fudge. So what?'

'A finger? Are you kidding? Her trolley's full of the stuff, it's like Willy Wonka on a busman's holiday. And she couldn't wait to get started. She's sucking the life out of a Walnut Whip.'

'Maybe she's depressed,' I suggested.

'Maybe she's pregnant.'

'Maybe the old sea dog's been cocking his leg somewhere else.'

'Living with Charlotte's all too much?'

'Missing London?'

'Eating disorder?'

'We can't stalk her all afternoon, love. We should go over.'

'And catch her in the act? Watch the whipped cream dribbling down her chin like a cheap porn star? Show some respect. We'll stay here 'til the coast is clear.'

'Fine. Now explain to the nice security man why we're hiding behind this pillar.'

We marked our final night at Susan's hilltop pile by donning glad rags and meandering into Yalıkavak for a trip down memory lane. As we passed the tatty tea house opposite the *otogar*, we recognised the figure sitting at a pavement-side table. A year earlier, we had encountered the flirtatious Ibrahim in a small *meyhane*, tucked away in a side street lined with oleanders. On a summer's evening crammed full of Eastern promise and sexual ambiguity, Ibrahim had climbed onto the bar, peeled off his tee shirt and looked to the drunken worshippers for adoration and cash rewards.

'Ibrahim?' I said. '*Merhaba!*'

Ibrahim looked up and smiled.

'No work tonight, Ibrahim?' asked Liam. 'Mehmet's bar?'

'No bar. Mehmet drink. No pay rent.'

'Oh,' said Liam. 'I'm sorry.'

A dishevelled Ibrahim shrugged his shoulders and dropped a sugarcube into his coffee. *'Problem yok.'*

'We should do something,' whispered Liam, tasting Ibrahim's embarrassment. Without work he was close to destitute and little more than a beggar. It was the way, the brutal truth for every village boy with high hopes, limited prospects and a family-full of expectations.

'How about a refill, Ibrahim?' I said. 'Or a beer at Berni's?'

'Thank you... I stay. Allah is with me. And with you.'

The famously fickle Yalıkavak breeze suddenly picked up as we passed through the arched gate of Berni's Bar and Grill. Babbling patrons flickered in semi-shadow and the restaurant was studded with a forest of tealights – a world apart from Berni's off-season offering of karaoke, quiz nights and the odd christening.

'Grand to see youz boys again.'

'We're house sitting in the hills,' said Liam.

'Chuck and Susan's. Aye, I know.'

'Not much gets past you, Berni,' I said.

'Pays to have yer finger on the pulse, Jack.'

'And how's little Josh?'

'The wee wean's got nappy rash.'

'Ouch!'

'Ach, it's nothing.'

Liam looked across at the restaurant kitchen. 'We've come to sample Alp's rump.'

'Then come say hi to my man.'

Berni's husband served up the best T-bone on the Peninsula, attracting takers from far and wide. His creamy sauce was the talk of the Aegean. Or so he told us. We poked our heads through the serving hatch of the kitchen. The restaurant's engine room was at full speed. Waiters rushed in with orders and out with plates, the air was thick with smoking chip oil and windows were fogged up with condensation from pots of steaming rice water.

'Alp!' shouted Berni. 'You have visitors!'

The *chef de cuisine* was sweating over a hot griddle and turned round to reveal an apron splattered with blood and grease. He grinned and we shouted quick hellos before Berni led us to the last free table in the packed restaurant. We looked across at the beach. Fuelled by the treacherous Meltemi winds blowing down from the Balkans, the summer breeze had turned nasty, battering gulets and propelling chips off dinner plates.

'Christ and all the saints in heaven!' said Berni, blessing herself with a hurried sign of the cross. 'That's all I need: a full house and the good Lord decides to throw a hissy fit. There's no pleasing Him sometimes.'

'Yoo hoo! Yoo hoo!'

Even before we had ordered, the curse of the emigreys struck our windswept table.

'Guess who's coming to dinner, Liam?'

'I'd hazard a guess it's not Judi Dench.'

'The ginger shipwreck from Susan's party. Deborah as in Deb-or-ah.'

'She who bumped off her husband?'

'He had a heart attack.'

Debbie Dog's orange perm flashed like a Belisha beacon as she jerked her head in the candlelight.

'Yoo hoo, boys! It's me! Look!'

She pointed at the handsome young man sitting opposite her, a broad-shouldered perky-pecked libertine with carved features and tombstone teeth. He was quite the dandy in his pristine tight white shirt, phoney designer jeans, fat buckled belt, and a waist so impossibly thin it was difficult to imagine where he stored his vital organs.

We smirked and mouthed 'hello.'

'It's fine,' said Liam. 'She won't be over. She just wanted to show off what she's caught.'

'Gonorrhoea?'

'Look at her, Jack. Sometimes, I just long to walk through the streets of a cold and anonymous city and get completely ignored.'

'Shouldn't be difficult, you've a very ignorable face.'

'Ta very much.'

'You're welcome. We'll do city next. Izmir. Okay, misery guts?'

As we tucked into Alp's juicy meat, the evening of doom continued along its fateful path when Blackpool Bobbi entered stage right, swivel-hipping through the gate with a face like Thor.

'Mind if I join you?' he said, pulling up a chair.

'Actually...' said Liam.

'Ask me how I am, go on ask me!'

'Hello Bobbi,' I said. 'How are you?'

'How am I? How am I? I've been robbed. Me, ROBBED, at knifepoint. In my own home, at KNIFEPOINT!'

'Good God,' I said, 'are you okay?'

'Am I okay? Do I look okay? No, I am not okay! And I need a drink.'

A *cin tonik* appeared courtesy of Bobbi's very own waiter, an enterprising lad who knew exactly what Bobbi needed and when he needed it. Bobbi downed the gin and gestured for another.

'So?' asked Liam. 'What happened?'

'Well, I was having my afternoon nap on my Louis Quatorze settee, you know, the one with the gold piping, when I suddenly woke up. I don't know why I woke up, something just stirred, to find this young man in my back salon. You know, the one with the palm leaf mural and the crystal chandelier.'

'No,' I said, 'I don't.'

'Oh, that's right, I've never invited you. It's not real crystal but you'd never know. Well, anyway. There he was, bold as brass, helping himself to my wallet, you know, my white Gucci continental purse.'

'So what did you say?' Liam asked.

'Nothing, I just screamed but he waved a kitchen knife at me, *my* kitchen knife, and told me to shut the fuck up.'

'No! What did you do?' asked Liam.

'I shut the fuck up.'

'I suppose you would,' I said.

'He lifted the cash, chucked the wallet at me, and scarpered with the kitchen knife, *my* kitchen knife.'

'He didn't keep the wallet?'

'I got it down the market. He probably guessed.'

Liam grinned. 'You must have been in absolute shock, Bobbi.'

'Oh, I was. It took a few stiff drinks to calm me down, I can tell you.'

'So did he take much?' I asked.

'Well, here's the thing. I'd just been to the bank. I had a thousand lira stuffed into my purse and the bastard knew it.'

'He knew? How would he know?'

'Well, I'd had tea with him earlier.'

'You knew him?'

'Oh yes.'

'Christ, Bobbi. Was he... did you...?'

'Well, yes, but that's not the point.'

We slumped back in our chairs in exasperation.

'I presume you've reported it?' asked Liam.

'I've just come from the *Jandarma*.'

'And what did they say?'

'To be more careful next time.'

'That's it?'

'His word against mine, apparently.'

'Bobbi, if you squeeze the lemons, you have to pay for the juice,' I said.

'Do you know what's *really* pissed me off? Now I don't have a full set of Sabatiers. Cost an absolute fortune at Argos.'

'At least you weren't murdered in your sleep,' said Liam. 'Be grateful for small mercies.'

'Grateful? The only thing I'm grateful for is that I'm a survivor. Always have been, always will be. It'll take more than a thieving farmhand with a penne penis to get one over on Bobbi Shuttleworth, I can tell you. There's Berni. Wait 'till I tell her. She'll be mortified, *mortified*.'

In the interests of our own sanity, we decided against dessert and opted instead for a full scale evacuation. Liam paid the bill and we tiptoed through the side entrance, listening to Berni's screams of disbelief as Joshua's fairy godfather relived his near-death experience.

'I'll tell you one thing,' said Liam. 'That Bobbi Shuttleworth's one Sabatier short of a knife block.'

'And I'll tell you another thing, Liam Brennan,' I replied. 'Someone up there has it in for us. That's Nancy's sea captain ahead.'

Irfan leapt up from the table at Bar Sandima, his lintel-shouldered frame casting a shadow the size of Belgium.

'*İyi akşamlar!* Come, we drink!' he said, gathering us up with his huge arms and dragging us to a small plastic table. Irfan's enormous tartan shorts fluttered about like gulet sails and a faded polo top was stretched like tight canvas across his whale gut. After an initial flurry of excitement and an order of large rakis, conversation dried up to nothing. Irfan's grasp of English had barely advanced beyond the 'enjoy your meal' stage and our Turkish was marginally worse. In the end, we were all content to watch the passing trade, occasionally raising a glass to toast happiness, Atatürk or Fenerbahçe's latest signing. It quickly became apparent that Irfan was a man on a midnight mission. The old gigolo ogled every bit of skirt passing by, regardless of age, size or shape.

'Irfan,' I said eventually. 'You are a slut.'

'Slut? What is slut?'

Liam's animated explanation, graphically illustrated by poking his index finger into a loose fist, provoked a loud baritone guffaw and a wobbling midriff.

'So… yes! I am slut!'

As if to drive the point home, when we finally staggered away from the roadside bar and looked back at the genial giant, Irfan was eating the face of a pencil-figured woman who had just joined him at the table.

It was Marianna. Nancy's arch rival was back in town.

CHAPTER NINETEEN

BEES AROUND THE HONEY POT

The drive to Izmir across the high plateau and down towards the city was a pleasurable jolly. We pit-stopped near Söke at a long line of designer outlet stores in the middle of nowhere and munched on Big Macs before continuing over the agricultural flatlands and hitting the toll motorway near Aydın. As we descended from the plain back towards the coast, Turkey's third city stretched out impressively before us, wrapping around the upper shores of the gulf and toppling precariously over a hinterland of low hills. If driving to Izmir was a dusty breeze, then driving through it was the perfect storm. The sprawling metropolis was dissected by elevated dual carriageways, and finding a way down was nigh on impossible, at least for Liam. He drove from one side of the city to the other and then back again, searching for an exit, any exit, cursing the death wish tailgaters who cut him up at every turn. Indicating, it seemed, was only for sissies. Two full hours of driving hell later, we landed at Kordon, Izmir's smart seafront boulevard, coming to rest outside the hotel we had both given up hope of ever finding.

Izmir wasn't beautiful. Much of it had been burned to the ground during the 1922 Greco-Turkish War and the city had been hastily rebuilt in reinforced concrete. Still, there was a sense of vitality about the city and within minutes of encountering the young trendies and the pavement cafés of Alsancak, Liam was peering into *emlakcı* windows checking property prices. We headed south towards Izmir's premier archaeological treasure, the Roman Agora, the largest market place ever excavated from the period. To get there we pushed through the modern *pazar*, a high decibel emporium of stalls and shops selling absolutely everything, including the kitchen sink. We confounded the catcalling spivs by responding in German, French, Spanish, and a little Turkish, anything to avoid being cornered by a lippy leather seller. The Agora promised much but was as disappointing as the unassuming residential street it ran along. We peered through the weathered railings to soak up the atmosphere, but a large irregular hole with piles of randomly scattered stones like a quarry on a tea break didn't quite set the pulse racing. We didn't bother going in.

That night, as we finished off our meze at an Alsancak waterside *kafe*, Liam retrieved a list of gay bars and an annotated street map of Izmir from his back pocket. Time, he said, to familiarise ourselves with the twilight world of Izmir's deviants. He promised a heady aroma of tinsel and testosterone, a light dusting of dancing queens vogueing round their bum bags, off duty taxi drivers twiddling with their tashes and the odd bi-curious tourist in search of furtive titillation. By the second after dinner macchiato,

I was hooked on the idea and we returned to the hotel to don our tap shoes and trip the light fantastic.

An hour later, and after a chilling exploration of the graffitied backstreets, we stood outside a dismal dive-bar hidden along a trashy alley on the wrong side of the tracks.

'Krüz Bar,' said Liam. 'The end of the rainbow.'

The small open door was plastered with ripped posters, and a single rectangular window had been painted black from the inside. The contents of several rubbish bags was strewn around the entrance and to the side, two feral kittens were battling for possession of a battered chicken carcass.

Liam tried the door. 'It's open. Unfortunately.'

'No secret knock then?'

'Things have moved on since the good old Seventies, Jack.'

'Ah, the happy days of thugs, blackmailers and honey traps.'

Liam looked up at the crumbling building and sighed.

'I'm not sure Turkey's moved on that much.'

'Just get on with it,' I said, pushing Liam through the open door. 'What's the worst that can happen?'

We climbed the dimly lit stairs and fell into the bar, a black and chrome clip joint pounded by deafening Turk techno.

'I guess you'd call it retro,' I yelled above the thumping.

Liam scanned the room with its blacked out windows and darkened alcoves. 'It's not exactly Istanbul, is it?'

'Or Bodrum,' I said, sniffing the air, a sickly mix of musky sweat and desperation. 'Let's just make the most of it, love. Grab a seat and hold onto your fez.'

We perched on barstools at the back of the room and looked for signs of life. On cue, a flabby bruiser in bad drag pitched up, took our order, returned with two small bottles of Efes and slapped the bill on the table. Liam picked up the tab and stared at the Laura Ashley frock, black beehive wig, three-inch lashes and pitted cheeks.

'How much! You gotta be kidding, sister.'

Miss Blobby crossed her tattooed arms. She wasn't kidding and Liam handed over the dosh. Moments later, she returned with a bowl of stale pistachios and another bill.

'Looks like her nuts come at a premium too,' said Liam, breaking into his wallet for the second time in as many minutes.

We focussed through the gloom. The silhouettes loitering in dark corners clearly weren't thirsty enough to keep Miss Blobby's ugly sister busy at the pumps. To relieve the boredom, she was pouring *votka* along the length of the countertop and setting it alight. Oh, how she screamed as the flames fandangoed along the bar.

Liam shuffled uncomfortably in his seat and looked around for a fire exit. 'I'm not enjoying this, Jack. Not one bit.'

'I'd watch that nylon wig if I were her. It'll go up like a Molotov cocktail. And who said anything about enjoyment? This is all about adventure.'

'A walk on the wild side, you mean.'

'Butch up, Liam. I need the loo.'

'You're not leaving me alone with this lot!'

I pinched Liam's cheek. 'Be my brave little soldier. And whatever you do, don't go snogging the hunter-gatherers.'

I made a beeline for the cockeyed *tuvalet* sign and banged my way through the saloon bar doors. Much like the clientele, they swung both ways. A covered granny leapt up from a stool and stretched out a wizened hand. She was clothed in traditional peasant weaves, a clashing riot of washed-out William Morris – the time honoured vestments of all God-fearing Turkish women up and down the land.

'You pay!' she snapped.

'Okay grandma,' I said, greasing her palm with a lira coin. 'I pay.'

The old woman smiled in gratitude.

'Tank you.'

'You're welcome, sweetheart. By the way, your arse looks like a hanging basket.'

'Tank you.'

'And you smell like the rear end of a donkey.'

'Tank you.'

'No problem. Been nice talking to you.'

The loo was empty and I could pee in peace without interference from a gay-for-pay Turk slipping in by the tradesmen's entrance.

'So, how was the *tuvalet*?' asked Liam as I remounted my stool.

'I wouldn't risk it. There's a psychogranny on the door. And a slash tax.'

As we became more accustomed to the dimmed lighting, a motley crew of purse-lipped, shiny-haired scallies in cheap shell suits and even cheaper trainers emerged from the shadows. The gyrating tracksuits circled like a pack of dancing hyenas, spinning in for the kill. Locking his sight onto Liam, one of the bolder apprentices unzipped his nylon jacket to expose a svelte, furry torso.

'Don't think much of yours, Liam. Not exactly *Magic Mike*.'

Liam bristled as the boy slowly advanced, squeezing his crotch like a rapper with nits.

'If he gets any closer, I'll put his lights out.'

'If he gets any closer we'll gag on his Brut 33.'

Liam's stalker winked, tweaked a nipple and inched a step nearer.

'Okay,' I said, 'the wild side just got a bit too feral, even for us. Bottoms up, love. Time to dig a tunnel.'

'And what if we're locked in?'

'Then we'll text Her Maj and get her to send a gunboat. Shift your arse, Liam. He's about to whip out his disco stick.'

Liam didn't need telling twice. We downed our beers, tore through the rent boys and I slapped a tenner on the bar.

'There you go, darling. Get yerself a decent girdle.'

Miss Blobby threw a bad smell look and snatched the tip as we quickmarched to the exit and sprinted down the stairs. The door was ajar and we tumbled out into the back alleys of Izmir, grateful for the sudden rush of fresh air.

'You know what?' said Liam, as we headed back to the safety of Alsancak.

'What, love?'

'I want you to know I blame you. For everything. For everything that has ever happened to me since the day I met you.'

'Oh, Liam. What a lovely thing to say.'

We woke to the sound of pneumatic drills pounding the street outside the hotel. Citied out, we jumped into the hire car and headed south to Ephesus, one of the most sophisticated cities of antiquity and home to the Temple of Artemis, another Wonder of the Ancient World. Or so the guide book bragged. Not that you would know it from the row of tawdry souvenir stalls outside the entrance where line upon line of plastic Madonnas vied for popularity with the multi-breasted Artemis. We were collared by a tour guide, a serious academic type who spoke English with a received Yankee drawl. When he dragged us along the main thoroughfare, darting around troupes of camera toting Koreans and stopping at strategic vantage points to deliver his well-rehearsed sermon, we soon regretted hiring him. The Ephesians were fine and upstanding, he told us, civilised, cultured and always kind to their slaves. We fancied the alternative history, the salacious version where the city fathers visited the brothel via the secret tunnel from the great Library of Celsus and where, during half time, rent boys assumed the position in the vomitorium of the amphitheatre. After an hour of deferential nodding we paid off our earnest but well-meaning chaperone and roamed the ruins unescorted.

A light went on in Liam's Catholic brain.

'Ephesus. As in Ephesians. As in letters to. As in St Paul's Epistles to the Ephesians. Why the hell did he write to the Ephesians?'

'To damn them for their debauched ways, I suppose. I've never read 'em. But I do know that Christianity was founded right here.'

'That's not what old Father Francis told me at St Ignatius. But then, he did have a lazy eye and wandering hands, so what did he know?'

As for the once celebrated Temple of Artemis, just one lonely, re-assembled pillar remained rising up precariously from a mosquito-infested bog on the edge of town. What a lunatic hadn't destroyed by torching the place, the Christians had finished off. That's the Christians for you. No respect for history.

The rest of the city was in impressively good shape after decades of digging and reconstruction. A highlight for Liam, like many thousands of visitors before him, was a visit to the public latrine, a chance to sit on the communal khazi and contemplate everyday life in the ancient world.

'The Romans loved a chinwag with their *caco*,' I said. 'And who can blame them?'

'Well I prefer *The Archers* and a good crossword,' said Liam, nesting on the ancient stone loo. 'I could sit here for hours.'

For an evocative slice of the ordinary, we stepped along the glass walkways above excavated terraced houses, intimate courtyards, domestic mosaics and frescos. Ephesus may have had 'monumental' carved into every stone, but for Liam, it was the glimpse into the mundane that really brought the place to life.

'Maybe that says more about me than it does about Ephesus,' he said as we climbed back into the car. 'Maybe I'm just common.'

'There's no maybe about it. My mother said I was marrying beneath me and I'll tell you something, Liam Brennan, the old girl is rarely wrong.'

CHAPTER TWENTY

THE HARLEQUIN AND THE CLOWN

Beril and Vadim returned from their six-week pilgrimage to Ankara with boundless energy and a crate full of antiques. For days, they carefully unpacked an assortment of curiosities, marvelling at each in turn and arguing vociferously about where to place them. On day three, I found Beril sobbing quietly at her patio table, an untouched breakfast platter by her side and her face buried beneath a tangled mesh of unbrushed hair. Bianco was on lookout high above the courtyard in the canopy of the olive tree. As I watched from a distance and sipped my coffee, Beril's sobbing ramped up to full scale wailing. Bianco whined in concert. Even when Liam tripped into the courtyard and dropped his bowl of *menemen,* Beril stayed focussed on her misery, oblivious to Liam's cursing and the plinking of broken porcelain as he cleared up the scrambled mess. As the minutes passed and Beril and Bianco continued their interminable caterwauling, Liam chewed on a *simit* and set about solving the mystery. Beril was on drugs, he surmised. Not the small, pink happy pills dished out willy-nilly by the nice local doctor, but the finest Afghan opium, smuggled across the frontier by Iranian drug mules in the dead of night. Vadim had been collared for crimes against the State (probably related to serial fornication and the befriending of sexual deviants) and his drug-dependent moll had turned to binge eating and prostitution. When Vadim strolled out to the patio with his *sucuklu yumurta* breakfast, Liam was forced to concede his fanciful theory was bordering on the absurd.

That evening, and with the mystery still unsolved, a scrubbed and gowned Beril rapped on our kitchen door.

'We eat, Jack!'

'Eat?' I asked.

'Actually,' interrupted Liam, 'we're a little tired, Beril.' He pressed his outstretched palms together and placed them against his cheek, pillow mode. 'See? Tired.'

'Tired? Bish bosh!' The imperious tones of Queen Sophia echoed across the courtyard. 'You cannot refuse me. I absolutely insist!'

A trace of Chanel No. 5 wafted through the leaden air and a harlequin dress floated into the garden, accessorised by twisted silver bracelets and a scarlet silk scarf hiding a sixty-five-year-old turtleneck. Sophia's reconstituted face appeared through the haze of candlelight accompanied by a dumpy bint slapped up like Coco the Clown.

'My darlings,' said Sophia. 'May I present... Elma...'

Elma's big backcombed hair gave her the look of a fairground hedgehog.

'... my daughter.'

'Oh!' I said. 'Hello.'

I held out my hand and Elma decided, without too much hesitation, to reject it. Liam appeared from behind my shoulder, startling Elma, who stepped back and stumbled into a flower bed.

'Hello Elma! Delighted.'

Elma kissed her teeth, glared at her mother and stomped into Beril's house, swinging her hips like a heifer on the way to market. Sophia's curious daughter would be a tough nut to crack.

'We should freshen up, Sophia,' said Liam, pulling at his clammy vest. 'We're a state.'

Sophia agreed. 'You look like a peasant, Liam.'

'That's a bit strong.'

'Nevertheless, it is the truth. We shall dine at Vadim's table in thirty minutes, a feast under the glittering stars of Allah. *Carpe diem* my darlings, *carpe diem.*'

Sophia joined Elma and we retreated into the house to regroup. Liam leaned up against the inside of the front door as if keeping back the hordes.

'Why us? Why is it always us?'

'Cheer up, my big gay serf. It could be worse.'

'We're cursed,' said Liam. 'Cursed.'

'Maybe we are. Or maybe that's what happens to the new kids in town. Particularly when they're a couple of self-opinionated old homos.'

'But the horrors. How come they always slither our way?'

'Some people think *we're* the horrors, Liam.'

'Us?'

'Well, you mainly.'

'That Elma's gonna be hard work.'

'Not to mention a bit broad at the beam. God, think of the carbon hoof print.'

'Mark my words, Jack. She's trouble. All of her mother's airs but none of her graces.'

We emerged into the garden refreshed, re-robed, recomposed and clutching bottles of Çankaya. Beril's chunky patio table had been polished to within an inch of its life and topped with an ornate candelabra housing twelve tapered candles. Silverware settings for six had been precisely positioned and long-stemmed wine glasses were placed next to mini kilim placemats. Sophia sat at one head of the table, her long diamante earrings catching the light like shards of glass. Her podgy sprog was slumped at the other end, mumbling to herself in Turkish.

'Sit! Sit!' shouted Sophia, taking possession of Beril's table as if it were her own. 'It is time.'

Beril took our wine and scuttled back into the kitchen where Vadim was busy dripping over a hot stove and managing the diplomatic mix of Turkish and Western mood music. Beril soon returned with her Sunday best crockery – cobalt blue Ottoman fritware – and checked and rechecked the table under Sophia's close supervision. We caught a heavy duty whiff of sautéed garlic and heard the sizzle and hiss of Vadim's pan-fried *chef-d'oeuvre*. Mouths watered and Sophia and Elma hit the *rakı*. Sophia sipped, Elma gulped and Beril replenished. Liam shuffled uncomfortably. He could smell something fishy. Liam didn't do fishy.

'So,' I asked Elma, 'you live in Bodrum?'

'Is*tan*bul.'

'Just visiting then?'

'Y*ars*.'

'And you like Bodrum?'

'*Yok.*'

I couldn't make out whether Elma's monosyllabic aloofness was a sign of underpowered English or complete disinterest. Sophia sensed my disquiet and intervened.

'Elma has just moved back from America, haven't you, darling?'

'Y*ars*.'

'The States? How wonderful. Whereabouts, Elma?'

'Tex*ars*.'

I pictured a posse of sweaty cowboys do-si-doing around the rodeo pit while Elma skulked at the barrier stuffing her face with Krispy Kremes.

'And how long were you there, Elma? In Texas I mean?'

'Ten *yars*.'

'Working?'

She pouted. 'My husband, big man in company.'

'Oh,' I said, shocked at the thought of anyone slipping a ring on Daisy the Cow. 'And your husband is with you in Bodrum?'

'*Yok*. Gone with whore. Bastard!'

Liam spat out a mouthful of wine, spraying his fritware. I slapped him under the table and Sophia shook her head in disgust. Beril and Vadim emerged from the kitchen. Vadim was holding a large bowl of steaming tagliatelle and set it down at the table.

'Thank the Lord,' whispered Liam. 'Pasta.'

Beril fussed indecisively, stacking large bowls to one side then moving them to the other. Sophia supervised loudly. Vadim picked up a dish from the pile, flopped out a serving of spaghetti and passed it to Sophia, who tucked in without ceremony. As the free-for-all turned into an undignified feeding frenzy, a spontaneous and lively Anglo-Turkish conversation broke out with Sophia acting as translator. Sophia talked over Beril, Beril talked over Vadim and we fought to get a word in. Elma didn't bother, preferring to gulp, gorge and pout. In the cross-cultural pandemonium, Liam picked out wet chunks of calamari from his bowl and slipped them into the side pockets of his freshly laundered cargo shorts. The more we chatted, the more Liam stuffed.

'Beril was acting very strangely this morning,' said Liam, turning to Sophia for a gossip.

'Yes, darling, I know. Do try the vine leaves, I stuffed them myself.'

'I'm a little concerned, that's all.'

'Oh, don't be. Beril is quite mad, you know.'

Bianco leapt down from the olive tree, crept under the table and began to weave between Liam's legs.

'But she was crying for ages, Sophia.'

'I know, dreadful wailing. Most unbecoming, don't you think?'

'And Vadim just ignored her.'

'Yes, dear, that's Turkish men for you. Heartless. The pasta is a little too *al dente*. What a pity.'

Bianco let out a piercing high-pitched meow and shot back up into the tree.

We all looked at Liam.

'The squid's divine!' he said wishing he hadn't kicked the cat quite so hard. 'What an absolute treat.'

'Are you alright, Liam?'

'Hunky-dory, Sophia.'

Liam went on to describe his racy theories about drugs and prostitution.

'My dear boy,' said Sophia. 'Beril is as likely to walk the streets of Bodrum as I am to run a brothel in the Vatican. Don't be ridiculous.'

The truth, he discovered, was rather more prosaic. Beril had been overcome by a dangerous mix of local gin and Ottoman romanticism. She had discovered an early Turkish novel amongst the box of tat she acquired in Ankara and for the first time in her life, Beril had single-handedly emptied an entire bottle of mother's ruin. *Tal'at and Fitnat In Love* was a work crafted with such overt sentimentality and Western sensibility, it had moved Beril to the brink of bohemian bliss. She had stayed up throughout the night reading and re-reading the first ever Turkish penny romance and had driven herself into a state of ecstatic exhaustion.

Sophia soon tired of talking about Beril and turned the conversation back to her favourite topic.

'When I was a young girl…' she announced to the table, '… a beautiful young girl, I was sent to England. You see, I was born with the desire to travel. It flows through my veins.'

Sophia stared up at the half moon and clasped her hands to her chest. 'The world is a book, my friends, and those who do not travel read only one page.'

'Talking of travel,' I said. 'I notice Turks call Britain, England. 'Why is that?'

'Darling boy, what do you mean?'

'Well, it can irritate the other occupants of our damp little island.'

Sophia shrugged her shoulders. 'England, Britain. It is all the same is it not?'

The conversation turned to national comparisons laced with stereotypes and schoolboy history.

'And what do you understand of the Kurds?' Sophia retorted. 'What does it say in your English history books?'

I stepped through the inquisition diplomatically if not compliantly. Experience had taught me not to stamp on Turkish sensitivities with Western steel-capped boots.

'Take the Welsh, Sophia.'

'No thank you, darling.'

'There was a time, and not that long ago, when the speaking of Welsh was discouraged, suppressed even.'

'And?'

'And today, the Welsh Language thrives. Welsh culture thrives. No one sees it as a threat.'

'Ah yes, but one day they will demand their independence.'

'Then they should have it.'

'And that would be the end of England.'

'Or the making of it.'

'The Welsh are not the Kurds, dear. The Kurds are mountain Turks who make trouble for my country.'

'But, Sophia, to be a modern, progressive nation, Turkey must embrace diversity.'

'Modern? You talk of modern? Turkey *is* modern! Atatürk saw to it. Am I not sharing my dinner with a homosexual? Did Turkish women not have the right to vote before their English sisters!'

It was my turn to shrug. It would have been crass and pointless to continue. Even if it were true, being told who to vote for by your father, your brother or your husband was hardly a right worth extolling. I decided against raising the Armenian question. Sophia and I spoke different languages and not even Kofi Annan's shuttle diplomacy could have bridged the divide.

Meanwhile, Liam had problems of his own. His pockets were bulging. As grease began to seep through the material of his shorts, he took evasive action and tipped a large glass of red onto his lap. Everyone leapt up from the table – everyone apart from Elma, who leered over at Liam before returning to her *rakı*. Beril rushed to Liam's aid and hovered hesitantly over his button flies.

'You'll need a squirt of Fairy on that,' I said knowingly. 'Best go change, eh?'

Liam left the table weighed down by a ballast of squid and waddled across the courtyard like a duck with rickets. Bianco leapt down from the tree, sprinted after him and darted into the house through his bandy legs.

'What can I do?' I said as Vadim and Beril looked over at me open mouthed. 'The man's a halfwit.'

Liam's departure appeared to energise Sophia's semi-detached daughter and as Beril cleared the empties, Elma put down her glass and delivered an unprovoked broadside in my direction.

'You!' she shouted, lurching forward in her chair and wagging her finger. 'You come to my country and you speak English. Speak Turkish! Enough of this English!'

The sudden outburst cloaked the table in a stunned silence. Elma had a point, of course, but I had tried, how I had tried, to master the local lingo. A humble apology and a promise to do better did nothing to placate her and even when Sophia stepped in to attempt a truce, the shellfire continued. Fresh out of apologies and emboldened by alcohol, I came to the conclusion that attack was the best form of defence.

'Enough!'

Elma stopped in her tracks.

'Sophia, please translate what I am about to say, word for word. There must be no misunderstanding.'

Sophia nodded and gulped her *rakı*.

'Elma, I'm sorry, truly, that my Turkish is poor. I know I must do better. I have said so, repeatedly. I have said I will try harder, and I will.'

Sophia translated and Elma nodded.

'But, you are a guest in *my* home. This is *my* garden and you insult me more than I insult you.'

'Oh, darling, I can't say that. Elma is my daughter.'

'Tell her, Sophia.'

Sophia bolted down the booze and delivered the message. Elma listened intently, her chins resting on a pair of painted hooves. When her mouth fell open like a discarded ventriloquist's dummy, I knew I had pressed the right cultural button. We all watched as Elma launched herself at me, an unguided missile in cerise lip gloss heading for the ornamental lavender. I leapt up to catch her and there I was propping Sophia's daughter up by her spare tyres as she fluttered her eyelids and simpered into my ear.

'Sorry, sorry, sorry... forgive, forgive, forgive...'

Elma's elaborate and obviously fake apology was only matched by my equally fake acceptance of it and, as she staggered back to her side of the Maginot Line, an uneasy ceasefire prevailed.

Liam returned to the table in a thin pair of sweat pants.

'Well? What have I missed?'

Elma looked across and hiccupped a smile.

'Oh, nothing. Just a re-run of the Cuban Missile Crisis.'

Beril restocked the table with a generous platter of cold mezes – salted aubergine, lemon-dribbled samphire, assorted white cheeses, savoury pastries, yogurt, hummus, pickled red cabbage, spiced boiled eggs, rocket salad, Black Sea bread and a fresh supply of Sophia's stuffed vine leaves.

'Who the hell's she expecting?' said Liam, topping up his glass.

'It is our custom!' said Sophia, starting to slur. 'A generous table is... generosity feeds the soul, etcetera, etcetera...'

Sophia clapped and a round of applause broke out in honour of Beril's gastronomic tour de force.

'Jack, my darling, how is your...'

Sophia paused mid-sentence as a cat skulked through our open door. Bianco was barely able to move and lumbered past the table into Beril's salon for an evening nap.

'How extraordinary,' said Sophia.

'Well there's one pussy with a well-fed soul,' Liam whispered. 'And a gutfull of squid, etcetera, etcetera…'

'Your delightful mother,' said Sophia. 'How is she, Jack?'

'Oh, the same. You know, alive and kicking.'

'Such an unusual woman, and… so very… charming.'

'She speaks highly of you, too, Sophia.'

In truth, my mother thought Sophia a 'pompous old dowager, way too big for her silver slingbacks', an opinion she formed at my fiftieth birthday party, a shindig held on the very same spot a year earlier.

'Beril must soon return to Ankara,' said Sophia, changing the subject abruptly. 'Her mother is old and her mother's mind… well, it is also old.'

'You mean Beril will move back to Ankara permanently?'

'Of course. It is her duty. She is, after all, childless and unmarried.'

'And what about Vadim?'

'What about him, dear boy? He is not her husband.'

Beril spoke to Sophia in Turkish and asked her to translate.

'Beril's fervent wish is that she should remain in Bodrum,' said Sophia. 'Remain free…'

Sophia attempted a toast to freedom but the small *rakı* glass missed her mouth.

'Of course, it will not last, this freedom.'

'Why won't it last?' asked Liam.

'Because it is not real!'

'For Beril or for Bodrum?'

'For Turkey, my dear boy, for Turkey! There is Bodrum and there is Turkey. This is Disneyland, all of it. This is not Turkey. This is all just… make-believe.'

Beril stood up from the table and screamed. 'No marry!' she shouted at Vadim. 'No çocuk, no child!'

And there we had it in a flash, the root of Beril's troubles, the reason for her anger and the reason for her crazed outbursts. The nonconformist wanted to conform after all. She wanted a ring on her finger, she wanted a child and she wanted the social respectability and legal status both would confer.

Vadim ignored the outburst and disappeared into the kitchen, leaving me and Liam to comfort Beril and anesthetise her with more alcohol. Minutes later, Vadim returned, holding aloft a large antique silver salver. When he ceremoniously presented its contents, the diners gasped. Vadim's crowning glory, set atop a plateau of lemon rice speckled with uncleaned shrimps, was an enormous grouper, a fat monster from the deep, bulging eyeballs, droopy mouth, fins, gills and tail.

Liam's heart raced, his face reddened and a line of sweat trickled down the back of his neck. 'For Christ's sake,' he hissed at me. 'Do something.'

'Calm down, Liam, it's a fish, not a nuclear warhead. We'll think of something.'

As Liam hyperventilated by my side, I knew there was little I could do. This was a top drawer menu of huge social significance and we were the guests of honour. Liam would have to face his oily nemesis.

'My darling boys,' said Sophia, 'have I told about my days at RADA?'

'You have mentioned it,' I said. 'Once or twice.'

Sophia spent much of her time reliving the glory days of her distant youth. Her life had been one long epic with a cast of one.

'I could have been a star, a huge star,' said Sophia, helping herself to a large scoop of rice. 'My life could have been so very different.'

Vadim expertly dissected the creature from the black lagoon, delicately filleting the flesh from the bones until only the head, tail and carcass remained. He passed the first helping to Liam.

'Ah! The Swinging Sixties,' said Sophia. 'Anything and everything was possible.'

'For half a dozen people along the King's Road, maybe,' I said.

'I may be mistaken, young man, but I don't recall seeing you there.'

'That's telling you,' said Liam, tucking his ration of fish flesh under a heap of leftovers. 'Go on, Sophia, tell Jack about your fling with Ringo.'

'It was not a *fling*, as you so indelicately put it, and it was not Ringo.' Sophia finished chewing her fish and picked the bones from under her false teeth. 'I first met Paul backstage at the London Palladium.'

'You mean Paul McCartney, don't you?' I said. 'And his unicorn.'

'You may mock, Jack, but it will not alter the truth.'

'I'm sorry, Sophia. So what is the truth?'

'The truth... everyone wants the truth...'

We waited as Sophia trawled the depths of her Walter Mitty mind.

'Paul was a rather uneducated boy but I gave him the benefit of the doubt.'

'You stepped out with Paul McCartney?' asked Liam.

'Not quite. That Eastman divorcee whisked him off before I got a chance. The rest, as they say...'

Sophia picked up a stick of celery and studied it hard.

'I have one piece of advice for all of you and it is a piece of advice you should never forget.'

'Oh?' I said.

'Never trust a vegetarian.'

'Let it be, Sophia,' said Liam. 'Let it be.'

I sniggered.

'Have I said something amusing?' asked Sophia.

Liam smiled, checked his fish was safely hidden under the debris on his plate and patted his stomach.

'What a banquet,' he said. 'I'll clear the plates.'

Sophia smiled. 'How kind. I bought the fish, only the best for this night of nights.'

'Of course,' I said, 'but what's the occasion?'

'The occasion? Presenting my beautiful Elma, of course.'

We all looked over at the semiconscious soak propped up at the end of the table cuddling an empty bottle of Yeni Rakı. As we raised a toast to Sophia's fatted calf, Elma fell face down and farted.

'Oh dear,' I said. 'Maybe the beautiful Elma should have stayed off the wine gums.'

'Yeah,' whispered Liam, carrying a pile of plates into the kitchen and scraping his fish into the bin. 'Not to mention the *baklava*.'

CHAPTER TWENTY-ONE

THE GATHERING STORM

Recep Tayyip Erdoğan, Prime Minister of Turkey, cut a rather pompous and belligerent figure on the international stage, but on home turf his colourful past as a streetwise political activist had equipped him well. His triumphalist version of democracy had closed his mind to balance and compromise; the man was not noted for his listening skills. Intellectuals who got above their station were pilloried, local politicians who refused to toe the party line were told to clear their desks, and rebellious journalists were locked up at the drop of a fez. It had not always been so. Erdoğan's tenure as Mayor of Istanbul delivered cleaner water, cleaner streets and cleaner government. Despite his religious bent, Erdoğan was a pragmatist and had even muttered some enlightened words about the theorised rights of gay people. Of course, when he landed the top job, he soon realised the best way to keep hold of it was to play shamelessly to the gallery. That meant harnessing the support of the traditional and conservative tractor class by wrapping the Prophet in the flag.

Earlier that summer, the result of the national election had unleashed loose talk of rolling back the secular state and idle chatter about another military coup. After all, time and again, the army had served as the traditional guardian of Atatürk's legacy, dispatching storm troopers whenever a threat was detected. Depending on your point of view, Erdoğan was either hellbent on taking a blunt knife to the secular republic and establishing a quasi-religious theocracy or was simply redressing anti-Islamic bias and guaranteeing religious freedom. To head the tanks off at the pass, Erdoğan cut the top brass off at the neck, and he did it with surgical precision. Within weeks of the election, the old guard was either retired early or arrested on charges of conspiracy, real or imagined. It was checkmate for the generals.

Erdoğan's autocratic style mattered little to the majority of Turks who settled for a strong man at the helm, particularly one who delivered spectacular economic growth and rising living standards. There was a new national pride and the enormous Turkish flags fluttering in the wind on top of every other hill seemed to grow bigger by the year. Whether this was a sign of confidence or insecurity, we weren't quite sure. There was no doubt that Erdoğan was a popular populist with a nice line in crude rhetoric, but unfettered cronyism and the darker side of the Arab Spring could well blow the good ship Turkey onto the rocks, taking Erdoğan with it. And then there were the colonels to worry about.

We spent much of our time checking the national temperature in the English-language press and watching reaction from around the world. Vadim, Beril, Sophia and the Belles had plenty to say about it too, little of it positive. From our perspective, the picture wasn't looking too rosy. The price of alcohol became the lightning rod of change and incremental tax hikes placed it beyond the reach of many. *Rakı* may have been the national tipple but it was quickly becoming a luxury only the rich and the infidels could afford. Despite being permanently plugged into Pinot Grigio on a drip, we decided not to panic but to keep a weather eye. Turkey was still a functioning democracy, not a blind despotism run by a mad mullah, a murderous dictator or a medieval monarch. Nor was it that other secular Turkic nation, Azerbaijan, lorded over by a ruling dynasty with an addiction to nepotism and vote rigging. In Turkey, there were at least some checks and balances to put a break on executive power, even if buying rural votes with new washing machines was par for the course. We figured if the going got tough, we could smuggle in contraband from Kos and open a speakeasy. And, of course, we could always leave.

Liam began to disappear upstairs, tinkling away on his electric piano and immersing himself in Sondheim and Bach for hours on end, isolated and separated by his Sennheiser headphones. All I could hear was the dull thump of the keys through the bedroom floorboards. I assumed he was unsettled by Turkey's political direction and the impact it could have on us; losing himself in music had always been Liam's way of working things through. He was born with an innate desire to bang and blow, something that first emerged at the tender age of seven when he learnt to play the descant recorder. A year later, he moved on to the oboe, an altogether more difficult discipline. By fifteen he had mastered the piano and by eighteen he was studying for a music degree. But at the age of twenty-one, Liam discovered the love that dared not speak its name and, with hormones raging and his creative juices flowing in an entirely different direction, his classical career lay in tatters. At the age of forty-seven, and about to escort me on a life changing move to Turkey, he rediscovered his oboe, sat in its frayed satin-lined box, broken and neglected. Unable to breathe life back into the lifeless, he sold it for a song on Ebay.

While Liam plonked away, I buried myself in my blog. News had travelled fast about the gay *yabancı* who courted controversy with his tongue-in-cheek exposition of expat life. The message had even leached from the whitewashed emigrey ghettos and a growing number of private messages had landed in my inbox, many of them from married Turks.

'Heello Jak. Im living close to Bodrum with wife in Milas. Wanna meet?'

'I lik man. Have hairy body. You want it?'

'I like Inlis boys. Am big man for you.'

Dinners were in front of the TV, an endless diet of BBC Entertainment repeats on a loop, mainly confined to the latest edge-of-seat clinical dilemma on *Casualty*, *Doctors* or *Holby City* and regularly interrupted by booming voices outside our salon window. Beyond Sophia's upper class gate, a lower class quarter was rented out to itinerant workers. Sophia took full advantage of the cheap neighbourly labour and hired boys by the hour whenever her dense thicket needed lopping. Judging by the constant ebb and flow of virile young men along Sentry Lane, the shabby boarding house was either the Tardis in breeze block disguise, or the waifs and strays were topping and tailing in sardine shifts. Understandably, such enforced intimacy presented privacy problems and calls home were reserved for the cobbles of Sentry Lane. Unfortunately for us, the boys screamed at their mobile phones so loudly, the proud mothers of distant Mardin could hear their sons without them.

As the days passed, Liam became more distracted and the conversations more subdued. I didn't ask why. He hated to be questioned. The moment would pass, I was sure. His calls to Sean were welcome pick-me-ups and every time his brother screamed down the phone in excitement, Liam would scream back, relieved that Sean was doing well and amazed at how smoothly everything had dropped into place. By all accounts, Liam's parents were finding life easier, if achingly empty, without their youngest son. Every Saturday, Sean would be taken to see Mammy and Daddy and would sit between them on the sofa, listening to their news and telling them, in his way, how much he missed them. When Liam was in London, he would visit Sean at his new home and rattle on about the latest misadventure on Turkey Street or the VOMIT in distress he sat next to on the plane. He'd catch Sean glancing around the communal lounge to gauge the reaction of his housemates, presumably thinking: *that's my brother. Bit mad. Lives half way around the world. What d'ya think?*

Liam stretched out on the sofa and yawned.

'Do we *have* to go to Musto's? Again?'

'Yes, Liam, we do. We're expected and we're going.'

Bodrum's main drag was not exactly blessed with gastronomic delights, at least not of the Ottoman variety. The standard Turkish offering was a service plate of rice, chips and a compost of limp shredded greenery with a kebab or plain grilled fish hurled on top. For better quality at half the price, it paid to venture behind the waterfront. Consequently, restaurants with an international flavour were especially popular with emigreys and the Turkish yachting fraternity. We had dipped our toes into most of the seaside venues and learned to steer clear of the flashy dives and their stratospheric prices. Our petty cash was spent in a small number of tried and trusted eateries where the menu was varied and our loyalty was repaid – a reduction in the bill and a complimentary *yolluk* at the end of a hard night. Musto's was top of our list and sat in a prime location on Marina Boulevard opposite the smart shopping parade. Its handsome young owner, Mustafa the Magnificent, was second cousin to our landlady and a generous and convivial host. The eponymous Mustafa learned his trade at Sünger, his uncle's legendary pizza parlour, a place that had been dishing up margheritas to the sailing squad since the early Seventies. Unlike some of his rivals, Mustafa never resorted to pressganging people in from the street. He courted the emigrey crowd with Italian seasoning, palatable wine, affordable prices and generous *yolluks*. It was a formula that attracted swarms of discerning diners, even out of season.

'All alone?' I asked Jess, pulling up a seat on Musto's outside terrace.

Jess looked up and swigged her drink.

'Where are the girls?' asked Liam.

'They're not coming.'

'So? Is Jessica Holt a little bit tipsy?' I teased.

'So what if I am?'

Liam took a seat at the table.

'Jess? What's wrong?'

'Cristal's in hospital. Doc and Victoria are with her.'

'Cristal? Why? What happened?'

'Murat splattered her across the kitchen floor. Beat the hell out of her.'

I poured Jess a glass of water.

'And guess what he did as she lay there bleeding? Kicked her phone away. She had to crawl on her hands and knees to call for help.'

'Well I hope the little shit's been arrested,' said Liam.

'Arrested! Don't make me laugh. He'll be off his head somewhere, guzzling *rakı* with his gangster pals. He's gonna kill her. Trust me. Next time she'll end up dead.'

Friday night in Bodrum was in full swing when we lifted Jess into a cab and walked back to Sentry Lane. Marina Boulevard had been transformed into a loud neon strip, rocking to earthquaking Turkopop as the rich kids of Turkey painted the town red. The children of the privileged were a strange breed: well-preened boys who would fit seamlessly into the gay bars of Soho and girls squeezed into very little looking like top drawer tarts. It all conveyed an emancipated image that was pretty much illusory given the deeply conservative nature of society, even at the highest echelons. Sophia was right, Bodrum wasn't Turkey.

When we finally closed the gate behind us and crept through the courtyard, I grabbed Liam and threw my arms around him.

'Liam, love, what's wrong?'

'Wrong?'

'Yes, wrong.'

'I'm just tired.'

'Of me?'

He pulled back.

'Where did that come from?'

'You're not yourself, Liam.'

'I am. I'm still me… sometimes I worry, that's all.'

'About Cristal?'

'Of course.'

'About Turkey?'

'Yes, a bit.'

'About us?'

Liam unlocked the front door, went into the kitchen and poured himself a large whisky. I followed.

'Well?' I said. 'Are you worried about us?'

'What's with all the fucking questions? Go to bed, Jack. There's nothing wrong.'

CHAPTER TWENTY-TWO

FOR BETTER, FOR WORSE

It was a horrible topsy-turvy night. Turkey Street was unusually busy and the dogs unusually vigilant. I lay awake, twisting and turning until the sun rose. Liam didn't sleep either and lay next to me in silence. When the morning light crept through the half opened curtains, he slid out of bed, quietly dressed and sneaked out of the house like a casual pickup catching the night bus home. I pretended to be asleep but heard him stir and listened to the catch of the front door as it clicked softly behind him. I rolled out of bed, staggered downstairs and pulled back the curtains. The sun flooded in, spot-lighting flecks of dust in the salon. Such was my disorientation that I almost didn't notice Onur, Sophia's fancy man, strutting down Sentry Lane, fixing his oily black wig as he passed by our window. It was six a.m.

I pulled the curtains closed. I wasn't ready for the day. Liam's gradual withdrawal had left me slightly unhinged and a sleepless night had loosened the screws a little more. His baffling outburst was entirely out of character. This was the man who had cried over Bambi for God's sake. And now he had stormed off to Neverland and slammed the door behind him.

I peered into the bathroom mirror and studied the lined face and greying temples. Maybe Jess was right. Maybe I was a VOMIT in waiting after all.

Nancy held her silver Manolo Blahniks in her right hand and crept through the backstreets of Yalıkavak towards the harbour. As she approached, waterfront cafés emerged from the morning shadows to service the breakfast trade, and night fishermen put-putted back to port to lay out their catch. Nancy's pneumatic chest heaved expectantly and her heart pounded like a virgin on her wedding night. Irfan's love boat was squeezed into its usual tight berth. She reached the stern, only to find the vessel rocking from side to side, breaking the glassy water and causing a wash that lapped up against the quay. The gulets either side swayed in rhythmic concert. Captain Irfan had already weighed anchor and this time he was on a different maiden's voyage. Not for the first time, Irfan was dredging Marianna's trench and Nancy was left high and dry.

The house glowed like an oven on regulo 8 but I kept the windows closed and the curtains drawn. Beril and Vadim pottered about in the courtyard and Ella Fitzgerald crooned through their open door. I was hardly in the mood for blues and sympathy. I opened a bottle of lunchtime wine and took a seat at the dining table. The phone rang.

Doc put down her phone, looked across at Liam and poured the tea. 'He's not answering.'

'I'm not sure I can do it anyway.'

'Don't be silly, Liam. He'll understand. Whatever it is. This is Jack we're talking about. He's been through worse. John wasn't it?'

'That was different.'

'I think we need something a little stronger, don't you? Wait there.'

Doc left Liam sitting under a pergola in a corner of her small courtyard plot. An old vine dripping with ripened grapes twisted around the sunbleached cane. Doc lived contentedly in a traditional Turkish house tucked behind a squeaky gate on Old Hamam Street. It hadn't always been so and, like many of her contemporaries, she had a ripe tale to tell. At the age of thirty-three, she sailed out of Tilbury, dropped anchor in Izmir Harbour and earned her keep teaching English to the eager to learn. Clever, keen and passionate, she sponged up the Turkish language and flourished in her adopted land. But Doc was on the lookout for love, and soon began a torrid affair with a respected local lawyer, a man with Banderas looks and the hots for Doc. There was a catch, of course. Her lawyer wasn't the marrying type, or rather, she wasn't the type he would marry. Mother's pride dictated he would have a Muslim bride, and when he wed his virgin and lined Doc up as his part time doxy, Doc had other ideas. She laced up her walking boots, hitched up her skirt and trekked south to Bodrum to lick her wounds and start afresh. Since then, Doc's romantic scuffles had failed to float her boat and she was content to bide her time as the wise owl of the Bodrum belfry. Until, that is, Mr Right came a-ringing.

Liam sat in the dappled shade, cheap market sunglasses protecting his puffy eyes from the sharp light of a late summer's day. Doc returned with a bottle of single malt, two tumblers and an ash tray.

'You're kidding, sister. Way too early.'

'It's never too early at a time like this,' she said, pouring a large glass of Dutch courage. 'Just the one. A large one. So what's the big drama, then?'

'I'm going back home. To London.'

'Okay. That's it?'

'I haven't told Jack.'

'And you haven't told Jack because?'

'Because he loves it here. Because I've handled it badly. Because everything's a fucking mess.'

He took a swig of scotch.

'Mum's got Alzheimer's.'

Liam recoiled at the sound of his own voice. He had never said the word out loud before, certainly not since his father had told him, all those weeks ago. Finding out hadn't been a surprise, not really. Siobhan had implied as much. It was just the word.

'Alzheimer's?' said Doc.

'Alzheimer's.'

'Does she know?'

'She's in denial. Dad's in a heap.'

'So you're going back?'

'Yeah. To help. Whatever that means.'

'And what does it mean, Liam? You can't always make things better. You're not God.'

'Well, I can't stay here, slapping on the sun cream. She's my mother, for fuck's sake.'

As a mummy's boy, Liam had always been a bit of a gay cliché. When they were kids, Liam would watch his father chase Siobhan across the grass at Finsbury Park. His sister would wince in pretend agony as Liam Senior rubbed his stubble across the soles of her feet. Liam would stay close to his mother, stretched out on the picnic blanket, staring intently at the perfect symmetry of the green stitching on her Dublin Castle scarf and watching her pour milky tea from a thermos.

'I'm sorry,' said Doc. 'I get it.'

She lit a cigarette and passed it to Liam.

'Smoke. It always calms you down. Go on.'

'Got anything stronger?'

'Sorry, we don't do spliffs on Old Hamman Street anymore.'

Liam gulped his drink and removed his sunglasses.

'God, put them back on, you'll scare the goats. Did you get *any* sleep?'

Liam puffed on his cigarette, Doc topped up the glasses and they sat back in their chairs as the midday *ezan* roared along the streets.

'I'm sorry,' said Liam. 'To dump this on you, I mean. What with all the Cristal stuff.'

'She's a lucky girl. She survived.'

'Yeah.'

'Cristal is Cristal. She'll go back to him. She always does.'

The two friends sat in silence, sipping their whisky until both glasses were drained.

'You've got a lot on your plate,' said Liam eventually. 'I should go.'

'Look, Liam. Stop being such a wuss. Just tell him. *For better, for worse*, wasn't that the line? Just grow a pair and get on with it.'

I flung open the salon windows, unable to bear the heat. The midday *ezan* roared along Sentry Lane and confusion turned to anger. I didn't deserve this. No fucking way. I had given up everything to rescue Liam from his perfidious boss, not to mention the midnight oil he regularly burned while she cocktailed her way to the top. I once had status, prestige, a few shillings in the bank and a pretty Victorian terrace in East London. And now all I had was a dwindling bank balance and a man with secrets.

I twisted the silver wedding ring round my finger. *Christ Almighty, Jack. Where's your Dunkirk Spirit? 'For better, for worse.' Wasn't that the line?*

The garden gate slammed shut and I threw open the front door.

'Liam? What the fuck's going on?'

CHAPTER TWENTY-THREE

'TIL DEATH US DO PART

Thin strands of wispy cotton clouds threaded the hazy skies above Torba. Foolhardy foreigners fried by the churning pool of the Kamelya Apartments while the less idiotic hid from the mugging sun under a dense canopy of pleached bougainvillea. All was silent except for the trickling of water and the hum of horny cicadas. Hidden from sight, a shovel-handed gardener surveyed his fiefdom from the broad shade of a sprawling fig tree, his muscular body honed by years of hard labour, his weathered face prematurely aged by the sun. Tariq Nejem was pleased with his lot. He had ridden the caravan of hope looking for casual work in boomtown Bodrum and after years of penury treading water in a pool of affluence, the hired hand from Hatay rose to the rank of resident caretaker at Tepe Heights. It was there, at one of the countless nondescript boxy developments crowding the ridges around Yalıkavak that Tariq had first encountered two exotic patrons from the West, a pair of dipsomaniac gay boys with rubbish that rattled and a penchant for Hollywood musicals. After a less than auspicious start coloured by Tariq's outright incredulity, our relationship with the likeable *kapıcı* had blossomed unconventionally. Tariq's mind had opened, his guard had dropped and he had taken to manhandling – me mostly. Though I feared his playful flirtation might spill over into a grope and a poke, he had never quite crossed the line. When we abandoned Tepe Heights and moved to Bodrum Town, Tariq shed a tear and we knew we had made our first Turkish friend. As fate would have it, our spunky outdoorsman was soon to follow, plucked by Victoria, our easy on the eye Belle, to become the cock of the walk at the Kamelya Apartments, a small development of select holiday lets, two miles west of Bodrum. A rise up the pecking order gave Tariq bigger digs, bigger lira and three young Kurdish flunkies to boss about, something he did with sadistic dedication. Tariq had arrived. Now, he could chain-smoke Western tobacco, put a little extra under the mattress for his daughter's education and splash out on that gleaming satellite dish for his pantalooned missus. Yes, Tariq Nejem was pleased with his lot. Victoria had been more than happy to offer Tariq a hand up. She herself had climbed the greasy pole from rep to tycoon and now ran her own holiday letting business. She spoke fluent Turkish without a hint of Sussex and against all the odds and obstacles, had made it big in a man's world. In the interests of self-preservation, Victoria had decided to forsake men for money. 'It lasts longer, doesn't shag around and gives far more pleasure,' she had said. Besides, Victoria's standards were high. Penniless waiters weren't her style and eligible doctors were few and far between.

Murat thumped the desk with his fists, tipping over a half-finished mug of Nescafé and spilling the contents over Victoria's bookings.

'Where is she? Where's my fucking wife!'

Marinated tanners looked up from their plastic sunbeds, straining hard to decipher the Turkish outburst. Tariq stubbed out his cigarette and hurried over to the site office.

'I don't know where your wife is, Murat,' Victoria replied, mopping up the mess with tissues. 'And I wouldn't tell you if I did.'

'You're lying! You foreign bitches are all the fucking same.'

Two by two, the Kamelya guests deserted their stations and withdrew to their air-conditioned apartments. Tariq stood guard outside the office and peered at Murat through the glass door. Victoria's finger was poised over the keypad of her mobile phone.

'I told you, Murat, she's not here. I'd like you to leave now. I'm busy.'

Murat leant over Victoria's desk, his eyes bulging.

'Look, slut, give me my fucking wife.'

'But Murat, I don't have your fucking wife.'

Tariq had heard enough and stormed into the office as Murat snatched Victoria's mobile and smashed it against the wall. He grabbed Murat's shoulders and swung him round.

'You may frighten her, you piece of shit, but you don't frighten me. Fuck off or I'll give you a dose of your own medicine.'

'You? Not before I kill you. And I will. I'll fucking kill you!'

Murat grasped a paper-knife from Victoria's desk and waved it around limply.

'Come on, big man,' Tariq beckoned. 'Try it.'

Not fancying his chances, Murat submitted and slipped the knife into the back pocket of his jeans. He turned to face Victoria, his eyes boring into hers.

'This isn't finished, bitch. I'll find her, and then I'll be back for you.'

Murat slammed the door behind him and Victoria shunted the coffee-sodden tissues into a wastepaper basket.

'Thank you, Tariq. It's over now.'

'He is weak, Miss Victoria. He is a coward.'

'Yes, Tariq, I know. You can go now. I'm fine.'

Two by two, the nervy residents returned to their damp beach towels and oil-stained holiday reads. Tariq swaggered through the borders, retrieved a Marlboro from the pack in his breast pocket and lit up. Yes, Miss Victoria was safe with Tariq Nejem around.

The rubber foot of a metal crutch pushed open a door at the back of the office and a battered redhead hobbled towards Victoria, her ankle encased in a boot-shaped plaster cast, her left forearm cradled by a cotton sling.

'I knew he'd come after me,' she whispered, flopping into a seat. 'I'm so sorry.'

Cristal's vision was blurred by the blood crusts around her eyes. Salty tears streamed down her cheeks and seeped into the sutures of her swollen lips.

It was a nice day for a funeral. Set in the foothills above Yalıkavak, the ruins of old Sandima delivered an atmospheric backdrop for a sudden passing. The parched cemetery was sheltered from the afternoon sun by an aromatic coppice of pine, cedar and juniper, and threads of light fanned the brittle scrub like a broken Venetian blind. The village itself was derelict save for a small house eccentrically renovated by a local artist and a handful of centenarians who refused to leave. Unlike most of the Anatolian ghost villages emptied by the 1923 trade in souls between Greece and Turkey, Sandima had been abandoned for sound economic reasons. Keen to raise their game and improve the prospects of their children, the villagers had gradually swapped their stony fields for the lucrative trade of sponge diving. As the years passed, the population drifted down the valley to the coast and by the Sixties, the village was all but empty. As Yalıkavak grew, Sandima decayed into peaceful wild oblivion, a tranquil resting place and the perfect spot to push up the daisies.

'Remind me why we're here?'

'I told you,' said Susan. 'To make up the numbers.'

She squeezed my hand. 'Promise me you'll behave, Jack. Promise.'

Liam sighed. 'So how did he… you know…?'

'It was all very quick. He was playing golf out by Lake Tuzla.'

We both looked at Susan.

'And?'

'Sudden Death Syndrome.'

'No!' said Liam. 'What happened?'

'Sudden death! He toppled into a bunker. It took a couple of caddies to drag him out.'

She stifled a laugh.

'Susan!' I chided. 'And you told *me* to behave.'

'Must be the shock, sorry. Poor old sod.'

The Mayor of Yalıkavak had given official dispensation for a Christian burial in the neglected graveyard. We joined the modest cortège of sombre-clobbered emigreys and slowly cracked through the clumpy grass past lopsided headstones of loved ones, long forgotten by long forgotten loved ones. A familiar off-the-peg pastor stood by the freshly dug grave, drowning in a heavy Singer-sewn cassock. He gestured for the congregation to gather round.

'Gordon was a well-respected member of the expat community,' he said, dabbing his brow with a lace handkerchief. 'Loved by his grieving wife and liked by everyone he touched.'

A bead of sweat dripped from the parson's nose.

'Gordon was generous to a tee, overflowing with Christian charity,' he continued. 'And so very kind to street dogs. The loss is keenly felt by us all. Not to mention the dogs.'

Liam hadn't seen Flesh Gordon as the pious type, more an unrepentant slum landlord with a nasty case of *schadenfreude*. Maybe Gorders had hedged his bets.

'And what would the vicar know?' Susan muttered. 'He never even met the old drunk.'

As the eulogy droned on, Liam and I focussed on a diminutive woman tucked into a little black number at the front of the flock. Her body was motionless, her head bowed and her face hidden from view by a black veil.

'Alexis Carrington does Turkey,' whispered Liam. 'Wanita the airmailed missus, I presume? Poor cow. What's she gonna do now?'

I sighed. 'Champagne and Club Class all the way back to Manila, I expect.'

'Have a heart, Jack. She's beside herself.'

How Liam came to that conclusion was beyond me. The mail-order bride hadn't so much as breathed. Intuition told me Wanita was more likely to dance around the grave than cry into it, and with youth on her side, a purse topped up with pesos and the old fart six feet under, who could blame her?

When the wittering pastor ran out of uplifting psalms ('*The pains of death surround me… let them go down quick into Hell*'), six strapping lads lifted up the makeshift coffin, a DIY affair cobbled together from roughly-sawn planks. The undertakers had broken with tradition and allowed Gordon to stay in his casket for the internment.

'They'd normally chuck him in wrapped in a cotton shroud,' said Susan. 'It's quite an honour.'

The unusual honour brought with it some unusual consequences. The apprentice pallbearers struggled with the heavy box, lost their footing and unceremoniously tipped it into the grave. Susan shrieked. Gorders came to a sudden halt, jammed at thirty degrees half way down the undercut hole. As the air filled with dust to dust, mourners shuffled in embarrassment, the parson's jaw dropped open and Liam held his fingers to his mouth. The horrified boys pushed, shoved, tapped and thumped, muscles strained and fingers splintered but it was all in vain. Gorders was going nowhere. Up came the casket, out came the shovels and in went the boys. When the coffin was eventually lowered into its final resting place, much to the parson's relief, an impromptu ripple of applause filtered through the tumbledown houses and echoed through the valley towards Yalıkavak. Wanita remained inscrutable throughout. Gorders was finally at peace and she was finally free.

The reception was a dry shift. Wanita didn't push the boat out. PG Tips, fish paste sandwiches and a few slices of Battenberg did little to raise the spirits at her High Chaparral pile on the Gökcebel road. We joined the obligatory 'sorry for your loss' queue and then retreated to a table in a corner of the front garden.

'You should have told me, Liam.'

'I panicked.'

'That's bloody obvious.'

'I thought you'd leave me.'

'Then you're an idiot, Liam Brennan. 'Til death us do part. Wasn't that the line?'

'Yeah, yeah. But what about the dream?'

'We knew it wouldn't be forever, didn't we?'

Liam pushed a curled up sandwich around his plate.

'We knew.'

'Things change, Liam. I'm glad we jumped ship when we did, but that's yesterday's script now.'

'You're right.'

'Course I am. Besides, Turkey will always be here and your Mum won't be.'

'Sensitive to the last.'

'You know what I mean.'

'It's just so complicated.'

'Your Mum needs you. Where's the complicated?'

Nancy rattled through the ranch doors with a bottle of Misli and three glasses on a plastic tray.

'There you are, boys. Been lookin' for yer everywhere. Like a bleedin' wake in there.'

Liam sniggered and looked about the garden. 'Where did you get that bottle?'

'The fridge. Ain't a crime, is it?'

'It's not your fridge.'

'Lighten up, luv, nobody died.'

Nancy filled the glasses and grinned mischievously.

'To Gorders. Gawd rest 'is bleedin' soul.'

'To Wanita,' I said. 'God bless her and all who sail in her.'

'And to me,' sighed Nancy. 'Fucked over yet again.'

'Oh? What's the old letch done now?'

'It's *who* 'ee's done. Marianna, the skinny German cow.'

'Ah.'

'Get this. The trollop's only bought 'arf his boat. She's got 'er claws in 'im good 'n' proper this time.'

'And he took the cash?'

'Course 'ee did. 'Ee's a Turk innee? All they fink about is the wonga.'

'A drunken sailor with a *rakı* habit to fund.'

'And a VOMIT in every port,' said Liam.

''Ee promised I was the only one.'

'He meant one at a time,' said Liam. 'Lie with dogs, Nans, and you're gonna get fleas.'

'It's like I'm playin' Pass the Parcel,' Nancy continued, 'and all I can hear is the bleedin' thing tickin'... I've really 'ad it this time. It's the last straw. I'm off.'

Nancy started to blubber. 'I wanna go 'ome, Jack. I wanna go 'ome.'

I held out my arms. 'Come 'ere, girl. Give Mama a hug.'

'Look at me,' she snivelled, 'I'm a bag of bleedin' nerves. How can one man do this to me?'

'Dry those eyes, sister. This may be a funeral but we can't have you wailing like some rustic washerwoman, now can we?'

'Or getting snot on Jack's best funeral shirt,' said Liam. 'It's Primarni.'

Nancy wiped her face with the sleeve of her black chiffon blouse.

'I mean it, Jack,' she sniffed. 'I'm done 'ere.'

As the rent-a-mourners buzzed about the garden trading hearsay like caustic hornets, we comforted our heartbroken Delilah wondering if, for once, Nancy would do the right thing.

CHAPTER TWENTY-FOUR

FOR WHOM THE BELLES TOLL

'Order! Order!' I shouted, ting-ting-tinging my glass with a fork and looking to Liam for reassurance. 'We have news.'

Musto's al fresco terrace was overflowing with grey-haired yachties in Tommy Hilfiger shirts, Blue Harbour chinos and tan loafers. A Turkish princess was shackled to each of them, bouffanted painted dolls with pert breasts, power pouts and fuck-me heels. Tables were spilling over onto the newly refurbished pavement and were huddled so close together, our favourite bistro was generating its very own microclimate. Liam scanned the sea of ivory table linen, tapered red candles and aluminium wine coolers and caught the attention of Cemal, head waiter, resident eye candy and the object of Liam's stirrings.

'Not yet, Jack. Emergency top-ups first.'

An extraordinary meeting of the Bodrum Belles came to order. The Belles were squeezed around a small oval table at the front of the bustling terrace, competing for attention with the moneyed marina crew and shouting to be heard above the motorised clamour of the street.

'So, what is it?' asked Victoria, looking to Jess for a clue.

'Don't ask me. Nobody tells me anything.'

'All good things come to she who waits,' I said. 'Patience is—'

'No it isn't. Patience isn't a virtue in my book,' said Victoria. 'You two sure know how to milk a moment.'

Jess tipped the last drops of an Angora red into her glass. 'I was in the middle of a Pilates class when I got the call. Nearly put my hip out.'

'Ah Cemal!' said Liam, smiling flirtatiously at the young tease, the kind of boy who would unbutton his flies for Satan himself if the price was right. 'One red, two whites and something to soak it all up please.'

Cemal grinned and threaded his way back to the bar.

'Ah Cemal! Cemal! The sun shines out of your bloody arse, Cemal!'

'Now, now, Jack, beware the green-eyed monster.'

'Well?' said Victoria, removing her shades as the sun finally set behind the town. 'When you've quite finished, can we get on with the big announcement. Sometime tonight would be nice.'

I smiled at Liam. 'Go on, love. You do it.'

Cemal returned with the wine and replenished the glasses.

Liam stood up. 'Thank you all for coming.'

'For pity's sake,' said Jess. 'Just get on with it.'

'A toast. To the Bodrum Belles!'

'The Bodrum Belles!' we rejoined, giggling as glasses were chinked a little too heartily and wine splattered onto the linen.

'Is that it?' asked Victoria. 'A toast to the Bodrum Belles?'

'No,' said Liam. 'There's something else.'

'Why don't you just ask the Belediye to broadcast it over the PA?' said Doc. 'It would be a damn sight easier.'

'Broadcast *what*?' asked Jess. 'What's going on?'

Liam opened his mouth, the Belles leaned forward and a yellow taxi screeched to a halt just feet from our table. The driver leapt out and threw open the rear passenger door. A crutch poked out, then a stiletto, then a boot cast. The cabbie grabbed the crutch and levered Cristal Cologne to her feet, running his eyes over her glitter-dusted bust.

'My, such big strong arms,' she purred as the couple entered an unplanned embrace, only separated by the girth of Cristal's pumped-up thrupenny bits. 'Enough to make a wench go weak at the knees.'

Cristal plucked a twenty lira note from her cleavage and passed it to the red-cheeked driver.

'Keep the change, bab.'

The silver rakes in the front row gawped at the voluptuous fancy and their po-faced companions tugged at the leash to bring them to heel. Even in plaster, Cristal scrubbed up well, jammed into a vintage black wiggle dress garnished with a floaty silk scarf. A wide, red glossy belt gathered her waist, accentuating her hourglass figure and underlining her factory-made frontage. Hair was Rodeo Drive, makeup was Blue Circle.

'Ooroyt, sisters!'

'You're just in time,' said Jess as Cristal hopped over to the table.

'In time? Fer what?'

'Liam's big announcement. He's got news.'

'Oh that. He's going back to England. Doc told me. Anyway, what does it take to get a drink round here? I'm as dry as a nun's gusset.'

'But it makes no sense, Liam,' said Jess. 'I thought you were happy here. You are, aren't you?'

'I have my moments.'

Cemal returned with a cheese platter and set it down in the middle of the busy table.

'What about Jack?'

'He's coming with me. Obviously.'

'Is it the Islamist stuff?'

'Not really. Actually, on a night like tonight, I'm not sure we've ever been happier.'

'Are you ill, is that it?'

'I need to go home, that's all, Jess. All of this… it was never meant to last forever.'

'Why ever not?'

'Because it's not real, Jess.'

Jess picked up an olive and squeezed it. 'Seems pretty real to me.' She popped the olive in her mouth and swallowed it whole. 'Tastes pretty real, too. Why don't you try?'

'It's Mum,' said Liam. 'Well, her mind.'

Jess sat back in her chair.

'Oh. You didn't say.'

'No.'

Cemal topped up the glasses and Liam took a swig.

'Don't say anymore. When are you going?'

'As soon as…'

'That soon? We'd better give you a bloody good send off, then, hadn't we?'

'Just listen,' I said. 'For once, just listen.'

Cristal removed her silk scarf and draped it over the back of her seat.

'You need to get away from that man.'

'That man loves me, Jack.'

'Men who love you don't put you in hospital.'

Cristal fiddled with her napkin.

'You don't understand,' she said, staring down at the table. 'I've got a reet gob on me.'

'You and me both. But Liam doesn't knock the crap out of me every time I piss him off.'

'I provoked 'im. I was asking for it. I always—'

'Look at me Cristal! You *asked* for it? What did you say? Beat me unconscious, Murat? I just adore hospital food?'

'It's his temper, Jack. It don't last. Yow don't know him like I do.'

'I know him alright. I know he's a thug in yob's clothing. Have you looked in the mirror lately? Plastering your face with concealer doesn't change a thing, Cristal. Next time he'll kill you.'

'Stop it, Jack! He knows he's done wrong.'

'Cristal, my darling, has that blow to the head made you simple? It's as clear as the broken nose on your face.'

'My nose ain't broke.'

'Not this time, no. I'm telling you. Call another cab, pack your bags, go to the airport and get the fuck out of here.'

'It's different fer me, Jack. I don't have a Liam. There's nothing fer me in England.'

'Just a daughter who loves you.'

Cristal baulked. 'How did you know?'

'Jess told me.'

'I don't have a daughter anymore,' Cristal said softly. 'She don't approve.'

'She doesn't approve of *him*. She doesn't approve of seeing her Mum getting used as a punch bag. You can hardly blame her. Go home, Cristal. Go back to your daughter.'

'I can't! How many more times? I love Murat. Leave me alone, Jack!'

Cristal picked up her handbag and looked across at the marina.

'I gotta go soon. Say something nice. Please, Jack. I don't want the night to end like this.'

'Nice? I can do nice. You're a unique woman, Cristal Cologne, a true original, a queen of hearts... despite the assisted tits, micro skirts and war paint.'

Cristal beamed. 'That's the nicest thing anyone's ever said to me... ever.'

'And that, my darling, is the bloody problem.'

Once the cross examinations were over and the news fully consumed, Doc brushed aside sentiment for things more matter of fact.

'What about your landlady?' asked Doc. 'Hanife isn't it? Have you told her?'

'Yeah. She threw her hands up in horror. After she took the rent, that is. When I dropped in the family thing she was absolutely fine.'

'No Turk would argue with the family thing.'

'And she invited us for dinner.'

'Christ, the last supper up at the manor. You *are* honoured.'

'And Beril and Vadim?'

'Ah, that's where you come in, Doc.'

'I've been thinking,' said Victoria, passing me a carafe of iced water. 'You'll offload the furniture, I assume.'

'I suppose.'

'Then I'll take the sofa.'

'And I'll have the patio table,' said Doc, 'and the chairs, of course.'

'I'll have your iron,' said Jess. 'Mine's knackered. It spits out shit all over the filigree. I'm forever dabbing my smalls.'

'And the big bookcase,' said Victoria, 'the one in the—'

'Ladies, ladies! Talk about the scavengers of Turkey Street.'

'And talk about short-lived emotions,' said Liam. 'What happened to the *please don't go, we couldn't cope without you*?'

'Shallow as a puddle,' I said. 'The whole bloody lot of 'em.'

Within minutes and in a tidy twist of fate, the furniture of No. 2 Sentry Lane was auctioned off to the Bodrum Belles – just as our fastidious old neighbour in London had bought our house and contents two years earlier. Lady Fortuna was still in our corner.

Cristal wrapped her scarf back round her neck.

'That's it. It's late. I have to go.'

It was last knockings at Musto's and we were the only guests standing, or rather slumping and slurring. As Cemal poured one final round of *yolluks*, his underlings stacked chairs and swept up around us. Like the old pro that she was, Jess had nodded off at the end of the table without spilling a single drop. Cristal said her final farewells and hobbled off to the Marina taxi rank without looking back. I sensed it was the last I would see of Miss Cristal Cologne, the glamour model who never quite made it to Page 3. For all her flaws, infuriating denials and bloody minded naivety, I was sad to see her go and even sadder to think where she might be heading.

CHAPTER TWENTY-FIVE

THE LETTER

Dear Beril and Vadim,

We have news. Sad news. We are leaving Turkey and returning to England. Liam's mother is unwell. We will be leaving as soon as arrangements can be made.

Our time in Bodrum has been magical and life-changing. In no small part, this is due to you, our remarkable neighbours. Thank you, truly, for your kindness. We will always remember our candlelit evenings, thumbing through that Turkish-English dictionary and drowning in rakı as Turkey Street buzzed on around us. Vadim, your bongos have changed our world and mostly for the good. Beril, your banquets have added inches to our waistlines and taken our bland English palates to places they have never been before.

We will miss you both. Maybe not quite as much as Hanife's tripe soup, but we will miss you. Thank you for teaching us a valuable lesson. In Turkey, or maybe in every country around the world, there are always people prepared to embrace difference. We only hope Turkey will accept you just as you have accepted us. You two are legends.

Your English friends,

Jack and Liam

Vadim placed the letter on his patio table. Beril ran into her house and slammed the door.

'Such histrionics,' said Sophia. 'The woman is deranged.'

Vadim smiled wryly and went to comfort his concubine.

'You write Turkish so much better than you speak it,' said Sophia, staring at the letter.

'You're too kind,' said Liam.

I arched my eyebrows at Liam. 'We had a little help.'

'You will return, surely?' she said. 'You must go, I understand. It is your duty, you must do what is right. But one day you will come back.'

'It's in the lap of the gods,' I said. 'Isn't that right, Liam?'

'Ah, yes, the gods,' said Sophia. 'Trust me, they are as fickle as autumn skies. In the end, I think it may be wiser to determine one's own fate.'

'And what's yours?' I asked, 'What does the future hold for the great Sophia?'

'My future is also my demise,' she said mysteriously. 'And it is short.'

'I hardly think so, Sophia. There's plenty of petrol left in that tank of yours.'

'What an ugly analogy, young man.'

'And think about the people who love you,' said Liam. 'Elma, Onur and Nuray, there will always be Nuray.'

'Yes, Nuray, there will always be my faithful maid. But as for Onur, I am not so stupid. I will be leaving also.'

Sophia turned stage right and extended her neck for a classic Norma Desmond shot.

'I shall sell my house. I shall leave Bodrum. I shall move to Istanbul and I shall live with Elma.'

'But why?' said Liam. 'You *are* Bodrum.'

'Elma insists. It is my duty. She says I must do what is right.'

'Ah,' said Liam. 'I see.'

I saw too. Sophia's daughter had sobered up just long enough to protect her inheritance from vultures like the oily-wigged Onur.

'Family can be a blessing, dear boy, but it can also be a curse.'

Bianco slinked into the courtyard and looked up wistfully at the olive tree, meowing pathetically.

'What *is* wrong with that stupid cat?' asked Sophia.

'He's just been separated from his family jewels,' I said.

'Jewels?'

'Snip, snip. At the vet.'

'Ah, another Ottoman eunuch. Just what Turkey needs.'

'And the poor pussy's been sore for days…'

Sophia frowned and lowered her chin.

'English humour,' she announced, 'is an acquired taste, and is most certainly not a taste I wish to acquire.'

Beril emerged into the courtyard and walked slowly to the table. Vadim followed behind, carrying a tray of glasses and his best bottle of *rakı*.

'And now,' he said, 'we drink.'

CHAPTER TWENTY-SIX

GORILLA IN THE MIST

Saddled with an underpowered hire car, we set out at first light on a farewell to Turkey road trip. The tyranny of summer was behind us and winter queued up impatiently out at sea. Clammy conditions had given way to bright warm days and cuddlier nights. It was a good time to stretch our cultural legs. In Bodrum, the hysterical nightlife had slowed to a lean trickle. The hordes were back in Istanbul and the whores were back in Kiev. In their place, bland Bavarians in straw hats and socked sandals meandered through town like train spotters and the thin-waisted hassle boys along Bar Street were out in force to squeeze one last pushy sale. Fink, the mother of all rich-bitch bars, had served its last overpriced vodka of the season and its huge swaying red chandelier, the most photographed patio light in all of Anatolia, had been dismantled and packed away for another year.

We took our usual route off the Peninsula past dreary Milas and swept north to skirt along the western shore of the perpetually beautiful Lake Bafa, a protected nature reserve, bubble wrapped from the free-for-all spreading along the coast, though not from the ever widening arterial highway.

'It's upside down, Jack.'

'I'm not a complete idiot.'

I turned the map around and ran my finger north to pinpoint a series of old relics. Liam had other ideas and screeched the car round a tight corner onto a narrow dirt track. He slammed on the brakes and the car came to an abrupt halt in front of a small hand-carved nymph cradling an overflowing wine jug. Above her, a large wooden sign was nailed to the trunk of an old juniper tree.

Otel Latmos. A retreat for discerning travellers. All welcome.

Liam grinned. 'Stuff the map, let's live a little.'

I stared up at the sign and wondered if we would qualify as 'discerning' travellers in this neck of the woods. Liam revved the car, swung left and bumped downhill along a lumpy road lined with twisted olive trees. We parked up against a row of overflowing bins in the car park of the lakeside motel and leapt out to take stock. Single-storey flat-roofed cabins poked through a copse of tamarisk trees, and cracked concrete paths tumbled over the edge to the lake below. To our right, a log-faced reception block announced in Turkish and English that Otel Latmos had vacancies, organic breakfasts and the 'Best views in Asia Minor.'

A woman the size of Asia Major appeared at the entrance and we both froze.

'Welcome, gentlemen, I am Grit. Come!'

'Well, well,' said Liam. 'The amazing bearded lady.'

There was no disguising it. Grit was a bit of a gorilla. Six feet and more in her cross hikers, she had the lumbering gait of a silverback. She beckoned us into the faux Tyrolean log cabin and we took our seats by an occasional table dressed haphazardly in camping leaflets and birding magazines. A large noticeboard covered in ripped felt hung on a wall. At its centre was a notice printed in bold red letters.

One tree can make 10,000 matches.
One match can burn 10,000 trees.
Burn the trees and we will burn you.

'You will have room ten,' Grit announced, towering over Liam as he fumbled in his manbag for his wallet. 'The *special* room.'

'Do you have wine?' he asked.

'Oh yes, we have *special* wine.' The edges of Grit's mouth quivered and almost broke into a smile. 'Organic.'

'So we're staying the night?' I hissed at Liam as we jumped up and followed Grit out the door.

'Unless you fancy a couple of rounds with Bigfoot, yes, we are. Look, it's a good base,' said Liam, tripping on the crazy paving as Grit dragged her knuckles ahead of us.

Grit swung open the door of number ten, a squalid concrete bunker with a low Artexed ceiling and walls splattered with the blood of a thousand squashed mosquitos like an early Jackson Pollock. Utilitarian furniture struggled to provide a little personality: a scratched Seventies-style Formica table, a single Van

Gogh chair and a small pine bed wrapped in greyish sheets so threadbare they could double up as voiles.

'Not exactly the Ritz,' said Liam.

'No,' I said, peering into the large bathroom with its seatless toilet, cracked sink and a tide-stained shower tray complete with a flaccid hose, drip, drip, dripping away. 'It's the Black Hole of Calcutta.'

'Special wine,' said Grit, gesturing at a recycled Coke bottle and two plastic tumblers on the knotted pine bedside table.

'So what do you know?' I said picking up the bottle. '*Special* wine. Whoopie doo.'

Oblivious to our obvious disappointment, Grit left us to it and clomped up the steep steps back to reception.

'This time, Liam Brennan, you've really surpassed yourself. I'd love to know what's so *special* about this dump?'

Liam grabbed the Coke bottle. We filed onto the terrace and looked out across the waters. The spurred ridges of the five-fingered Beşparmak Mountains loomed over the pine-trimmed north shore of the lake, and serrated islets sprinkled with holy remnants rose from the brackish depths. Huge boulders loosened by long-forgotten earthquakes cluttered the lake's jagged edge. The silence was deafening.

'Well, well,' said Liam. 'That answer your question?

He took a slug from the bottle.

'And I'll tell you one thing for nothing,' he said, replacing the cap and wiping tears from his eyes. 'It's no wonder Grit's got balls. This little concoction would put hairs on the chest of a cherub.'

'Euromos,' I said to Liam as we hit our first ruin, 'houses one of the best preserved classical temples in all of Turkey.'

'You don't say?' he replied, staring up at the Corinthian columns of the Temple of Zeus and taking a quick selfie for a few hundred of his closest Facebook friends.

'Yes, Liam, I do say.'

'It's all about to end, isn't it, Jack?'

'Don't fret Gunga Din, it's only midday, we've got hours.'

'You know what I mean.'

He pointed his camera at the horizon and clicked.

'Look at us. We've barely scratched the surface.'

'We'll be back,' I said. 'Stop moping and take me to Apollo. We've kept that nice young man waiting for far too long.'

We drove in silence across miles of tedious treeless flatlands broken only by occasional heaps of building rubble, skeletal buildings and solitary wind turbines rotating slowly in the breeze. It was not the best Turkey had to offer, an unappealing gateway for the truckloads of tourists who flocked to the coast during the summer scurries. It was small wonder Thomas Cook flew them in under the cover of darkness. We eventually passed through Didim, an unfinished urban sprawl built over the Sacred Way, the processional route that led pilgrims to the Temple of Apollo at Didyma. We arrived at the site and found it caged in by a scruffy shanty town overrun with pushy hawkers, but once through the gate, we were instantly converted. Despite the modern encroachment, Christian vandalism, earthquakes and the plunder of dressed stones, the vast temple was breathtaking. We spent the afternoon drifting through the precincts, weaving through the sentry of giant columns, posing for photographs in the grand inner court and peering at the remains of a small shrine where the sacred spring once flowed, a babbling brook for the babbling oracle that once rivalled Delphi. Liam explored erratically, one minute hopping up and down the ceremonial staircase like the Von Trapp children on the *do-re-mi* steps, the next, staring quizzically at two thousand years of graffiti.

'You don't get that in Londinium,' said Liam, tracing a carved plinth with his fingers.

'Nice to see you appreciating a bit of history for once. Just a shame the oracle's out of order.'

'Yeah. She might have told us where we go from here.'

'We know where we go from here, Liam. If we stand still and watch the world go by, it will. It's time to move on.'

It was late afternoon and we took a slow saunter around the perimeter of the Temple. As Liam took snaps of the soaring columns, a high-pitched grunting escaped from the undergrowth, quickly followed by a rat-a-tat-tat. We stepped around a stack of upturned drums and peered through the brittle fronds of desiccated ferns like a brace of David Attenboroughs. A mottled tortoise was pursuing a smaller mate with all the determination of a spring-loaded waiter chasing a VOMIT. When he caught his flighty paramour, he headbutted the back of her shell and barked like a velociraptor. She pulled away, teasing him shamelessly just as he thought his luck was in. As the barking and banging continued, the hit and miss tryst drove Romeo into rapturous frustration until, in the end, a nonplussed Juliet relented and played dead as he mounted. Seconds later, job done, he slipped out and crawled off into the long grass for a post-coital nap.

'Is that it?' asked Liam.

'That's what *she* said. Typical bloke – hop on, hop off, then leave the girl holding the baby.'

We headed back towards the exit and held hands until it was unsafe.

'Jack?'

'What?'

'Do you think we'll ever grow up?'

'Not a chance. People don't grow up, love. They just learn how to behave in public.'

We arrived in Altınkum – Didim-on-Sea – just as the evening's festivities were kicking off. The sandy beach was edged by a pageant of competing clamour and naff neon. Bar Street was buzzing with a noisy garrison of tattooed bingo wings, pussy pelmets and beer-bellied Umbro tops serviced by pushy patrons and their vested underlings. We snatched a quick kebab, ate in the car and returned to the wilderness to drown our sorrows at our lakeside hideaway. Grit's fruit-infused paraffin was more potent than any wine I had ever imbibed. As the night sky glittered and the crickets pumped up the volume, we settled down outside our cell, huddled together on a bench overlooking the lake, supping the organic gut rot from plastic beakers and gazing up at the stars hunting for UFOs.

'Liam.'

'What now?'

'According to the legend, it was right by this very lake that the goddess Selene fell in love with Endymion, a young shepherd boy.'

'Fancy.'

'Zeus kept him in perpetual sleep so Selene could mount him nightly.'

Liam rolled his eyes and looked out to the lake.

'If you think I'm playing Selene, you can think again.'

The following morning, Liam and his mozzie-punctured legs wobbled to breakfast, more in need of a blood transfusion than an almond croissant. I sat him down at the nearest table to sample the delights of Grit's special food, Go Cat cereal and slabs of high fibre lino. The pine-clad restaurant had been invaded by an industrious troupe of Teutonic trekkers with highlighted mullets, each of them kitted out in identical walking boots and oatmeal shorts, presumably in preparation for a thigh slapping day of hiking and twitching. We watched in wonder as lunches were deftly packed into plastic Tupperware boxes with all the efficiency of an Audi production line. *Vorsprung durch Technik.* When we finally escaped to the car and bundled our things into the boot, Grit stomped over and invited us to an escorted walk of the wetlands. We declined. We weren't especially interested in a five hour eco trail through the bog. Not unless there was an organic bar at the end of it.

We were both ruined out by the time we got to ancient Miletos and we took tea in a rickety roadside *kafe* to admire the imposing amphitheatre from afar. The rush-covered terrace was strewn with a ragbag of tatty wooden tables and plastic garden chairs.

'It's round the back,' said Liam. 'I assume that look on your face means something?'

I hurried along the sun-baked mud path towards the toilet block and pushed open the door of the less than fragrant little boy's room. It was bad news. I stared down at the *alaturca*, a stinking ceramic hole flush with the tiled floor, and glanced across at the bucket of cold water. Memories came flooding back. I had my first encounter with a squat loo as a young army brat living in Malaysia. It was the time before the rise of the Asian Tigers and the reawakening of the Middle Kingdom when Britain still had a blue-water fleet and a stiff upper lip. All military personnel, except lowly squaddies in their airless billets, had a standard issue amah courtesy of Her Maj. Our married quarters came with a back extension for her use, equipped with a ground-level toilet. Obviously, our family pan was of the standard pedestal variety. She used hers and we used ours – *East is East and West is West and never the twain shall meet.* In short, my mother toilet-trained me to sit, not crouch.

I decided not to panic. After all, I had wet wipes, O Levels and a certificate in Home Economics. In the end, it was a masterful game of solo twister: shorts and Y fronts yanked over trainers, legs lifted, one and then the other and a panting body contorted to avoid contact with the slippery floor. With my clothes clutched in clenched teeth, my consignment hit the drop zone with perfect precision. The Luftwaffe couldn't have done a better job.

'So?' asked Liam as I returned in triumph. 'How was it?'

'An inconvenience.'

My mobile phone rang and I left it to vibrate in the pocket of my cargo shorts.

'Jack.'

'What?'

'Are you *really* sure you're okay about going back?'

'Christ, how many more times! Look, Liam, I'd walk to the end of the Earth with you.'

'Then push me off, I know.'

'Look, life can't all be Snow White and Julie Andrews.'

'Are you going to answer that bloody phone?'

Nancy screamed.

'What's this about you and bleedin' England and why the fuck am I the last to know?'

'Ah,' I said, nodding at Liam, 'The jungle drums.'

'Well? Is it kosher? Are you off to England or ain't yer?'

'It's true.'

'For good?'

'Nothing's for good.'

There was a silence at the end of the phone.

'Nans? Are you still there?'

'Yeah. I'm thinkin'.'

'And?'

'And… I'm comin' wiv yer. Get me a ticket.'

'What about Irfan? What about Charlotte?'

'Yeah, and what about me? I want me bleedin' life back. Just do it, Jack. Just do it.'

We ordered more tea, digested Nancy's call and watched unsuspecting visitors run from the ruins, flailing their arms about like Tippi Hedren as the mozzies of Miletos blitzkrieged their victims. So, Nancy had finally come to her senses. She was heading for the lifeboat.

CHAPTER TWENTY-SEVEN

THE EXILES

'And what if they don't drink?' I asked, fingering the plonk in Tansaş.

'We'll get chocolates as a backup,' said Liam. 'Even the ayatollahs like chocolates. Anyway we'll need the booze to dull the senses. You know what her cooking's like.'

There was a tap on my shoulder. I turned round to face an immaculately pressed short-sleeved shirt with a badge in the shape of a shield sewn onto the breast pocket. The face was partially overshadowed by a military style peaked cap, a razor-sharp crease ran down each leg of the bum-hugging trousers, and a crackling walkie-talkie was strapped to a wide leather belt.

'Mr Jack? You *are* Mr Jack?'

I looked at Liam and then back at my young interrogator.

'Yes?' I said defensively. 'So what?'

'Only a suggestion,' sighed Liam, 'How about being nice?'

I cleared my throat and tried again. 'Good afternoon, officer. How may I help?'

The uniform shook his head, retrieved a notebook and pen from his breast pocket and began to scribble.

'It's that bloody blog of yours,' Liam whispered. 'What the hell have you been writing?'

A small group of nosy shoppers gathered around anticipating an arresting moment but Liam sensed something wasn't quite right. The uniform raised his head and winked.

'It can't be,' said Liam. 'Ibrahim? Is that you?'

'*Evet!* Is Ibrahim. Is good joke, no?'

This was a newly improved, fattened up, freshly laundered Ibrahim, so different from the sunken-eyed vagrant we had last encountered outside a tea house in Yalıkavak. We double kissed and the crowd quickly dispersed, disappointed the stocks would remain empty.

'God, Ibrahim,' I said. 'Look at you.'

'Yes, Mr Jack. I am security now.'

Ibrahim had finally bucked the hand to mouth trend of the waiter class and landed a plum job in a large national chain. The position came with a regular salary paid on time, a Third Reich uniform and the respect of his friends and family. Ibrahim's English had improved immeasurably since our last meeting and when he teased us about our worsening Turkish ('Is very bad, no?'), we shrugged in embarrassment.

'All's well that ends well,' I said as Ibrahim strutted down the aisle. 'And if it doesn't work out, he can always get a job as a kissagram.'

'I'd sit on his lap,' said Liam.

'And talk about the first thing that pops up?'

'Precisely.'

We queued up at the checkout with two bottles of Majestik and a tub of Cadbury's Celebrations, attracting the curiosity of the shopper ahead of us. She was loading her groceries into a large tartan shopping trolley, her eyes darting quickly between me and Liam as if she had suddenly recognised long lost friends. I contemplated smiling but thought better of it.

'You're Jack Scott, aren't you? I've been reading your blog.'

'Oh,' I said, blushing like a pubescent teen caught coming out of a backstreet massage parlour. 'I suppose I should apologise.'

'Actually, it's rather good.'

Liam rolled his eyes.

'Well,' I said, 'would you mind telling *him* that?'

She grinned at Liam, almost in sympathy, paid the cashier and pulled the flap down over her trolley.

'I'm Eve. Thrilled to meet you both. You've caused quite a stir, you know. And don't worry, I'm not about to stalk you, but I hope we meet again. We're practically neighbours after all.'

We climbed two flights of stairs to the top floor of the inner sanctum, a modern flat-pack building on Turkey Street, yards from Sentry Lane. We were apprehensive. And not just about the food. Hanife and her unassuming husband had always respected our privacy and kept their distance, showing appropriate gratitude when Liam handed over the monthly rent. They would wave and smile as we passed in the street and Hanife would drop by with inedible gifts from her kitchen. In many ways they were the model landlords just as we were the model tenants, paying on time and sprinkling a little fairy dust over their family seat. But in truth, we had no idea what they really thought about the gay *yabancılar.* Liam had ordered me to man up just in case.

'*Hoşgeldiniz!*' said Hanife as we emerged from the stairwell into a broad rooftop terrace. 'Welcome to our home.'

'Come, come,' said Levent, Hanife's husband, beckoning us to a candlelit table covered by an ornate lace tablecloth and a bewildering array of mezes. A selection of soothing American crooners serenaded from two speakers set up in the corner. We took our seats while Levent shuffled off in search of a corkscrew. The terrace overlooked an extensive mandarin grove stretching as far as the eye could see and, closer to the house, neat lines of orange, lemon and plum trees competed for room around a large rectangular vegetable garden tilled to perfection. By its side, a restive coop of roosting chickens clucked and cackled as they bedded down for the night and a small dark cat kept watch, one eye half open, its tail quivering like a rattlesnake.

'It's stunning, Hanife,' I said taking in the view. 'I never would have known.'

I offered the tub of Cadbury's.

'Is secret garden,' she said, accepting the chocolates and placing them at the centre of the table. 'My Eden.'

Levent returned with wine and a tray of tumblers. Two young children were by his side, a boy of six or seven and a younger girl, a dainty little thing in a floral tunic dress gathered at the waist. Her straight shoulder-length hair was swept back by a crimson Alice band.

'And who do we have here?' I asked, the pitch of my voice rising inexplicably.

Hanife beamed. 'Ah! Grandchildren. Our son is in Paris with wife.'

The boy was smartly dressed in a blue Pringle sweater and tan shorts, ears protruding slightly from a spiky mop of black hair. He approached the table and grinned.

'Well?' said Hanife. 'Say hello, Mikail.'

Mikail duly obliged and firmly shook my hand and then Liam's.

'And this is Lale, our little tulip.'

The tiny girl poked her head out from her grandfather's flank and fixed her gaze on the chocolates. Liam looked to Hanife for approval, passed the tub to Lale and the two children ran back into the house giggling.

'They're adorable, Hanife,' I said.

'They are future…'

Hanife paused, staring into the mandarin grove and then across to her husband.

'But now, we eat. Please…'

The eating bit was a relaxed affair. Our hosts held back as we picked a bit of this and a slice of that from the lavish spread. This was Ottoman cuisine at its finest and a step up from Hanife's standard offering of tripe soup, chicken jelly and sheep's anus. Maybe Beril had done the catering. Conversation flowed as best as it could given the cultural and generational divide. Levent and Hanife were an impressive couple, generous, warm and completely in love. At five feet tall, they shared the same stature and the same deep olive skin. Hanife told us her tale while Levent looked on admiringly. They were childhood sweethearts and by the time they reached adulthood, Levent and Hanife were inseparable. They graduated from the same Izmir University, married soon after and both became teachers at the same Bodrum school. She taught English, he taught history, though, ironically, his English was better than hers. It always made them laugh. As a bourgeois couple with money and connections they could easily have relaxed into a comfortable lifestyle with all the usual trappings. But Levent and Hanife were freethinking left-of-centre mavericks and were considered a minor threat to the military junta during the rope-swinging Sixties. They marched, they demonstrated and they got noticed by all the wrong people.

'No,' Levent interrupted gently. 'The *right* people.'

In many ways, they were just bit players in the counter-revolution and their punishment was relatively light, nothing so vulgar as trumped-up charges, show trials or hard labour. Even so, their sentence was designed to inflict the utmost cruelty. At the age of twenty-three and heavily pregnant, Hanife was purged from her job, and on the same day Levent was exiled to the East to teach in a remote village school. The inseparable couple were separated for eighteen months. They wrote to each other every week without fail, but a third world postal service meant few letters got through. Hanife clung to her family for support while Levent batted off isolation and depression. Despite the distance of time and space, they kept faith in the cause and in each other. When Turkey next flirted with democracy, they were finally reunited.

'Since that time,' said Hanife, 'we never apart. Not day. Not night.'

To a couple of soft-living Brits, their tale was barely comprehensible.

Even in her seventies, age had not tempered Hanife's feistiness or her strong opinions. She was resolutely opposed to the governing AKP which she thought 'worse, far worse than the generals'. Her views were well known in local political circles and she would repeat them to anyone who cared to listen.

'Mr Erdoğan and his people, they want Sharia Law,' she said. 'They will make us another Iran. You understand?'

'Be careful, my love,' said Levent. 'We are too old for all this... business.'

Hanife stroked the palm of her husband's hand. 'We must think of grandchildren, Levent.'

The sound of a stuttering piano spilled onto the terrace and everyone strained to listen to the faltering medley of chords and bum notes.

'Mikail is learning,' said Hanife looking at Liam. 'You play too, yes? You play for us?'

Liam needed little encouragement and disappeared into the salon to join Mikail and Lale at the piano. After the shuffling of a piano stool and a crack of his fingers, he began.

'He plays good,' said Hanife, placing her hand on my knee as Liam rattled off a Bach partita. 'You are proud, yes?'

I was.

Mikail studied Liam's fingers as they hopped across the keys and placed his hands on top of Liam's to sense the vibration and speed. He giggled as Liam gradually picked up the tempo and when Bach transitioned into a jazz version of *Twinkle, Twinkle, Little Star*, little Lale danced around the room.

'Mr Liam?' said Mikail. 'When I am big, I will play like you.'

'No, Mikail,' said Liam. 'You will play better.'

When the night drew to an end and we stood up to make our short journey home, Hanife kissed her guests goodnight and led us to the staircase.

'You know,' she said. 'I born in Beril and Vadim's house. Yes. I play in garden as girl.'

'It's a magical place,' I said.

Levent rested his hand on my shoulder. 'We are sorry you must go.'

'Me too.'

'Thank you for tonight, Hanife,' said Liam.

'Is pleasure. Take care of mother.'

'Come, Hanife,' said Levent, 'it is late. Let them go home. Goodnight, gentlemen. And good luck.'

With that, we climbed down the steep stairs and walked in silence onto a lamp-lit Turkey Street. We had just found another remarkable corner of a remarkable country and its discovery had made our imminent departure all the more poignant.

CHAPTER TWENTY-EIGHT

ALL ABOUT EVE

Eve was no ordinary vetpat. The woman we had encountered at the Tansaş checkout had a look of Kristin Scott Thomas about her. She was quite the role model with a fearless sense of adventure, Michelin-starred hands and a profound interest in all things Turkish.

'And now,' she said, snapping her chocolate spoon in Kahve Dünyası. 'I've taken a leaf out of your book. I've started a blog.'

As we sipped our frothy cappuccinos, Eve confessed all. As a pretty slip of a girl back in the early Eighties, she had stuffed her antiquities degree in her old kit bag and bought a one way ticket to Izmir. Like you do.

'I've always been a bit of a rebellious madam.'

Happenstance and a fair wind had carried her to a thirty-foot sloop moored in Bodrum's new marina and so began a life on the waves as a salt-sprayed deckhand, apprentice galley cook and trainee archaeologist. For as long as she could recall, Eve had always held a fascination for things nautical, ancient and culinary and had managed to indulge all three with a devil may care combination of rigging, digging and bottle washing. In the romance stakes, Eve knew precisely what floated her boat and, unlike many of her sisters, she didn't cream her knickers at the sight of a dumb waiter with a Jagger swagger, biblical attitudes and a herd in the hills. Eve was no VOMIT. A year into her maritime probation, she met and fell overboard for Erdem, a shipshape stockbroker from Istanbul, learnéd, urbane and a child of the Establishment. The young couple courted, he proposed, and she accepted. He wed for love, not for passport. She wed for love and the secrets of the Ottoman kitchen. It was the perfect match, a marriage of equals. With a newborn daughter in tow, they sailed back to England for liberal schools and lucrative careers. And so, for nearly two decades, the Anatolian dream was put on hold and trips to Turkey were reserved for holidays and family reunions. Eve had approached the extended hiatus with resigned pragmatism in the certain knowledge that one day she would return. With offspring schooled and careers spent, the time had finally come. And now Eve and her crew were back for good, a two-centred family with a town house on Halfway Square and a rural retreat on the edge of Mumcular, a small and traditional settlement off the tourist trail.

'I always knew we'd come home,' said Eve, flushing at the sudden rush of memories. 'It was inevitable.'

Anatolian life suited her. Whether it was raiding the chicken coop in wellies and waxed jacket or slipping into that little black dress for the captain's table, Eve fitted right in.

'And now I've decided to blog about it,' she said. '*Back to Bodrum.* A kinda then and now exposé.'

'Should do well judging by the success of my silly old nonsense. People have lapped it up.'

'Not everyone.'

'Oh?'

'You've rattled a few cages, that's all.'

Eve ordered another round of coffees and explained. For some senior members of the emigrey politburo, my blog had gone down like the Hindenburg. Bodrum may well have been a place where exiles were once banished and the unconventional had come to live unconventionally, but to some Brits abroad, rules were rules and I had broken most of them. Bodrum, it seemed, was like St. Mary Mead, a place where twenty years' probation was needed before flogging homemade chutney at the bring and buy stall. I had shone a satirical light on our corner of the expat forest and, by doing so, had committed the gravest sin.

'You haven't served your time, Jack. You're not entitled to an opinion.'

'No one said.'

'No. They suffer in silence. Some flagellants enjoy the pain. Some of the blue rinse emigreys… see, I'm using your words now… aren't exactly fans. And the gay angle hardly helps with the BNP abroad lot.'

'Maybe they just need to get out more.'

On that, we were agreed. Disappointment and negativity haunted the home from home bars, toxic chat rooms and *Come Dine with Me* circuit.

'I suppose it's all about balance,' she said, toying with her amber necklace. 'The familiar and the foreign.'

'Turkey light and Turkey full fat,' I said less poetically.

'Precisely, Jack. If Ramsey, Bell and Fellows could rough it for God, glory and plunder, I'm sure we can do it in air-conditioned comfort for fun and enlightenment.'

Eve was an impressive but modest woman. At the merest hint of her taking the limelight, she would turn the conversation back to me, resting her head in the palm of her hand, her eyes flashing with interest. I talked of John, his sudden death, his grand passion for Turkey and how he had been drawn to her like a lodestone. How, on our inaugural visit, John and I had survived two sweaty weeks in a whitewashed villa nestled on a craggy headland near the tiny hamlet of Taşbükü on the Datça Peninsula. How we had spent lazy days splashing about in the warm sea and how at night we'd sat on the beach to watch the shooting stars.

'It really was like that,' I said. 'Sometimes we could just make out the lights of Bodrum blinking on the far side of the gulf and we said we would visit one day. We never did, of course...'

Still, it had started a chain of events leading to that afternoon with Eve, and as we argued over the bill and laughed at my comical Turkish, I knew I had uncovered a bit of an expat rarity. Just as we were about to leave.

'You must miss him, John?' she said, as we window-shopped along Marina Boulevard.

'I've got this tree,' I said. 'An olive sapling in a clay pot. I planted it after we arrived. Not exactly something I can slip into the hand luggage, but... oh, we're here, it's my turning.'

'Well, it's been lovely,' said Eve, as we said our goodbyes at the top of Spring Lane. 'Really. And don't worry about John's tree. I've got an idea.'

CHAPTER TWENTY-NINE

ERDEM AND EVE

Erdem broke the surface of the summer-hardened ground with a large pickaxe and when the baked crust gave way he attacked the stony soil with a broad-bladed shovel. Wider and longer than the common or garden British variety, in the hands of an expert it made short work of the excavation.

'I do feel bad letting him do all the digging,' I said disingenuously.

Eve looked across at her husband and set down a tray loaded with hot and cold mezes.

'It's fine. It appeals to his sense of machismo.'

Erdem removed his fishing hat, wiped his brow and thumbed up to the poolside terrace. I squinted across the scrubland and shouted back some praise.

'For heaven's sake, don't encourage him,' said Eve. 'I'll never hear the end of it. Feed a Turkish man's ego at your peril, Jack... Tuck in both of you, I'll get the drinks.'

Erdem strutted over from the clearing and handed me a muddied trowel.

'Here,' he said. 'It's done. The rest is up to you.'

'That would have taken me an absolute age. Thank you.'

'You see, Erdem,' said Liam. 'Jack only has the one functioning muscle. He's a medical curiosity. Joining us for lunch?'

Erdem looked at his watch. 'Thank you, no. There's a tennis racket with my name on it.'

'I feel sorry for your opponent,' said Liam, flirting with the striking six-footer. 'He doesn't stand a chance.'

Eve returned carrying a wine cooler in one hand and a hillock of bread in the other.

'I hope you're right,' she said. 'Erdem's a sore loser. Good luck, dear. And remember. It's the taking part that counts.'

Erdem scoffed at the quaint Old Etonian notion and said his goodbyes. 'Now boys, don't go leading her astray. She's just a little ingénue, my wife.'

After a five star lunch we were given the grand tour. The country estate was surrounded on three sides by an arc of dense pine-forested hills and on the fourth, a swimming pool overlooked a dusty olive grove. The house itself was centred round a striking dome-capped circular room, an architectural nod to the traditional yurts used by ancestral Turkic tribes as they migrated west from the Asian Steppes.

'Unlike the tents, it's hell to heat,' said Eve. 'It's why we decamp to Bodrum after Christmas.'

'Is it time?' I asked Liam as the sun began to set.

'Yeah. It's time.'

Liam clasped the base of the sapling, prized it from its green glazed pot and laid the plant on its side at the edge of the freshly dug hole. Eve set down a watering can and returned to the house. I eased John's tree into position, fell to my knees, ladled loose soil around the roots and pressed down the dirt with my fingers, fussing until all the gaps were filled.

Sensitive boy, good with his hands.

When the tree was firmly in place, I froze. The sun released ribbons of orange, red and yellow as it set behind the hills and I muttered like a man on the edge, allowing tears to flow for the first time in years. When I was done, Liam passed the watering can. I soaked the soil and stood up to admire my handiwork.

'That's that,' I said, like a Queen at an opening. 'It's done.'

Liam put his arm around my shoulder and looked down at the little olive tree.

'You've done him proud.'

Eve returned with a tray of four bubbling Champagne flutes.

'One for John,' she said. 'It's time for a toast.'

'You know what?' I said as we raised our glasses. 'Now there's a corner of Turkey that's forever John.'

I took Liam's hand and wrapped my fingers around his. The sweet froth of chilled champagne trickled down my throat and I laughed out loud. John had made it to Bodrum after all.

CHAPTER THIRTY

THE WINDS OF CHANGE

Trial and error modernisation continued to batter Bodrum. Turkey Street failed to escape the assault and a new street lamp appeared outside our garden wall. The upgraded model was a weak aluminium thing, unlikely to survive the constant bombardment from passing traffic and hapless house martins. Halfway Square was refurnished with a flashy playground for the local nippers – a mishmash of metal-tubed swings, slides and climbing frames spray-painted in bright primary colours. No doubt unsuspecting children would be soldered to the glowing pipes by the forty-five degree summer heat. Simultaneously, the town dashed headlong into superfast broadband along its narrowband lanes. A battalion of dusty navvies carved out mini trenches and laid fibre optic cables, rolling them out from huge wooden drums as gridlocks and frayed nerves built up around them. To the pungent aroma of burnt tar, Bodrum's twisted streets were scarred by shallow furrows backfilled with lumpy tarmac.

Liam threw down the phone.

'Typical. Bloody typical.'

The removals van was caught in a jam.

'It's a sign,' I suggested. 'Something or someone's telling us to stay.'

'This is hard enough as it is, Jack.'

I looked up from my laptop. 'I'm just saying it's never too late. There's more than one way to skin a goat.'

The gate squeaked open and hurried footsteps clip-clopped along the path. A petite figure appeared at the open door, a ghostly apparition silhouetted against the brilliant morning sun.

'Well if it ain't the Mother of God herself,' said Liam, peering into the blinding light at a white cotton dress topped with a crest of tousled hair, freed from its usual bun. Sophia was draped against the doorframe, posing like a Caravaggio reject. Liam narrowed his eyes and took a closer look.

'Is she drunk, do you think?'

'I am most certainly *not* drunk,' said Sophia. 'Well? May I come in?'

Sophia stepped into the salon and looked about the room.

'Elma is waiting in the car so I must be quick. I am here to say goodbye. Istanbul calls.'

'You're leaving?' asked Liam. 'Now?'

Sophia breathed melodramatically and placed her hand to her chest. 'Never to return.'

'I don't believe it,' said Liam. 'I thought you'd *never* go.'

'Liam meant that in a good way, didn't you Liam?'

'No matter. Elma has insisted. I must go to Istanbul to live with her. I have no choice.'

'But Sophia,' I said. 'You're part of Turkey Street, you always have been.'

'The winds of change are blowing, Jack. For me, for you and for my beloved Motherland. Besides, if nothing ever changed there would be no butterflies.'

'Right,' I said hesitatingly. 'Butterflies.'

'And where would we be without butterflies?' asked Liam.

'Precisely, my sweet boy, precisely.'

Sophia kissed Liam on each cheek.

'Or moths,' said Liam.

'Or moths,' Sophia agreed.

'Or horny toads,' I said.

'That's quite enough, Jack.'

Sophia turned back to Liam and ran her perfectly manicured index finger across his cheek.

'You must always be happy, my darling boy. But most of all, you must always be in love.'

Liam smiled awkwardly as if his mother had spat on a tissue and used it to clean a smudge from his cheek.

'He'll do his best,' I said. 'But it's not easy with a face like that.'

'And so, to you, my darling Jack. You will miss me terribly, I know.'

She buried herself in my chest and I gasped as her nails dug into my spine.

'Please don't forget me, Jack. Promise me.'

I looked across at Liam and prised Sophia away.

'As one door closes…'

'No Jack, all my doors are closed now. I shall grow old gracefully.'

'Disgracefully,' I said. 'Surely?'

Sophia's laugh was exaggerated and unconvincing. 'We shall meet again, I am sure of it. Perhaps I shall visit you in England.'

Liam glanced at me in panic.

'Perhaps you shall,' I said, grinning. 'Wouldn't that be something, Liam?'

A car horn sounded from the street.

'Elma is impatient to leave,' said Sophia dabbing her eyes with the tips of her fingers. 'It is time.'

The camera zoomed in for one last close up, and Sophia turned on her heels and swan-sang her way to the front door.

'My heart,' she said, 'is heavy with the burden of goodbyes. *À bientôt, mes amis. À bientôt!*'

'Exit Sophia stage left,' said Liam. 'And… cut!'

It was as if Sophia had always worked towards that moment and as she bangle-jangled down the path towards the fuss and flurry of Turkey Street, we resisted the urge to whoop.

Within seconds, the gate squeaked open again and footsteps clip-clopped along the path.

'She just couldn't resist a curtain call, could she?' said Liam. 'That's one helluva Dame.'

A large figure sweating like a goat at the butchers appeared at the door carrying a clipboard and briefcase, its bulky frame plugging out the sun. It spoke.

'Mr Jack?'

'Yes. Come in,' I said. 'You're a sight for sore eyes, I can tell you.'

'You need doctor? My nephew is doctor.'

'He means for the sore eyes,' explained Liam.

'No, I don't need a doctor. Look, can we just get on with it!'

Fatman slammed his case on the dining table, extracted a small forest of red tape and set to work, scrawling, checking and crosschecking document after document.

'And now,' he said loudly as if we were deaf, daft or both. 'NOW YOU SIGN.'

There followed an unending series of barked commands to sign here, sign there, initial this and initial that. Naturally, we had no idea what we were signing for but we signed nonetheless. It had become our habit.

'It's at times like this,' said Liam as his aching fingers scrawled a final signature with a flourish, 'I wish I'd paid more attention to those *Turkish for Idiots* CDs. For all we know we're handing over our worldly goods to his grandma in Bursa.'

Once the formalities were over, Fatman summoned his trio of stick-thin lackeys and they filed in silently, balancing flattened boxes, bubble wrap and packing tape like a well drilled circus troupe. They set to work. Packing up the family silver was done with such zeal and speed that the entire house would have been stripped of everything, fixtures and fittings included, had we not kept an eagle eye. The Belles had delivered on their promise to buy every stick of our Ikea housepack – beds, sofa, cabinets, dining table, chairs, wardrobes – the whole kit and caboodle, everything but the Chinoiserie cocktail bar.

We had promised faithfully their acquisitions would be left in the house under Hanife's charge until they were ready to collect them. In a little under three hours, with only the obligatory midterm stop-for-tea-to-cool-down-and-light-up break, our happy packers were gone and our prized belongings had hit the Silk Road. Without the personal touches – hangings and displays, knick-knacks, cushions and curtains – the sterility was instantly depressing.

'I thought I'd feel better once our bits were gone,' said Liam. 'Well, I don't. And what did you mean earlier about more than one way to skin a cat?'

'I said goat, not cat. And it doesn't matter now.'

'But our stuff's on its way to Felixstowe and we've nowhere to live.'

'A cardboard box made for two?'

'And a shrinking bank balance.'

'I'll rent you out by the hour.'

'They'll be queues along skid row.'

'For richer, for poorer, wasn't that the line?'

Our final night at Sentry Lane was a restless affair. Yellow lamplight flooded in through the drapeless windows, casting fractured shadows across the lumpy stone walls. We rose early and crept onto the first floor balcony as dawn was breaking. Farting mopeds buzzed along Turkey Street, shackled dogs yawned lazily and municipal workers did their best to wake the whole ward as they emptied the rubbish bins. When the call to prayer drifted over from the mosque on Halfway Square, Liam filled up.

'I don't know why we didn't do this before,' he said. 'Isn't it incredible?'

'It'll always be here, Liam.'

'Yes. But we won't.'

'No,' I said. 'We won't. We'll be happy somewhere else.'

'Hope so. I promised Sophia I'd be happy.'

'You also promised you'd be in love.'

'Promises, promises.'

Waterman pulled up at the top of Sentry Lane.

'Your boyfriend's here.'

'He's not my boyfriend, Jack.'

'I'm glad to hear it.'

'He's my lover.'

'Liam.'

'What?'

'These mugs are chipped.'

'Get used to it. Our best china's on the road to Bursa.'

We were still on the balcony nursing cold Nescafés when Vadim, Beril and an enormous cloud of un-lanced tension returned from a boozy pyjama party in Turgutreis. When their door was flung open, Bianco shot out of the house and rocketed into the olive tree, relieved to be released from his kiln-like quarantine and maybe sensing what was about to go off. We had seats in the upper circle when the curtain went up. Beril swung open the kitchen window, filled her lungs and let out a high-decibel scream, dispersing a flock of roosting crows and shocking Sentry Lane into a momentary silence. The stillness was quickly pierced by a full scale humdinger of a recital. Dogs bayed in sympathy, Bianco fell from his perch and we took cover inside the house.

'Aah,' said Liam. 'Some things never change.'

'Aah? Don't tell me you'll miss that racket.' The sound of smashing glass crashed around the courtyard. 'Expensive business, Turkish tempers.'

Liam looked at his watch.

'One hour to D Day and we're nowhere near ready.'

'We're all packed up, what's the problem?'

'Just the little matter of our feuding comrades.'

Of all our goodbyes, this was to be the most difficult scene to play. Ditzy, edge of the cliff Beril and browbeaten Vadim had become family of sorts, even though we might as well have communicated by semaphore for all the difference it made. In some ways, the language barrier hadn't mattered. They'd got our number from day one and hadn't flinched an inch. Perhaps it had something to do with Vadim's flighty days as the drummer in a blues band. Maybe Beril's unconditional love for her unconventional brother had played its part too. Certainly, in one way or another, we were all estranged from the mainstream, outsiders swimming against the tide. Of course, we now knew Beril was deeply troubled by her pariah status as an unmarried hussy. She longed for that elusive ring on her finger but Vadim was an unrepentant rebel and wasn't about to drop to one knee and make an honest woman of her. Having set them apart, maybe societal pressure would eventually pull them apart. For us, Vadim and Beril represented Turkey's progressive side. For others, they threatened the very meaning of what it was to be a good Turk. We knew it was only a matter of time before

Beril too would leave Sentry Lane. Family obligations would drag her kicking and screaming back to Ankara. But would her old rockabilly follow?

We wandered around the house for the last time, paying homage to the moody cistern that only flushed when it felt like it, the rutted walls that refused to let a picture hang straight and the windows that let the rain in without a fight. Through one of them, we caught sight of Beril and Vadim sitting quietly at their table. Hostilities, it seemed, were over. Above them, a large banner had been strung up between their balcony and a branch of the old olive tree.

Bye bye Jack – Bye bye Liam.

We met in the middle of our shared enclosure. Vadim pulled Liam close for a man hug and Beril hurled her arms around my neck. We embraced.

'Friends!' said Beril. 'Yessss!'

'Friends,' I said. 'Big friends.'

We swapped partners like mucky swingers and, as hug begat hug and Beril took farewell selfies, the seconds turned into minutes.

When the love-in was done and dusted, Vadim wheeled our fake Louis Vuittons to Doc's four-by-four and heaved our fat luggage into the boot.

'For Hanife,' said Liam, shaking Vadim's hand for the last time and handing him two sets of house keys.

'*Güle güle*, Liam.'

'Bye, Vadim. Look after that woman of yours.'

'Where *is* Beril?' I asked Liam as we piled into the back of the car.

'Dunno.'

'She gets madder by the minute, that girl.'

'I think she's just fabulous.'

Doc turned the ignition. As the fancy engine purred into life and we pulled away into a line of slow-moving traffic, crazy Beril dashed out with a bucket of water and hurled it onto the road behind us.

'Bye bye, Jack!' she screamed. 'Bye bye, Liam, bye bye!'

'Quite an honour,' said Doc, smiling. 'A Turkish tradition. She obviously likes you. Lord alone knows why.'

We cruised past the end of Sentry Lane and took one last look down the alley. High above Sophia's upper class gate, a wooden 'for sale' sign was swinging in the breeze. Sophia was right. The winds of change were blowing through Turkey Street.

CHAPTER THIRTY-ONE

THE RINGING OF THE BELLES

Quality hotels in the centre of Bodrum were as rare as a bottle of so-so plonk for less than fifty lira. This was surprising given the popularity of the town with Turkish toffs. The Marina Vista was the best of a meagre bunch, an old Bodrum staple opposite the armada of sloops, ketches and gulets. It came with a lavish travertine foyer, a gleaming pool and surly staff. It was to be home for our final night in Turkey and as Doc chauffeured us and our luggage through the congested streets, all was quiet in the back of her four-by-four.

'Obviously, they feel bad about it,' said Doc, checking us out in her rear view mirror. 'Not seeing you off, I mean.'

'Oh?' I said, looking out to sea. 'They didn't say.'

'Jess is back at work and Victoria's got business in Torba. They'll call in the morning before you leave.'

'And there was me expecting a proper send-off. It's not every day your favourite fairies leave the continent for good.'

Liam grabbed my hand.

'Oh, I just remembered,' said Doc, opening the car windows and letting in a rush of warm air. 'Jess asked me to give you something. We'll swing round to my place first and pick it up.'

'A leaving present,' Liam said softly. 'That's more like it, eh, Jack?'

Doc darted off Marina Boulevard and sped up Old Hamam Street, screeching to a halt outside the gate of her house. A familiar humpbacked pedlar and his handmade pushcart creaked past the car and stopped to adjust his embroidered pillbox hat.

'Wait there, boys,' said Doc, slamming the car door shut and smiling at the cussing rag and bone man. 'Won't be long.'

She wasn't. As we watched the old man shuffle down towards Marina Boulevard, a gang of screaming groupies poured out of the gate and ambushed the car – Jess, Victoria, Susan and Eve, each of them dressed up to the nines for a parting of the ways.

'About time,' shouted Jess, flinging open the passenger door and dragging me out onto the street. 'We're gagging.'

Victoria snatched Liam from the car and the Belles manhandled us through to Doc's sun-dappled courtyard. A large table was squeezed into a corner and covered with a Ken and Barbie tablecloth. At its centre, a miniature minaret constructed entirely from pink cupcakes took pride of place and a small cameo of Zeki Müren lollypopped out of the top. Powder-pink helium balloons were tied to the backrests of two chairs and a classic medley of

Eurovision ding-dingy-dong songs was bouncing through Doc's kitchen window.

'Camp enough, Jack?' asked Liam.

'You knew?'

'Sometimes, Jack, you are more dense than even I give you credit for.'

'And sometimes you are a deceitful old bastard.'

'Oh, do stop mithering. What more could you want? Seven tarts, tequila cupcakes and the campest table since the Mad Hatter's tea party.'

'Did you say *Tequila* cupcakes?'

'And vodka jellies,' said Jess sliding a tray of wobbling shots onto the table.

'Not to mention the rum and bum punch,' added Victoria, 'just to add a splash of Roger the Cabin Boy.'

'And make that *eight* tarts,' said Berni, cantering into the courtyard carrying a magnum of pink Cava. 'And this one's got a crate of bubbly courtesy of me lovely fella. Not that he knows anything about it, of course. Sorry I'm late, girls.'

'Well go on,' said Susan, pointing to the his and his seats. 'Take a pew!'

Doc turned up the Samantha Janus and I glanced across at a glassy-eyed Liam.

'*Stop worrying,*' I mouthed. '*We'll be fine.*'

'*I can't stop crying, what's wrong with me?*'

'*You're a gay man. It's in the job description.*'

Susan fell onto the seat next to me and grinned.

'Surprise!'

'But I hate surprises.'

'Just drink the bubbly, honey, we ain't in no mood for a wet blanket.'

'Any news on Charlotte and Alan?'

'Oh, it's just a car crash. Nothing any of us can do now.'

'I wish they were here.'

'She finds it difficult. She thinks we all let her down.'

'Even me?'

'Especially you, Jack.'

'Oh.'

I looked across at Liam as Jess stuffed a cake in his mouth with the palm of her hand.

'We tried to help, Susan.'

'I know, honey. We all did.'

'And Alan?'

'Gone fishing.'

Jess reached across the table and grabbed another boozy cake.

'Easy, girl,' said Liam. 'The afternoon's still young.'

'I hate to say it, but I'll miss you two.'

'Oh don't, Jess. We'll soon be forgotten. Footprints in the sand and all that.'

'I think you'll find your footprints are set in concrete.'

'You say that as if it's a bad thing.'

'Do I?'

Jess tapped the table with her fingers and hummed the chorus of *Save All Your Kisses for Me*.

'So where's that handsome man of yours?' I asked Susan as she fiddled with her paste earrings.

'Chuck? Getting his annual Yankee fix in the good old You Es of A. You know what he's like… needs to escape the ramshackle charm from time to time.'

'Well, give him one from me.'

Susan choked on her Cava.

'You get worse every time I see you, honey.'

'It's a gift.'

'Anyway, no men allowed today. Just us sisters.'

'So what does that make me?'

'Oh, you're just one of us with an extra leg.'

'So how's your kid brother doing?' asked Doc.

'Sean? He's fine,' said Liam. 'No, he's much better than that. I couldn't have hoped for more.'

'And Mum?'

'Early days. We'll see.'

Doc raised her voice to compete with Séverine belting out the final reprise of *Un Banc, Un Arbre, Une Rue*.

'I told you Jack would be okay.'

'Nothing fazes that man. He's not normal.'

'Bulldog spirit, Liam. Everything will be fine. I can feel it in my water.'

'That'll be the cystitis, Doc.'

'I'm so glad you came,' I said, sidling up to Eve at the kitchen sink. She washed, I dried.

'Wild horses, Jack.'

She looked through the window at Liam.

'Your man seems happy. In between the tears I mean.'

'He wants to stay.'

'But he can't, can he?'

'No, he can't.'

Eve flicked the suds and dried her hands on a Bodrum Castle tea towel.

'And you?' she asked.

'It's time to move on.'

'So, no regrets?'

'I wish we'd done Cappadocia.'

'That place gets worse with every year that passes. Biblical to boutique in fifty years.'

'And we never did the lubed-up lads in lederhosen... smack downs and dodgy hand insertions... rough and tumble in a field.'

'You mean Turkish wrestling, don't you, Jack?'

'Yeah.'

'They're called kisbets.'

'What are?'

'The lederhosen.'

'Oh.'

'See, now you're learning Turkish.'

'Eve? Look after John's tree for me.'

'Of course. Just make sure you come back and taste the olives.'

I smiled.

'Wild horses...'

'So how was the farewell to Turkey road trip?' asked Victoria.

'Oh, hit and miss,' said Liam. 'Mostly miss. Our hearts weren't in it.'

'You'll come back though, won't you?'

'To live? Dunno. It's all about butterflies.'

'Is it?'

'Apparently. So, what about you?'

'What about me?'

'What do the coffee grinds predict for our dolly drop Belle?'

'Oh, a tall dark stranger with a fat wad and talented hands.'

'That's my girl. Pass the vodka jellies, would you?'

Back at the Barbie table, Susan moved closer and whispered in my ear.

'You heard about Irfan and the German slut?'

'Yeah, we heard.'

'Nancy's in bits. Why the hell does she bother with that fat sailor?'

'He presses all the right buttons, I guess.'

'There's more to life than wham, bam, thank you ma'am.'

'Is there? Who knew? Anyway, she says she loves him.'

'They're hardly Brad and Angelina.'

'I wouldn't give up on Nans, just yet. She might end up surprising us all.'

Doc shoved Susan out of the way and slid onto the seat next to me.

'So where *is* Nancy?' she asked. 'I thought she was a fan?'

'Packing, probably,' I said.

'Packing for what? A midnight flit with Captain Pugwash?'

'You'll find out soon enough.'

'Anyway, I've got a bone to pick with you, Jack Scott. About the VOMIT thing on your blog. You've got us wrong. We're not *all* victims or washed up old slappers. And we don't *all* chase pretty boys and drop our drawers at the first smile.'

'I didn't say you—'

'Some of us learn. Evolve. We're not *all* goldfish!'

'I just say what I see, Doc.'

'Maybe, but there are bastards everywhere and I for one would rather be single in the sun than on a shelf in London. For every Cristal there's an Eve, for every Nancy there's a Berni. Give us a break!'

'You're very impressive, fortified by the fizz. Has anyone ever told you that?'

'We're just a bunch of women trying to make our way, Jack. Credit some of us with a bit of nous.'

'Or a lot, in your case.'

'Flattery isn't gonna dig you out of this hole, Jack Scott.'

'No?'

'Well try again, you never know your luck and while you're at it, pour this ex-VOMIT another glass of that pink stuff.'

As Doc's cup bubbled over, I raised my glass. 'To the Sisterhood.'

'The Sisterhood?'

'Ex-VOMITs. Ladies who learn.'

'That works for me.'

As the Belles rang out into the night, the chatter gushed and the wine flowed. Happy confusion reigned and our trollied wake descended into mayhem. There were no grandstand speeches, just giggles, gossip and glassy eyes embellished by the sauce. It was a simple moment in time when two world weary rascals were once again to alter the course of their own insignificant history.

CHAPTER THIRTY-TWO

SCHOOL'S OUT

The *İstiklâl Marşı* ringtone blared out from the sweet and savouries scattered across our Marina Vista breakfast table. Liam hunted for his mobile phone among the breads, cheeses and jams, and a skittish waiter fussed around the table working his tip.

'I don't think so,' I sighed as the young flirt cruised by. 'I couldn't raise a smile.'

'Fine,' said Liam, pacing up and down by the table. 'We'll pick you up at the Torba Junction. And don't be late, okay?'

Liam sat back at the breakfast table and squinted.

'I thought I told you to turn that bloody sun off.'

'She's going through with it, then?'

'Yeah. If she can squeeze the Manolo Blahniks into her luggage.'

'And for God's sake, Liam, put your shades on and stop moaning.'

'That's alright for you to say. You haven't got terminal wine flu.'

I chucked him a napkin.

'Eat something, Liam. Before I kill you.'

Doc and her tank cruised along Marina Boulevard, ascended into the western end of Bodrum Town and zoomed past the British Consulate.

'Well, boys, this is it, time to go home. All set?'

Liam moaned. 'Do we have to go quite so fast?'

Doc looked in her rear view mirror and slowed the car. 'Dear me, Liam. That's some face. This little sister knocked it on the head after the second bottle.'

'Praise be to the Motherfucking Superior.'

We got stuck in traffic at the Gümbet roundabout. Mustafa Kemal on horseback bore down on us from the centre of the traffic island, brandishing his sword-like olive branch. Turkey had a lot to thank Mustafa Kemal Atatürk for. This was the man who saved the Ottoman heartlands after the feckless Sultan backed the wrong greyhound in the Great War. This was also the man whose towering personality and single-mindedness swept away many of the old sclerotic ways and dragged his country into the Twentieth Century. He cherry-picked the best from the West, and Turkey took its rightful place at the European table.

As we sped past the castle for the last time, I wondered what The Father of the Turks would make of Turkey now. Would he approve of the personality cult that had developed since his death and the laws outlawing even the mildest criticism of him? And what would he think of his monumental tomb and the thousands of statues in his image adorning every town square and a Gümbet traffic island? And then I wondered what he would make of the two old gay boys who dropped by for a while. What a conversation that would be.

And so to the people we had lived among. What had *they* made of us? Gaining acceptance from the landed gentry of Bodrum Town had been a wholly unexpected windfall, but getting to grips with the diehard emigreys had been a much tougher gig. We had spent the first six months getting to know our fellow expats and the following six trying to get rid of most of them. In time, of course, we had found our footing and discovered tulips among the weeds, even if one or two were wilting under the ruthless Turkish sun.

'So what's next for my boys?' said Doc as the car sped towards the airport. 'What will you do now?'

'Sleep or throw up,' said Liam. 'Not sure in which order.'

'The blog's done well,' I said. 'Maybe there's a book in it.'

'A book?'

'Jack's developed delusional tendencies,' said Liam. 'It's the heat.'

'Well then,' said Doc. 'I've got to be in it.'

'Be careful what you wish for,' said Liam. 'Chances are he'll crucify you.'

Liam checked his watch and gestured for Doc to slow down. 'We need to stop at the Torba Junction.'

'You didn't say.'

'No. We're picking up a stray.'

Doc took the slip road down towards the roundabout.

'Are you sure this is the right place? There's no one here.'

'Over there,' said Liam. 'Look.'

She was hugging the shade of a bus stop. An oversized floppy hat and large sunglasses all but covered her face and a yellow polka-dot frock was so low at the cleavage, her bountiful bosom was bursting out to greet the day. It was not a dress in which to run for a bus. Two silver suitcases stood guard by her side, flashing in the sun like Aldis lamps.

Doc swung the car round to the lay-by and Liam jumped out.

''Bout bloody time,' she said, clambering into the back of the car. 'Been sweatin' me arse off out here!'

'You made it, then?' I said. 'What's with the posh frock and no knickers look?'

'Just making the effort, now I'm completely crutchless.'

'So how's our favourite trollop?' asked Liam.

Cristal Cologne removed a small compact from a lizard-skin clutch and checked her make-up.

'Oh, you know, bab. Like me face. Reformed. Take me home, boys.'

Some people are stalked by happenstance. Others have to grab fate by the throat. We were the grabbing kind and we clung to our place in the sun for as long as we could, living the seasons and doing our best to make it a memorable run. In the end though, even for Cristal Cologne, nothing competes with the ties that bind. Where next for the tent? I hear Norwich is nice.

Bedlam in Bodrum

The Stone Cottage

Halfway Mosque

The Mausoleum

Sentry Lane

Turkey Street

the Balcony

Bianco

TURKIPENDIX ONE

EXPAT GLOSSARY

Expatriates, like everyone else, come in all shapes and sizes – the mean and the mannered, the classless and the classy, the awful and the joyful. The abbreviated epithet 'expat' doesn't adequately express the myriad folk who have chosen to live in Turkey. Jack coined or purloined a few expressions to add spice to the mix.

Emigreys

Retirees serving out their twilight years in the sun, most of whom seem to be just a little to the right of Genghis Khan. Many have bought a jerry-built white box in Turkey because it was cheaper than Spain (well, it was at the time). Everyday emigrey life operates within a parallel universe of neo colonial separateness preoccupied with pork products, property prices and Blighty bashing.

VOMITs (Victims of Men in Turkey)

Vintage desperate ex-housewives with a few liras to spare, who shamelessly chase younger Turkish men.

Predictably, such relationships rarely last once the money runs out. A subgenus of the species is the MAD ('My Ahmed's Different'): delusional VOMITs who think their Turkish man is somehow unlike the rest because 'he really loves me'. As a general rule of thumb, they are kidding themselves.

The Sisterhood

A new addition to the Expat Glossary, the Sisterhood is the antidote to the VOMITing sickness afflicting the many Shirley Valentines who wash up like driftwood on the beaches of Turkey. Many of the Sisters are reformed VOMITs who've been through the ringer, some more than once, but have emerged to tell their tale stronger and wiser. The Sisters stick together (like birds of a feather), because men are rubbish.

Bodrum Belles

Single ladies of a certain age, rollercoaster pasts and plucky presents. To qualify as a bone fide Belle you must live in Bodrum Town. Anywhere else just doesn't cut the mustard. The male equivalents, the Bodrum Beaus, are thin on the ground.

Semigreys

Those too young to retire in the conventional sense, and who are living the *vida loca* on the proceeds of property sales from the boom years. Plunging interest rates present quite a fiscal test to those trying to maintain a hedonistic lifestyle on dwindling assets while waiting for the pensions to kick in. Assuming there will be a pension to kick in, of course.

Vetpats

Veterans who have lived in Turkey for many years. Usually better informed than their peers and with a less asinine view of the world, vetpats have taken the trouble to learn Turkish and are better integrated into the wider community. Some have even acquired Turkish citizenship through marriage or toil and are fortunate to have found gainful employment on the right side of the Law.

Emiköys

A rare breed of seasoned pioneers, Emiköys have forsaken the strife of city life and deodorant for the real köy McCoy. They eke out a life less ordinary in genuine Turkish villages. They get down, dirty and dusty with the locals, contribute meaningfully to their small rural communities, keep chickens, get unnaturally close to nature and talk Turkish to the trees (well, not always, but I'm sure some do).

Hedonistas

Those who enjoy a carefree existence of total self-indulgence, liberated from the binding ties of responsibility or the worries of tomorrow. They spend, spend, spend because 'you can't take it with you.' Typically, they have no children to fret about. That was Jack and Liam.

The Ignorati

A collective term for those who live in utter ignorance of

the history and culture of their foster land, shout loudly in English, and see the world at large through the narrow minded pages of the Daily Mail (known as the Daily Bigot in more enlightened circles).

Note: The term VOMIT was first coined by former vetpat Cathy Crawford and originally described a select group of Bodrum Belles who had survived their encounters with Turkish men. Subsequently, the word shifted to its current meaning as it spread across the Bodrum Peninsula. Jack first came across the term during his brief residency in Yalıkavak.

None of these terms are mutually exclusive. It is perfectly possible for an emigrey to also be a vetpat VOMIT and a fully paid up member of the ignoble ignorati, and many are.

TURKIPENDIX TWO

A WORD OR TWO IN BRITISH

*'We (the British and Americans) are two countries
separated by a common language.'*
George Bernard Shaw

English is a funny old foreign language. *'Turkey Street'* is littered with British cultural and geographical references, slang, phrases, idioms and place names that may fly over the heads of our cousins across the seven seas. Cue, Jack's tongue-ever-so-slightly-in-cheek guide to Brit talk. Readers will also find here some non-British expressions that may need deciphering too.

Ach! – An exclamation in Ulster English (and Scots English). Sounds like a goat clearing its throat.

Alaturca – Squat toilet, from the Italian 'alla Turca' – as the Turks do.

Amah – Maid or housekeeper, a loan word from traditional Chinese. Used across the Gulf, Indian Subcontinent and Southeast Asia. Widely adopted by the British Raj and now considered politically incorrect.

Archers (The) – A long running soap on BBC Radio 4 about a dull farming community. Popular with those who prefer their beer warm and their neighbours white.

Argos – One of the largest high street retailers in Britain where customers flick through a fat catalogue, write their order on a little slip, pay at a till point and queue up at a warehouse counter to obtain their purchases. Weird.

Aye – Ulster English (and Scots) for 'yes'.

A wee dram – A small alcoholic drink, usually whisky, in Ulster English (and Scots). The *wee* bit can seem ironic when presented with a half a bottle of Bell's in a large tumbler.

Barney – A quarrel.

Beak (The) – Judge or magistrate, so called because of the primitive gas masks stuffed with herbs and spices that medieval judges wore on the bench to ward off the plague. Little good it did them.

Belisha beacon – An amber-coloured globe lamp atop a black and white pole. It marks a pedestrian road crossing.

Betting shop biro – A half size ballpoint pen supplied free to punters who like a flutter on the horses. Millions of them end up in the bottom of handbags and manbags.

Bint – Bitch, originally a racist term (and still hardly complimentary) derived from the Arabic word for daughter and used by British soldiers in the Great War.

Bigwig – An Eighteenth Century VIP, the bigger the wig, the more important the person.

Blackpool – A trashy British seaside resort in northeast England famous for fish 'n' chips, kiss me quick hats, loose morals, brash illuminations and even brasher bottle blondes.

Blimey – An exclamation of surprise and an abbreviation of 'gorblimey', 'God blind me.' Blimey, who knew?

Blue Circle – A former cement company that, like so much of British industry, was closed down or sold off to the highest bidder.

BNP – The British National Party and a nasty bunch of neo-Nazi nutters they are too.

Bob – Old slang for a shilling (one twentieth of the pre-decimalised pound).

Bruce Forsyth – Britain's favourite all-round entertainer and a man older than the dinosaurs. Brucie is famous for his soft-shoe shuffle, catch phrases, dodgy wig, lantern jaw and marrying women young enough to be his granddaughter.

Bung – Bribe, not to be confused with the abbreviation for 'bung hole'.

Cadfael – A series of murder mysteries set in the Twelfth century written by Edith Pargeter under the name of Ellis Peters and featuring the eponymous Benedictine monk as the medieval sleuth. The books were turned into a TV series in the Nineties. You will never see Cadfael and the Chancellor of Germany in the same place at the same time.

Carpe diem – Latin for 'seize the day'.

Cheesy Wotsits – A brand of 'cheese' flavoured corn puffs that stick to the teeth for days.

Chelsea tractors – The large four-by-four vehicles clogging up the streets of rush-hour London while Camilla drops little Hugo off at his private prep school.

Cherry Bakewell – A tart of shortcrust pastry with a layer of jam, ground almond sponge, topped with fondant and crowned with a glacé cherry. The very thought of it hardens the arteries.

Children of the Damned – A 1964 science fiction film about a group of evil children with psychic powers with the strapline 'Beware the eyes that paralyse!'

Chips – French fries. What the Yanks call chips, Brits call crisps.

Clap clinic – An STD clinic, from the Old French word 'clapoir', meaning a venereal bubo – an enlarged gland in the groin associated with sexually transmitted diseases. Ouch.

Clare Balding – A TV sports presenter with short hair and big bones.

Cottage – A public toilet visited by men seeking men, from Polari, a slang language used in Britain by sinners on the social margins – actors (when acting was considered no better than whoring), circus and fairground showmen, criminals, prostitutes, and, up to the early Seventies, gay people.

Council Tax – A property tax that helps pay for local services. It's never been popular but then Brits are reluctant to pay for anything that isn't related to booze, fags, the gee-gees and footie (that's liquor, cigarettes, horse betting and soccer).

Craic (pronounced crack) – An Irish term for fun, conversation and entertainment. The word is a Gaelicised version of the Middle English word 'crak' meaning 'loud conversation'.

Croydon – A soulless south London suburb famous for its high-rise centre and Sixties shopping mall. Also one of the chaviest places on Earth (see Vicky Pollard below).

Cumberland Sausage – A delicious pork sausage shaped like a dog turd originating in the historic county of

Cumberland. Cumberland is in the English Lake District (where it rains 364 days a year).

Delia – Delia Smith, the matriarch of British celebrity cooks and, just like Nanny, not a woman to meddle with.

Dip his wick – Now come on, what else could it mean?

Dosh – Money, derived from God knows what.

Earls Court – A district of West London and the Capital's gay village back in the day (today, no more than a couple of shabby dive bars and a seedy club: no match for Amsterdam or San Francisco).

Eejit – Idiot in Ulster and Southern-Irish English.

Eton Wick – A village in England close to the college town of Eton, home to the famous private school, the alma mater to a political class that has absolutely no idea about the price of a pint or a line of coke.

Fag[1] – Cigarette (not a derogatory term for homosexual as it is in Yankee). Gives a whole new meaning to the phrase 'sucking on a fag'.

Fag[2] – A young pupil at an English public (i.e. private) school who provided a personal service to one or more older boys. Well, you can just imagine what that involved.

Googie Withers – Veteran British actress who died in 2011. She was perhaps best known for playing the plum-voiced Gov'nor of a women's prison in the Seventies' drama *Within These Walls*. There was definitely no lights-out lettuce-licking on Googie's watch.

Harry Judd – The dangerously horny drummer in the boy band McFly. Women (and some men) across the land wet their panties at the very thought of him.

Hi De Hi – The title and catchphrase of the strangely entertaining Eighties BBC TV sitcom set in a fictional holiday camp featuring hammy acting, corny plots and slapstick humour.

Hobnob – A popular and very moreish biscuit made from oats. A minute on the lips, a lifetime on the hips, especially when covered in thick milk chocolate.

Home Counties – The shires ringing London, often characterised as prosperous, middle-class and terminally boring.

I frutti proibiti sono i più dolci – Italian for 'forbidden fruit is the sweetest.'

Isle of Wight – A diamond-shaped green and pleasant island off the south coast of England. It's where people go to die and where Jack lost his virginity (though not with a pensioner).

Jammy Dodgers – A round shortbread biscuit with a raspberry-flavoured jam filling, popular with children. To badly paraphrase the Jesuits, 'Give me the boy until he is seven and I will give you the obese man with heart disease, high cholesterol and type 2 diabetes'.

Khazi – A toilet, possibly derived from the Swahili word 'm'khazi' meaning a latrine.

Kirk – A church in Scots and similar to words all over northern Europe – *kirkja, kyrka, kyrkje, kirke, kirche, kerk, tsjerke, kirik, kirkko*. I blame the Vikings.

Knacker's yard – A place where old animals unfit for human consumption are taken for slaughter. Also known as an old people's home.

Knocked off – Stolen or fake, like most of the goods sold in the East End markets of London and *pazars* all over Turkey.

Knocking shop – A venue to meet people for casual sex (for consumption on or off the premises). What was your name again?

Laa-Laa – One of the four Teletubbies, a popular children's BBC programme. The series was attacked by Bible Belters in the States who accused Auntie Beeb of turning the children of the world gay because Tinky Winky, one of the other characters, carried a handbag.

Lancashire – A historic county in northeast England. It has the dubious privilege of counting Blackpool amongst its treasures. Also home to Lancashire Hot Pot, a dull and tasteless lamb stew requiring little skill and no imagination to prepare.

Last knockings – See *Knocking Shop* above. The last men standing at the end of a hard night.

Loo – Toilet, possibly from the cry 'gardyloo' (from the French *'regardez l'eau',* 'watch out for the water'), which was shouted by medieval servants as they emptied chamber pots from upstairs windows into the street.

Looker – Someone nice to look at. Like Jack when he was younger. Much younger.

Louie Spence – A very, very camp British choreographer and TV personality, grandma's favourite and a man who is way beyond gay.

Malarkey – Nonsense. There's a lot of it in this book.

Marks and Spencer – A clothes and food retailer, the cornerstone of the high street and as British as the Queen (except Her Maj is German and most M&S products are imported).

Marmite – A sticky dark brown food paste made from yeast extract with a distinctive and powerful flavour. It is truly disgusting and quite rightly banned in Canada on health grounds.

Midnight flit – To leave secretly, popular with people trying to avoid the rent.

Milk Tray – One of Britain's favourite boxes of chocolates. Targeted at desperate women who think that stuffing their mouths with cheap confectionary will send a James Bond lookalike swinging through their bedroom window on a rope (or so the ad implies). Dream on, ladies.

Miss Blobby – A variation on Mr Blobby, a character on an old Saturday night TV variety show, a ridiculous fat pink monstrosity covered with yellow pox spots.

Mother's ruin – Gin, so called because of its popularity with Eighteenth Century washer women trying to blot out their wretched lives with home brew.

Mucker – Best friend in Ulster English. Also a farm hand who shovels shit.

Nice to meet you, to meet you Nice – Bruce Forsyth's most famous (and most irritating) catchphrase (see Bruce Forsyth above).

Nicker – From nick, *to steal*. The verb is also slang for being arrested and the noun is slang for a prison cell – crime, apprehension and punishment all wrapped up in the same word. Has a poetic ring, don't you think?

No. 6 – Cheap brand of Seventies' cigarettes that first got Jack addicted to the dreaded weed.

Nookie – An abbreviation of 'Nook and cranny', cockney rhyming slang for sex. Cranny rhymes with fanny which in British is a lady's front bottom (not her booty as in Yankee).

Norfolk – England's breadbasket and most easterly county, a place where the gene pool has been badly damaged by centuries of inbreeding and marriage to livestock.

Norwich – The county town of Norfolk and a city with more medieval churches than any other north of the Alps. Most have been boarded up or converted into coffee shops.

O Level – An end of year subject-based examination taken by sixteen-year-olds across all parts of the United Kingdom except Scotland. In the Eighties it was scrapped and replaced by the GCSE (dumbed down and much easier to cheat in).

Old Roedeanian – A former pupil of Roedean, arguably the most famous public (i.e. private) girls' school in Britain. The filthy rich intern their female offspring for seven years to perpetuate the class system. You get less for murder.

Ooroyt – 'All right' in Brummie, the irritating accent of Birmingham (Britain's sprawling second-largest city).

Page 3 – The Sun 'newspaper', once Britain's undisputed champion red top, featured images of topless busty babes on Page 3. All good clean fun and not intended to objectify women in the slightest.

PG Tips – Britain's favourite brand of tea. As everyone knows, tea drinking is a national addiction. Actually, the consumption of tea has plummeted in recent years in favour of crappifrappuccinos and other fancy brews.

Portobello Road – A poncy (i.e. showy or affected) street in the Notting Hill district of West London with a pretentious street market and shops selling overpriced 'antiques' to gullible tourists.

Primarni – An oxymoronic amalgamation of *Primark* (the British chain famous for cheap disposable fashion) and Armani (where shopping requires a second mortgage). A term used to describe those with champagne tastes but beer bottle pockets. That'll be Jack and Liam then.

Putney – A smug little suburb in southwest London famous for the annual Oxford and Cambridge Boat Race and where Jack misspent his youth relying on the kindness of strangers along its moonlit towpath.

Quid – Slang for a British pound, possibly derived from the Latin 'quid pro quo' – to exchange something for something else.

Ragamuffin – A dirty, shabbily-clothed street child. Straight out of Dickens.

Reet (Right) little earner – Brummie for something that pays well, like fixing the LIBOR Rate or laundering money through a Caribbean tax haven.

Saga – A company that specialises in servicing the over-fifties. Libel laws prevent further comment.

Samantha Janus (now Womack) – Represented the UK at the 1991 Eurovision Song Contest. She sang so flat, ears bled and dogs howled. Samantha now plays the unhinged Ronnie Mitchell in EastEnders, Britain's most depressing soap opera.

St. Mary Meads – The fictitious village featured in many of Agatha Christie's *Miss Marple* whodunits. It is depicted as the epitome of tight-arsed Middle England and, judging by the murder rate, a more dangerous place to live than Baghdad.

Saveloy – A sausage with no discernible natural ingredients, hence the bright red colour. The genuine article glows in the dark.

Scallies – A term derived from 'scallywags' to describe a UK subculture of working class youths of uncertain parentage who have adopted street fashion as their uniforms. And no, they're not all muggers from broken homes.

Séverine – Won the 1971 Eurovision Song Contest for Monaco with a belting ballad entitled *Un Banc, Un*

Arbre Une Rue (A Tree, A Bench, A Street). Great tune, ridiculous lyrics. That's the French for you.

Shagging – Sexual intercourse. One of those wonderful words that does what it says on the tin but is less offensive than the F word.

Sink estates – Grim and poor quality social housing schemes from the Sixties and Seventies that have remained in public ownership (because you can't give them away). Generally used to corral those at the bottom of the social heap.

Sitges – An elegant seaside resort near Barcelona in Spain popular with the gays, particularly those who like to wear tight pants for a night on the tiles then drop them on the beach at four a.m.

Skiver – Scottish slang for the idle.

Slag/Slapper/Slut – A person of generous disposition who drops them at the first smile, like the young Jack.

Slough – Ugly sister to Windsor and Eton. 'Come friendly bombs and fall on Slough!' wrote the former Poet Laureate, Sir John Betjeman. Sir John had the right idea.

Sparky – An electrician. Obvious, really.

Spiv – A dealer in black-market goods, typically during the rationing years of World War Two and its aftermath.

The term was the nickname of Henry Bagster, a small-time London crook in the 1900s frequently arrested for illegal street trading.

Spud – Potato, probably derived from a tool used for digging and related to 'spade'.

Strongbow – A brand of cheap cider. It helped Jack onto the slippery slope of alcohol dependency and cirrhosis of the liver.

Sussex – The beautiful historic county on the south coast of England sitting on top of vast reserves of gas ripe for the fracking. Also home to the Rude Man of Cerne, a well-hung giant with a magnificent morning manhood cut into the chalk down.

Swan Vesta – The brand name for the most popular kind of strike-anywhere matches in the UK. Especially popular with arsonists.

Tea Leaf – Cockney rhyming slang for 'thief', the preferred occupation of those living in the East End of London along with dressing up as pearly monarchs, eating jellied eels and brawling on a Saturday night.

Tenko – An early-Eighties BBC series chronicling the fate of a mixed collection of imperious women interned by the Japanese after the fall of Singapore in World War Two. Appalling living conditions, malnutrition, disease, violence and even death failed to dent the superiority of some of the magnificent dames of the Empire. Comes from the Japanese for 'roll-call'.

The only gay in the village – The proud lament of Daffyd Thomas, the Welsh character from the BBC comedy sketch show, *Little Britain*. Like all the gays of Harlech, he minced round a former mining town in PVC and rubber fetish wear.

The Smoke – London, so called because the huge metropolis was once afflicted by smog, a thick and deadly carpet of coal smoke and fog that once killed people by the thousand. The title has now passed on to a choking Beijing.

Tiffin – A slang term for a light meal originating in India during the good old days of the British Raj (before the Brits lost an empire and miserably failed to become good Europeans).

Toff – Upper class, rich and often stupid, possibly derived from the Anglo-Saxon 'toforan' (superiority) or 'toffee nosed' from the toffee-like nasal mucus that leaked from the snouts of Nineteenth Century snuff sniffers. Yuk.

Tooting – A suburb of South London, shabby no chic.

Twat – An idiot. Yes an idiot. What else could it mean?

Vicky Pollard – A character from the BBC comedy sketch show *Little Britain* and the epitome of the British female chav – poor white trash in fake designer wear, usually up the duff (i.e. pregnant) by the age of thirteen.

Wads – Bundles of banknotes, often illegally obtained.

Walnut Whip – A cone of hollow, thick milk chocolate filled with vanilla fondant and topped with a walnut. Impossible to eat without looking like a cheap slut.

Wean – Ulster English for 'child', pronounced wain.

We're grand – Ulster and Southern Irish English for 'we're fine'.

What about ye? – Ulster English for 'how are you?'

William Morris – A Nineteenth Century English textile designer, poet, novelist, translator, and revolutionary socialist with a very long beard. As a designer, he adored floral designs. Just like the village ladies of Turkey.

Willy-nilly – Haphazardly from the Old English 'wile hē, nyle hē,' literally: 'will he or will he not?'

Wonga – Money, possibly from the Romany for 'coal' and now the name of a payday loan company lending to the feckless at stratospheric interest rates.

TURKIPENDIX THREE

A WORD OR TWO IN TURKISH

Turkish words and phrases appearing in Turkey Street (some are phonetic versions of familiar words):

Arkadaşlar – Friends
Aşkım – My love, my darling
Baklava – A sweet pastry made of layers of filo pastry filled with chopped nuts and sweetened with honey
Bay/Bayan – Male/female
Berber – Barber
Bodrum, Bodrum – An iconic modern folksong by popular Turkish trio, MFÖ
Bugün – Today
Bulgur – A staple food made from durum wheat, similar to couscous
Butik – Boutique
Caddesi – Street
Çankaya – A superior Turkish wine named after the central district of Ankara
Çay – Tea

Cin – Gin (C is a hard J in Turkish)

Çocuk – Child

Darbuka – Traditional Turkish goblet drum

Dekorasyon – Decoration

Dizayn – Design

Dolmuş – A minibus used as public transport (literally 'filled')

Efes – Ephesus and the brand name of Turkey's most ubiquitous lager

Ege – Aegean

Elma – Apple

Emlakcı – Estate agent

Eş – Wife

Evet – Yes

Ezan – Call to prayer

Fenerbahçe – One of Turkey's top-flight soccer teams

Görüşürüz – See you (later)

Güle güle – Bye-bye

Gulet – A traditional two or three-masted wooden sailing vessel

Hellim – Turkish version of halloumi cheese

Hoşgeldiniz – Welcome

İngilizce – English

İşkembe çorbası – Tripe soup

İstiklâl – Independence

İstiklâl Marşı – Independence March, the Turkish National Anthem

İyi – Good

İyi akşamlar – Good evening

İyiyim, sağol – I'm fine, thanks

Jandarma – Provincial police (and part of the military) as opposed to the civilian *Polis* (police) who operate in the larger cities

Kafe – Café

Kâfir – Non believer

Kahve – Coffee

Kahve Dünyası – Coffee World

Kapıcı – Caretaker

Kardeş – Sibling

Kardeşler – Siblings

Kilim – A flat-weave rug

Köy – Village

Kuaför – Ladies hairstylists

Lezzetli – Delicious

Lokantalar – Restaurants

Londra – London

Market – Convenience store

Menemen – Scrambled eggs with tomato and green peppers

Merhaba – Hello

Meze – A small dish, similar in concept to Spanish tapas

Milli Piyango – National Lottery

Misli – A Turkish table wine

Muhtar – The elected head of a village or ward

Mutlu yillar – Happy New Year (literally, 'happy years')

Müezzin – The man appointed to recite the call to prayer

Nasıl anlatsam? – How can I explain?

Nasılsınız? – How are you?

Nerden başlasam? – Where do I begin?

Noel Baba – Father Christmas

Otel – Hotel

Otogar – Bus station

Para – Cash/Money

Park – Park (as in public space)

Pazar – Public market

Peki – Okay

Problem var – There is a problem

Problem Yok – No problem

Rakı – The Turkish national tipple, an aniseed-flavoured alcoholic drink made from grape pomace. Similar to ouzo

Ramazan – The Muslim Holy Month (Ramadan)

Şarap – Wine

Şekerli – Sweetened

Shahada (Anglicised Arabic) – The Islamic Testament of Faith ('there is no god but Allah, and Muhammad is the messenger of Allah')

Sigara – Cigarette

Siktir git – Fuck off

Simit – A circular bun with sesame seeds similar to a bagel

Su – Water

Sucuklu yumurta – Eggs with Turkish sausage

Süper – Super, excellent

Sumak – Middle Eastern spice made from the crushed fruit of the Sumac bush

Taksi – Taxi

Tamam – Okay

Tavuk Göğsü – A traditional Turkish dessert made from chicken breast and milk

Telefon – Telephone

Teşekkürler – Thanks
Teşekkür Ederim – Thank you
Tonik – Tonic
Tuvalet – Toilet
Votka – Vodka
Yabancı – Foreigner
Yabancılar – Foreigners
Yağmur – Rain
Yarın – Tomorrow
Yavaş – Slow
Yeni – New
Yok – No/there is no…
Yolluk – A local Bodrum expression for a complimentary
drink. Literarily, 'provisions' or 'expenses for a journey'.
Zafer Bayramı – Victory Day

A word or two about the Turkish alphabet.

Ç – *Ch* as is change
Ş – *Sh* as in shot
Ü – *Oo* as in nude
I – (i without the dot) *Er* as in number
C – Hard J as in jam
J – Soft J as in treasure
Ğ – Silent but extends the preceding vowel
Ö – *Ur* as in urge

A word or two about street names

Jack has played fast and loose with the street names featured in this book, sometimes because they are fiendishly difficult to pronounce, sometimes just for the hell of it. The anglicised versions and their real life Turkish equivalents are shown here.

Turkey Street – Turgutreis Caddesi. Turgut Reis was a famous Ottoman admiral.

Sentry Lane – Çavuşlar Çıkmazı. Roughly translated as 'Sergeants' Cul de Sac'.

Bar Street – Cumhuriyet Caddesi (Republic Street). Commonly known as Bar Street, so not one of Jack's dubious inventions.

Old Hamam Street – Hamam Sokak. Called 'old' in the book because the hamam has long gone. The building is still there, but houses a dress shop, *Kuaför* and a butcher's.

Marina Boulevard – Neyzen Tefvik Caddesi. Well, can you blame Jack?

Spring Lane – Türkkuyusu Caddesi. 'Turk's Well Street' (the main source of artesian water in Bodrum).

Halfway Square – Has no Turkish name. The square is halfway between the bus station and Sentry Lane.

Tavern Alley – Meyhane Sokak. Meyhane actually means 'tavern'.

POSTSCRIPT

THE GIRL IN THE RED DRESS

When Jack and Liam left Turkey, the nation was on an economic roll and the popularity of the ruling AK (Justice and Development) Party and its charismatic but dour leader, Recep Tayyip Erdoğan, seemed unassailable. The nation was fêted (not least by Erdoğan himself) as a template for the popular revolutions sweeping through the old Ottoman lands, the so called 'Arab Spring'. Across the border, Syria had begun its tragic descent into murderous civil war and Erdoğan's attempts at mediation were casually rebuked. His newly acquired taste for international statesmanship appeared amateurish and the limit of his influence was humiliatingly transparent. On the home front, a lively demonstration in Istanbul against the destruction of a clearing in the urban jungle (to make way for yet another shopping mall) quickly spread into a wider national protest against creeping government authoritarianism. To the banging of pots and pans by disapproving housewives hanging out of kitchen windows, riot police dispersed the Gezi Park occupation with water cannons and rampaged through the surrounding streets, tear-gassing everything that moved. If there was a single image more eloquent than a thousand headlines or a million tweets, it was the picture of a young woman in a red dress, armed only with her handbag, being tear-gassed at close quarters by a policeman in full riot gear. The photograph circled the world faster than the Gulf Stream. The violent clampdown was nothing new for Turkey, of course. Turks at the top always got tough with those snapping at their heels. But this time, the target was different – the bourgeois, the educated, the secular and the children of the upper crust. Tables had turned. Erdoğan's predictable hard line played well to the party faithful but quickly unnerved the markets. As foreign investment took flight, the stock market crashed and the lira nosedived. Global capitalism has no morals and social instability is bad for business. Erdoğan's paranoid nonsense about foreign devils and domestic subversives conspiring to wreck the Turkish economy served only to stoke the fire.

In March 2014, the AKP consolidated power in municipal elections which were mired in accusations of vote rigging. Weeks later, Turkey suffered its worst ever industrial disaster when an electricity distribution unit exploded deep underground at the newly privatised Soma Coal Mine. Lifts and ventilation systems failed, tunnels filled with smoke and three hundred and one miners choked to death. Cost cutting, cronyism and profiteering were widely blamed for the catastrophe. All of a sudden, the Justice and Development Party's economic miracle appeared to deliver precious little justice and way too much development. Ironically, when the doughty old bruiser stood for election as Turkey's first executive president in August 2014, he won by a landslide. The outcome was never in doubt.

Erdoğan's time will pass. In the final analysis, Turkey is much more than his crude sound bites and so much more than lazy Western clichés. As an openly gay couple, Jack and Liam demonstrated that even the avant-garde can enjoy the Turkish good life without compromising too much. Thousands of *yabancılar* who now call Turkey their home would agree and continue to add colour to the cultural kaleidoscope. Turkey is changing.

ABOUT THE AUTHOR

Jack Scott was born on a British army base in Canterbury, England in 1960 and spent part of his childhood in Malaysia as a 'forces brat'. A fondness for men in uniforms quickly developed. At the age of eighteen and determined to dodge further education, he became a shop boy on London's trendy King's Road: 'Days on the tills and nights on the tiles were the best probation for a young gay man about town'. After two carefree years, Jack swapped sales for security and got a proper job with a pension attached. In his late forties, passionately dissatisfied with suburban life and middle management, he and his husband abandoned the sanctuary of liberal London for an uncertain future in Turkey.

In 2010, Jack started an irreverent narrative about his new life and *Perking the Pansies* quickly became one of the most popular English language blogs in Turkey. Within a year, he had been featured in the Turkish national press, had published numerous essays and articles in expat and travel magazines and had contributed to the Huffington Post Union of Bloggers. As the blog developed a head of steam, a growing worldwide audience clamoured for a book. Jack duly obliged and his hilarious (well, he thinks so) memoir, '*Perking the Pansies, Jack and Liam move to Turkey*' was published in 2011.

Jack's critically acclaimed debut book won two Rainbow Book Awards, was shortlisted for the prestigious Polari First Book Prize and was featured in *Time Out*. The critical success of his book opened up a whole new career for Jack. He now works as a freelance writer and author. In 2012, Jack and Liam ended their Anatolian affair and paddled back to Britain on the evening tide. They currently live in Norwich, a surprising cathedral city in eastern England.

Other books from Summertime publishing
and Springtime Books

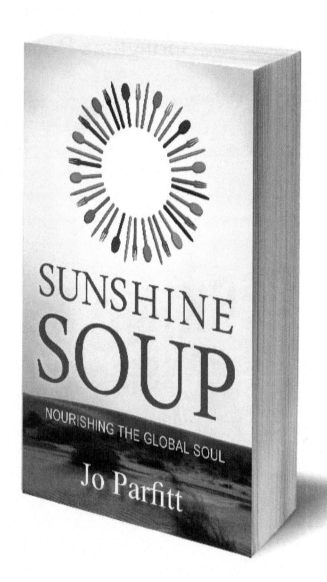

All available at

FINDING YOUR FEET IN
CHICAGO

THE ESSENTIAL GUIDE
FOR EXPAT FAMILIES

Véronique Martin-Place

expatbookshop.com

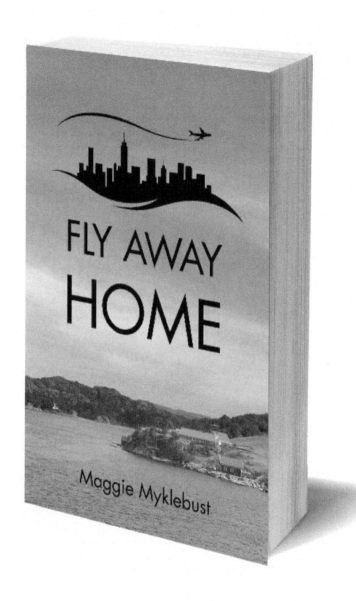

FLY AWAY
HOME

Maggie Myklebust

All available at

Anne O'Connell

@home
in
Dubai

GETTING CONNECTED
ONLINE AND ON THE GROUND

expatbookshop.com

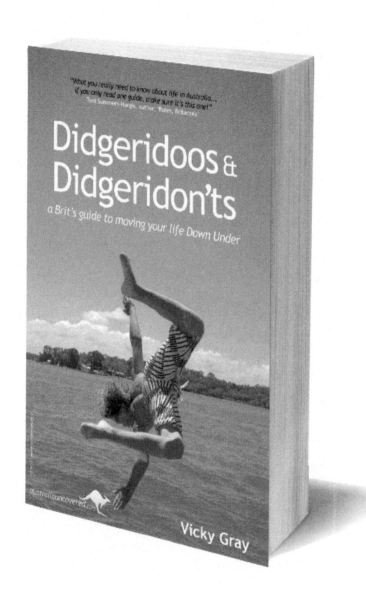

"What you really need to know about life in Australia...
if you only read one guide, make sure it's this one!"
Tom Summers-Hargis, author, 'Rules, Britannia'

Didgeridoos &
Didgeridon'ts

a Brit's guide to moving your life Down Under

australiauncovered.com

Vicky Gray

All available at

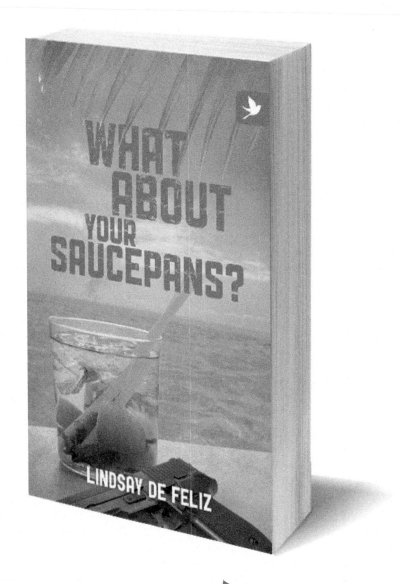

WHAT ABOUT YOUR SAUCEPANS?

LINDSAY DE FELIZ

expatbookshop.com

BITTEN BY SPAIN

THE MURCIAN COUNTRYSIDE
– A BAPTISM BY FIRE

DEBORAH FLETCHER

... had me chuckling from the first page till the last"
Vanessa Rocchetta, Expatica.com

Lightning Source UK Ltd.
Milton Keynes UK
UKOW01f1013171017
311121UK00001B/323/P